D1085039

Faith of Our Mothers, Living Still

Faith of Our Mothers, Living Still

Princeton Seminary Women Redefining Ministry

Abigail Rian Evans
and
Katharine Doob Sakenfeld

WESTMINSTER
JOHN KNOX PRESS
LOUISVILLE · KENTUCKY

© 2017 Westminster John Knox Press

First edition
Published by Westminster John Knox Press
Louisville, Kentucky

17 18 19 20 21 22 23 24 25 26—10 9 8 7 6 5 4 3 2 1

All rights reserved. No part of this book may be reproduced or transmitted in any form or by any means, electronic or mechanical, including photocopying, recording, or by any information storage or retrieval system, without permission in writing from the publisher. For information, address Westminster John Knox Press, 100 Witherspoon Street, Louisville, Kentucky 40202-1396. Or contact us online at www.wjkbooks.com.

Scripture quotations from the New Revised Standard Version of the Bible are copyright © 1989 by the Division of Christian Education of the National Council of the Churches of Christ in the U.S.A. and are used by permission.

"Faith of Our Mothers"/BETSEY STOCKTON, text by Mary Louise Bringle and music by Sally Ann Morris; text and music © 2017 GIA Publications, Inc., 7404 S. Mason Ave., Chicago, IL 60638. www.giamusic.com. 800-442-1358. All rights reserved. Used by permission. For congregational reprint permission, including overhead projection, contact OneLicense.net, 1-800-663-1501. "Tongue-Cut God" by Huengkyum Kim is used by permission of his estate.

Unless otherwise indicated, photos are reprinted by permission of the individual pictured; however, the following photos are copyright and used by permission—Thelma Adair (p. 30), Sang Chang (p. 32), Jane Dempsey Douglass (p. 33), Freda Ann Gardner (p. 35), Patricia Budd Kepler (p. 37), Inn Sook Lee (p. 38), and Anna May Say Pa (p. 42), courtesy of Princeton Theological Seminary; Amy Julia Becker (p. 141), © Christopher Capozziello; Carrie L. Buckner (p. 90), © Terry Lorant Photography; Pam Driesell (p. 56), © Marcus Krause Photography; Cecelia Evelyn GreeneBarr (p. 71), © AP Johnson; Kimberly Hyatt (p. 158), © Tiffany Manning; Hyun-Sook Kim (p. 110), © Yeon Jin Bang; Carol E. Lytch (p. 130), © Lori Stahl; Charlotte Ruth Mallory (p. 80), © The Portrait Gallery: PCH International Inc.; Julia M. Robinson (p. 95), © JCP Portraits; Catherine Rutledge-Gorman (p. 178), © Hannah Gustin; Ester Pudjo Widiasih (p. 146), © Joanna Lindén-Montes/WCC.

Book design by Sharon Adams
Cover design by Lisa Buckley

Library of Congress Cataloging-in-Publication Data
Names: Evans, Abigail Rian, author. | Sakenfeld, Katharine Doob, 1940- author.
Title: Faith of our mothers, living still : Princeton Seminary women
   redefining ministry / Abigail Rian Evans and Katharine Doob Sakenfeld.
Description: First edition. | Louisville, Kentucky : Westminster John Knox
   Press, [2017] |
Identifiers: LCCN 2017005495 (print) | LCCN 2017026328 (ebook) | ISBN
   9781611648072 (ebk.) | ISBN 9780664261917 (hbk. : alk. paper)
Subjects: LCSH: Women in church work. | Women clergy. | Pastoral theology. |
   Princeton Theological Seminary.
Classification: LCC BV4415 (ebook) | LCC BV4415 .E93 2017 (print) | DDC
   277.3/08082--dc23
LC record available at https://lccn.loc.gov/2017005495

PRINTED IN THE UNITED STATES OF AMERICA

∞ The paper used in this publication meets the minimum requirements
of the American National Standard for Information Sciences—Permanence
of Paper for Printed Library Materials, ANSI Z39.48-1992.

Westminster John Knox Press advocates the responsible use of our natural resources. The text paper of this book is made from 30% post-consumer waste.

Most Westminster John Knox Press books are available at special quantity discounts when purchased in bulk by corporations, organizations, and special-interest groups. For more information, please e-mail SpecialSales@wjkbooks.com.

To all Princeton Seminary women, past and present,
whose faithful ministries have inspired and encouraged women
across the globe to follow God's call.

FAITH OF OUR MOTHERS, LIVING STILL
Commissioned by Princeton Theological Seminary

8.8.8.8.8.8

Faith of our mothers, living still,
through gifts derided, calls denied,
striving undaunted through the years,
till bolted doors have opened wide:
    faith of our mothers, firm and strong;
    voices long silenced rise in song!

Faith of our sisters, serving still,
with towel and basin, cup and bread,
tending earth's needs with patient care,
till hurts are healed and hungers fed:
    faith of our sisters' art and skill,
    loving with heart and mind and will;

Faith of our daughters, hoping still,
venturing pathways yet untrod,
partners in witness to the world,
seeking a living, moving God:
    faith of our daughters, bold and true,
    restless till Christ makes all things new;

Faith of our families, growing still,
varied in gender, class, and race,
patchwork of patterns, shapes, and hues,
vast as the mantle of God's grace:
    faith of our families, growing faith,
    we honor you in life and death.

Mary Louise Bringle
© 2017 GIA Publications, Inc.

The complete hymn, with text and music commissioned by Princeton
Theological Seminary, can be found on pp. 262–63.

Contents

PART I

Breaking New Ground: Pioneers and Trailblazers

PART II

One Ministry, Many Forms: Women's Voices

PART III

Explorations in Ministry and Theological Education

Foreword

A portrait of Sarah Miller hangs on the wall of the president's conference room at Princeton Theological Seminary. It has a rightful place in watching over the daily deliberations that occur in that room, for she was one of the early pioneers of faith to whom we owe so much. Sarah Miller was a writer, teacher, fundraiser, and community leader, as well as a daughter, a mother, and the wife of the seminary's second professor, Samuel Miller. Sarah had her own ministry in the Princeton community as the founder and president of the Female Benevolent Society of Princeton, which served the poor and the sick in the community and raised scholarships for children to attend school, and as the superintendent of a weekly Sabbath School for children, which she ran from her home. She also helped to establish and raise significant funds for an orphanage near Princeton, and the endowment that she raised for that project eventually helped to fund Ashmun Institute, which was the nation's first degree-granting historically black college. It continues today as Lincoln University.

The story of Princeton Seminary's founding and early history is incomplete without noting the substantial contribution of Sarah Miller and her contemporaries to the flourishing of the young seminary and its students and faculty. But she is just one example of the many women connected to the seminary who were leaders in their own right in the church and in the community long before women were students or faculty members. This book tells the stories of these women and those for whom they paved the way, each of which is a narrative of calling, intelligence, perseverance, imagination, and deep Christian faith.

Over the last two hundred years since the days of Sarah Miller, women faculty and alumnae of Princeton Seminary have been faithful leaders in the church, in theological education, and in the world. They have served as seminary presidents, professors, pastors, and public leaders. They are missionaries, counselors, and writers. While their collective impact is impossible to quantify, their stories highlight the transformative role that they have had for individuals, communities, and even nations as they have responded to the call of God in their lives. With the publication of this volume, we celebrate the remarkable achievements of generations of women who have been faithful servants of Jesus Christ in many extraordinary and ordinary ways. Princeton Theological Seminary is incredibly proud of their legacy of service.

Among these stories is an astounding record of "firsts"—first woman graduate, first woman president of the American Historical Society, first African American woman elected as moderator of the Presbyterian Church, first woman appointed acting prime minister of South Korea, and the list continues. Yet the path to such achievements has not always been easy. Behind these impressive accomplishments are the realities of perseverance, sacrifice, and commitment. The stories collected here are profound testaments to the courageous and visionary leadership of women who frequently faced skepticism, resistance, or serious obstacles to fulfilling their calling. These women are pioneers who demonstrated strength and resolve. Their persistence and faithfulness despite such opposition are an inspiration to us all.

Yet their stories are only the beginning of a narrative that stretches into the future. As we celebrate the great gifts of these women, we know that God continues to call women to lives of ministry and leadership, and we eagerly anticipate the generations of women to come who will carry on the legacy of these pioneering mothers of the faith.

One of the most critical insights woven into the narratives of this book is the discovery of how instrumental women have been to the formation of our seminary's own identity and mission. And that is just another reason why this book is so important. The stories of these women are woven into our school's common story of faith and scholarship. As a Presbyterian seminary we join others celebrating the 500th anniversary of the Reformation by remembering that the church is always being reformed. Through their hard work, tenacity, various personalities, and faithful response to God's calling in their lives, these women helped reform Princeton Seminary into what it has become and shaped the trajectory for what it will be.

The seminary owes a particular debt of gratitude to the coordinators of the Women in Ministry Initiative and the authors of this book, Abigail Rian Evans and Katharine Doob Sakenfeld. This project would not have come to fruition without their vision, commitment, and boundless enthusiasm for sharing the stories of the women of Princeton Seminary. They have tackled this project with the relentless zeal that characterizes their scholarly work.

Not only have they led a research project to celebrate the history of women in ministry, but they themselves have made history at Princeton Seminary. Abigail Rian Evans, who is herself an alumna of the seminary, was the first woman to serve as the chair of the Practical Theology Department at the seminary. Katharine Doob Sakenfeld was the first woman to celebrate Communion in Miller Chapel and, with Freda Gardner, taught the first course in women's studies at Princeton Seminary. Professors Evans and Sakenfeld have been trailblazers in their own fields of study, and they have also been a source of inspiration to generations of students. Indeed, many of the women who are profiled in this book credit the influence of women faculty members as instrumental in their education and development as scholars, pastors, and leaders.

From the era of Sarah Miller until the present day, the women of Princeton Theological Seminary have responded to the call of God with courage and faith. The church, our seminary, and the world have clearly been shaped by their leadership. Thanks be to God.

M. Craig Barnes
President, Princeton Theological Seminary

Acknowledgments

Preparing this book has given us the opportunity to journey with Princeton Theological Seminary women of faith through two centuries and into the present. This is truly the roll call of the faithful. We are thankful to all the women whose faithfulness and courage have inspired us in our writing, including in the early years when the ministry of faculty wives, women administrators, philanthropists, and many unsung women was vital to the health and well-being of the seminary, church, and world. We extend a special word of appreciation to those who have shared their stories here and to those who found time to respond to our survey. We are most grateful to President Craig Barnes, whose support has been outstanding. His advocacy has made it possible to write this book as well as to develop the seminary's Women in Ministry (WIM) project. There are many others in the PTS administration to whom we owe great thanks: Jaime Zamparelli, Vice President of Advancement, and her staff, especially Lorelei Zupp; John Gilmore, Senior Vice President; Shane Berg, Executive Vice President, and his staff; Bill French, Chief Technology Officer, and his staff, especially Scott Saletta; James Kay, Dean of Academic Affairs, and others in his office; Martin Tel, Seabrook Director of Music, for commissioning Mary Louise Bringle and Sally Ann Morris for the composition of the text and music for a new hymn, "Faith of Our Mothers"; and additional administrative and faculty colleagues too numerous to mention lest someone be inadvertently omitted. We appreciate the hard work of our research assistants Grace Vargas, Melissa Martin, Jillian Marcantonio, Brandon Watson, and Beatrix Weil, and especially that of William Stell, who worked diligently throughout this project. Our work would not have come to fruition apart from our editorial assistants

Janet Jacewicz and particularly Linda Day, who worked tirelessly on the final version of the manuscript. We are especially grateful to Kenneth Henke, the seminary library's Curator of Special Collections and Archivist, for his outstanding chapter on women pioneers. In addition, his diligent research on the history of PTS women both present and past has put our work within a broader context. Staff members of multiple offices of the PC(USA) and the Association of Theological Schools have graciously responded to our many telephone and e-mail inquiries.

A special debt of gratitude goes to our families, who listened patiently to our endless updates about our progress and cheered us on to the finish line.

Story Contributors

Amy Julia Becker is an author who has published three books and many articles. As the mother of a daughter who was diagnosed with Down syndrome, Amy Julia writes at length about children with disabilities, most notably in her book *A Good and Perfect Gift: Faith, Expectations, and a Little Girl Named Penny* (2011). She is a 2010 MDiv graduate of Princeton Theological Seminary.

Rev. Esther M. Berg is the founder and president of Zeteo Missions, a mission project that is committed to alleviating poverty in the Philippines. She has also served in multiple churches. Currently, she lives in the Philippines with her daughter Kate. She is ordained in the Presbyterian Church (U.S.A.) and is a 1988 MDiv graduate of Princeton Theological Seminary.

Dr. Kathryn D. Blanchard is Associate Professor and Chair of Religious Studies at Alma College in Michigan. She is the author of *The Protestant Ethic or the Spirit of Capitalism: Christians, Freedom, and Free Markets* (2010) and the coeditor of *Lady Parts: Biblical Women and* The Vagina Monologues (2012). She is a 1997 MDiv graduate of Princeton Theological Seminary.

Rev. Carrie L. Buckner is Director of Chaplain Services at Alta Bates Summit Medical Center in Berkeley, California. Previously, she worked at California Pacific Medical Center in San Francisco. She is ordained in the Presbyterian Church (U.S.A.) and is a 1994 MDiv graduate of Princeton Theological Seminary.

Rev. Pam Driesell is the senior pastor at Trinity Presbyterian Church in Atlanta, Georgia. Before serving at Trinity, she founded and pastored Oconee Presbyterian Church in Watkinsville, Georgia. She is ordained in the Presbyterian Church (U.S.A.) and is a 1998 MDiv graduate of Princeton Theological Seminary.

Donna J. Garzinsky is the director of music and organist at St. John's Lutheran Church in Summit, New Jersey. Previously, she has served as a music director and organist at many churches. She is a 1987 MA (Christian Education) graduate of Princeton Theological Seminary.

Rev. Dr. Cecelia Evelyn GreeneBarr is the pastor of Smith Chapel African Methodist Episcopal Church in Inkster, Michigan. She is the president of Sharing Faith Ministries and of GreeneHouse LLC. She is also a producer and broadcaster of "Your Sunday Worship," a television production in the Detroit area. She is ordained in the A.M.E. Church and is a 1996 MDiv graduate of Princeton Theological Seminary.

Heather Sturt Haaga is a California plein-air artist with more than twenty-five years of experience in nonprofit board leadership. Currently, she serves as a trustee of Vassar College (her alma mater), as chair of the Salzburg Global Seminar, as a member of the board of the African Wildlife Foundation, and as a trustee of Descanso Gardens. She is a trustee of Princeton Theological Seminary and served as the cochair of its bicentennial campaign.

Rt. Rev. Dr. Helen-Ann M. Hartley is Bishop of Waikato for the Anglican Church in Aotearoa, New Zealand, and Polynesia. Elected in 2013, she is the first woman to hold this office. Previously, she worked as the dean of Tikanga Pakeha Students (i.e., students of European heritage) at the Anglican College of St. John the Evangelist in Auckland, New Zealand. She is a 1996 ThM graduate of Princeton Theological Seminary.

Rev. Elizabeth Barry Haynes is an adjunct professor of both world religion and business law at Flagler College in St. Augustine, Florida. Previously, she worked as the pastor at Northside Presbyterian Church in Jacksonville, Florida. She is ordained in the Presbyterian Church (U.S.A.) and is a 1997 MDiv and 1998 ThM graduate of Princeton Theological Seminary.

Rev. Karen Hernández-Granzen has been the pastor at Westminster Presbyterian Church in Trenton, New Jersey, for over two decades. She is also the chaplain and coordinator of Bethany Presbyterian House of Hospitality in Trenton. She is ordained in the Presbyterian Church (U.S.A.) and serves as the vice chair of the United Mercer Interfaith Organization (UMIO). She served for many years on the advisory council of the School of Christian Vocation and Mission at Princeton Theological Seminary and has been serving as a field education supervisor for numerous PTS students through several decades up to the present.

Rev. Kimberly Hyatt is the president and CEO of the Cathedral Arts Project in Jacksonville, Florida. Previously, she served as a pastor in Florida and worked as a lobbyist in Washington, DC. She is ordained in the Presbyterian Church (U.S.A.) and is a 1996 MDiv graduate of Princeton Theological Seminary.

Dr. Hyun-Sook Kim is Dean of Academic Affairs and Professor of Christian Education at Yonsei University in Seoul, South Korea. She has published many articles on religious education, multiculturalism, and other topics. She is a 1993 MA (Christian Education) and 1999 PhD graduate of Princeton Theological Seminary.

Rev. Dr. Karla Ann Koll is Professor of History, Mission, and Religions at Latin American Biblical University in San José, Costa Rica, and is supported through Presbyterian World Mission. Previously, she taught in Guatemala at the Evangelical Center for Pastoral Studies in Central America and in Nicaragua at the Evangelical Faculty for Theological Studies. She is ordained in the Presbyterian Church (U.S.A.) and is a 2003 PhD graduate of Princeton Theological Seminary.

Rev. Dr. Carol E. Lytch is the president of Lancaster Theological Seminary in Lancaster, Pennsylvania. Previously, she has worked in both the church and the academy, including as assistant executive director of the Association of Theological Schools. She is ordained in the Presbyterian Church (U.S.A.) and is a 1980 MDiv graduate of Princeton Theological Seminary.

Rev. Charlotte Ruth Mallory is a chaplain supervisor at Edna Mahan Correctional Facility for Women. She also serves as an associate minister of Fountain Baptist Church in Summit, New Jersey. In addition, she formerly served as vice president of the New Jersey Institutional Chaplain's Association. She is ordained in the American Baptist Church U.S.A. and is a 2005 MDiv graduate of Princeton Theological Seminary.

Rev. Taryn Mattice is chaplain of the Protestant Cooperative Ministry at Cornell University, a campus ministry program supported by the Presbyterian Church (U.S.A.), the United Methodist Church, the American Baptist

Church U.S.A., and the United Church of Christ. She is ordained in the Presbyterian Church (U.S.A.) and is a 1986 MDiv graduate of Princeton Theological Seminary.

Rev. Dr. Cynthia S. Mazur has worked at the Federal Emergency Management Agency since 1991. Currently, she serves as Alternative Dispute Resolution Director, and previously she was Associate General Counsel for Program Law. Before her legal career, she served as a church pastor on Fort Berthold Indian Reservation. She is ordained in the United Church of Christ and is a 1980 MDiv graduate of Princeton Theological Seminary.

Rev. Dr. Linda A. Mercadante is the B. Robert Straker Professor of Theology at Methodist Theological School in Ohio. Among her five books is *Beliefs without Borders: Inside the Minds of the Spiritual But Not Religious* (2014). She is ordained in the Presbyterian Church (U.S.A.) and is a 1986 PhD graduate of Princeton Theological Seminary.

Gail McArthur Moody serves as Director of Christian Education at Westminster Presbyterian Church in Salem, Oregon. She has served in Christian education roles in many churches over the years. She is a 1977 MA (Christian Education) graduate of Princeton Theological Seminary.

Rev. Julie Neraas is Associate Professor of Religion at Hamline University in St. Paul, Minnesota. Previously, she has served as a solo pastor and as a chaplain at various locations. In addition, she is a certified spiritual director. She is ordained in the Presbyterian Church (U.S.A.) and is a 1979 MDiv graduate of Princeton Theological Seminary.

Rev. Sonja Gall Pancoast is the copastor, with her husband, of Zion Lutheran Church in Loveland, Colorado. Previously, she served as the solo pastor of St. Bartholomew Lutheran Church in Trenton, New Jersey. She is ordained in the Evangelical Lutheran Church of America and is a 2001 MDiv graduate of Princeton Theological Seminary.

Rev. Dr. Julia M. Robinson is Associate Professor of Religion at the University of North Carolina at Charlotte. Previously, she taught at Western Michigan University. Her publications include *Race, Religion, and the Pulpit: Rev. Robert L. Bradby and the Making of Urban Detroit* (2015). She is ordained in the Presbyterian Church (U.S.A.) and is a 1994 MDiv graduate of Princeton Theological Seminary.

Rev. Catherine Rutledge-Gorman is an instructor at Oregon Health and Sciences University in the School of Nursing, Monmouth Campus. Previously, she served as an interim pastor in the Portland area. She is ordained in the Presbyterian Church (U.S.A.) and is a 1989 MDiv graduate of Princeton Theological Seminary.

Rev. Ruth Faith Santana-Grace is Executive Presbyter for the Presbytery of Philadelphia, the first woman and first person of color in this role. Previously, she worked as Executive Presbyter for the San Gabriel Presbytery, as an associate pastor in Pennsylvania, and as Executive Director of the Bridge Association in Rome and Florence, Italy. She is ordained in the Presbyterian Church (U.S.A.), is a 1994 MDiv graduate of Princeton Theological Seminary, and currently serves as the vice chair of the PTS Board of Trustees.

Rev. Dr. Barbara K. Sherer is a U.S. Army chaplain who has deployed to combat four times, including for Operation Iraqi Freedom in 2003. Previously, she served as the assistant and associate pastor of First Presbyterian Church in Stillwater, Oklahoma. She is ordained in the Presbyterian Church (U.S.A.) and is a 1982 MDiv graduate of Princeton Theological Seminary.

Rev. Danielle Shroyer served for eight years as the solo pastor of Journey Church, a multidenominational emerging church in Dallas, Texas, and now is pursuing writing full-time. She is the author of three books, including *Original Blessing: Putting Sin in Its Rightful Place* (2016). She was ordained at Journey Church and is a 2002 MDiv graduate of Princeton Theological Seminary.

Rev. Dr. Ester Pudjo Widiasih is Program Executive for Spiritual Life at the World Council of Churches. Previously, she worked as a lecturer in worship and church music at Jakarta Theological Seminary in Indonesia. She is also a composer, choral director, and artist. She is ordained in the Christian Churches of Java and is a 2000 ThM graduate of Princeton Theological Seminary.

Introduction

Faith of Our Mothers, Living Still forms part of a larger project of Princeton Theological Seminary (PTS), the Women in Ministry (WIM) Initiative. WIM was established in 2011 to honor all women associated with PTS since its founding and also to offer ongoing support to, and advocacy for, women in their different ministries in service to God, the church, and the world. It is led by cocoordinators and a twenty-member committee that includes pastors, educators, executives, administrators, and chaplains, both laity and clergy. They organize (especially for alumnae) conferences, programs, women's networking, and archival library collections. The third floor of the PTS library features the Women in Ministry Room.

This book provides the first overview of the ministry of women associated with PTS over the last two hundred years, with an emphasis on the seminary's living graduates. It introduces a cross section of women, including international and multicultural women, and reaches beyond graduates and faculty to include others related to the seminary. By reflecting on these PTS women now and through history, we hope that this book will become an occasion for rethinking ministry in the changing church as well as inviting new reflections on theological education from the wider church. This book is only a snapshot of all the wonderful ministries of PTS women. There are thousands more stories that could be told, and we anticipate developing a larger collection in the Women's Archives in the PTS library.

The book's ten chapters are divided into several parts:

> *Part I—Breaking New Ground: Pioneers and Trailblazers.* Chapter 1 tells wonderful stories of the early women of the seminary who—as faculty

wives, daughters, early students, and faculty—broke the mold of women's assigned roles in the nineteenth and early twentieth centuries to serve in numerous and creative ways by answering God's call. Chapter 2 introduces ten women, from the United States and abroad, who seized the opportunity to change the church and society through education, the pastorate, and administration, taking risks to overcome prejudice to redefine women's leadership and to pave the way for women today.

Part II—One Ministry, Many Forms: Women's Voices. Chapters 3–8 feature first-person stories by women in their own voices, selected to reflect a diversity of ministry settings and to show how the church is being reshaped by the innovative ways in which women are responding to God's call. While honoring the importance of parish ministry and traditional specialized ministries, the breadth of these stories also helps to redefine ministry within a broader interpretation of God's call to congregation, marketplace, community agency, seminary, nonprofit agency, prison, university, government, and other diverse settings where Princeton women have served and are serving today.

Part III—Explorations in Ministry and Theological Education. Chapter 9 develops an expanded understanding of ministry grounded in a biblical and theological context, where Christians serve God both inside and outside the church. The chapter then discusses the situation of clergywomen in the context of women's changing place in U.S. society. Women's experiences presented here and in the prior sections of the book inform the concluding chapter 10, which proposes a new vision for theological education for the whole person. Appendixes are provided with information on American women's church leadership and statistics on PTS alumnae.

The methodology for this book was quite complex and lengthy. One of our principal research tools was an online survey developed by the authors and sent to a sample of PTS alumnae selected from twenty different categories of ministry as well as a random sample of alumnae pastors, to learn what PTS alumnae are doing and thinking, especially regarding call, ministry, and theological education. This survey is best described as qualitative rather than quantitative research and does not purport to be a scientific survey of PTS women's views on a variety of ministry-related subjects. Rather, it provided a general overview of alumnae perspectives. The thirty-nine-question survey (including twelve essay questions) was sent to 428 individuals; numbers were assigned by the IT department to ensure confidentiality. The 208 surveys returned (a 48.6-percent return rate) generated over three hundred pages of narrative data. To complete the entire survey took approximately eighty minutes.

In addition to this survey, we interviewed countless PTS women, both graduates and current students, as well as trustees, faculty, administrators, current and past staff, and experts on theological education. Additional resources included numerous books and articles, material from the PC(USA) Board of Pensions and other denominational offices, and from the Association of Theological Schools. All this material enriched the findings of this book, which grew from our own previous writing, research, and teaching on these subjects in our decades of ministry at the seminary and in the church, both here and abroad.

Perhaps the most important finding of this book is how PTS women's firm, vibrant Christian faith shines forth even in the face of difficulties and challenges, giving witness to the strong power of the Holy Spirit. This does not mean that all PTS women's experiences are happy and victorious ones, or that some have not suffered prejudice just by the fact of being female. But at the end of the day, so many praise God for the privilege of ministry wherever they find themselves, often in unexpected places and callings. For any small ways that PTS was able to help them on their faith journeys and preparation for ministry, we give thanks to God.

It has been a privilege in the writing of this book to give voice to some of these women, both sung and unsung, and to share their stories with you. It is our gift to PTS and the larger church, with the hope that it will help to encourage and inspire future women, and the men who support them, to respond to God's call to ministry wherever it may lead. Faith of our mothers is living still, in spite of struggles, pain, and tears.

PART I

Breaking New Ground: Pioneers and Trailblazers

INTRODUCTION

The first chapter in this section, written by Kenneth Woodrow Henke, begins with the stories of early Princeton Theological Seminary (PTS) women up to 1960 and how they were engaged in ministry from the seminary's founding. It sets the stage for our broader definition of ministry, which follows throughout the book to embrace more than those who are ordained. The aim is to bring these women out of the shadows and into the center in order to honor and appreciate all they have done in service of Christ, the church, and the world. These pioneer women found creative and groundbreaking ways to do their ministry in a culture that did not always recognize women's leadership. Many of their ministries in music, hospitality, education, and nursing also shine through in the stories of contemporary women in subsequent chapters.

Chapter 2 introduces the trailblazing work of contemporary women from the 1960s forward who also were pioneers in their ministries and illustrate the diversity of women and women's ministry. These trailblazers have been among the first women in significant positions over an extended period in this country and abroad, women who have been breaking in and breaking out, game changers who have paved the way for subsequent women in ministry. We highlight how their leadership has demonstrated their vision, advocacy, prophetic voice, and compassion.

1

Princeton Theological Seminary Women Pioneers, 1812–1960

Women did not come to Princeton Theological Seminary as students or faculty until the twentieth century.[1] (James Moorhead, in his book on the history of the seminary, can speak of Princeton Seminary as "overwhelmingly a bastion of male dominance" for most of its history.[2]) Yet women played an important supportive role from the very beginning—as members of the households of the male faculty members, as contributors and benefactresses who helped to keep the seminary afloat financially and looked to its needs for scholarships and buildings, and as providers of services to the students, such as infirmary care, and, later in the nineteenth century, as cooks and house mothers of the various eating clubs. They also carried on their own important ministries, broadly defined.

FACULTY WIVES

Of most of these women we have little record, but for some we can tell more of their stories. In the spring of 1801, Archibald Alexander, a young Presbyterian minister who had recently resigned his pastoral charge and the presidency of Hampden-Sydney College in rural Virginia, started off on a journey, the ultimate destination of which he was not yet sure. It had not begun as a

---

1. This chapter was written by Kenneth Woodrow Henke, Archivist, Princeton Theological Seminary library, based on his research in the PTS archives.

2. James H. Moorhead, *Princeton Seminary in American Religion and Culture* (Grand Rapids: Eerdmans, 2012), 497.

very auspicious journey. The first night after leaving home, he was robbed. Now he was sick, seized with a chill so violent that he determined to find some friendly nearby home where he could ask permission to simply lie down and rest for a while. In this state he came to the home of James Waddel and his daughter, *Janetta Waddel* (who will become his wife). She was born in Ireland and educated in Pennsylvania; her father, the Rev. Dr. James Waddel, was one of the most revered clergymen of his day. Known for his powerful preaching, in later years his sight failed, and by 1801 he depended on Janetta to read to him—Scripture passages, biblical commentaries, and even learned Latin tomes—as he prepared his sermons in his mind.

Archibald had visited the home before, but this time, when he had recovered enough to resume his journey a few days later, he proposed to the attractive, intelligent, and caring Janetta, and she accepted. His journey took him north to Philadelphia, Princeton, New York, and New England, and again back through Princeton, where, arriving in time for the commencement exercises, he was unexpectedly awarded a Master of Arts degree. Upon his return back home, he and Janetta were married on April 5, 1802.

Janetta's father died in the fall of 1805, and in 1807 the Alexanders moved from Virginia to Philadelphia, where they took up work in the important Pine Street Presbyterian Church. Sentiment had been growing in the Presbyterian Church for the establishment of a seminary similar to the seminary the Congregationalists had established in New England, one that would provide more adequately for the needs of the young and still growing nation. The old system, whereby college graduates intending to enter the ministry would apprentice themselves for a period to some senior minister to prepare for their licensing and ordination examinations before the presbytery, was simply not meeting the needs of the growing cities along the Atlantic coast and the new territories being settled to the west. Young Archibald Alexander joined with those calling for the establishment of such a seminary, and when the General Assembly of the church voted to do so in 1812, they chose him as its first professor.

Janetta and Archibald Alexander moved to Princeton to take up the new duties, and Princeton became their home for the next forty years until the death of Archibald in 1851 and Janetta's own death not long after in 1852. At the time of their deaths, seven of their children were still living—six sons and a daughter. Three of their sons had become ministers, two of these serving as professors at Princeton College and at the seminary; two had become lawyers; and one had taken up the medical profession. Looking back on those Princeton years, their son James remembered the way his mother had made their home a place of real hospitality. He remembered her conversation, "full of vivacity and humour," as well her quick mind, her strong memory, and her good taste in religious literature. He recalled the poverty of the first years of the seminary, and how his mother had been active in obtaining financial support for needy students. Above all, he remembered what a support she had been to his father. "When his spirits flagged, she was always prompt and skillful to cheer and comfort. And as his days were filled with spiritual and literary toils, she relieved him from the whole charge of domestic affairs," he wrote. "She was such a gift as God bestows only on the most favored."[3]

Another of the early women of Princeton Seminary was *Sarah Sargeant Miller*, the wife of Samuel Miller, the second professor at the seminary. She was the great-granddaughter of Jonathan Dickinson, the first president of the College of New Jersey (as Princeton College was first called), and was related to the famous Presbyterian missionaries David and John Brainerd. Her father, Jonathan Dickinson Sargeant, was a Princeton attorney and a member of the revolutionary Continental Congress. Her maternal grandfather was a Presbyterian pastor in Trenton and a trustee of the College of New Jersey.

The family of Sarah Sargeant moved to Philadelphia after her father was appointed attorney general of Pennsylvania, but in 1787, when she was nine years old, her mother died. The following year her father remarried, and from then until age fifteen Sarah attended a series of boarding schools. Of most of these she did not later retain a good opinion, though she did remember fondly her time at the Moravian Female Seminary in Bethlehem, Pennsylvania, where she felt that she had been surrounded by piety and good influence. In 1793 her father died in the great yellow fever epidemic that swept through Philadelphia that year. During the summer of 1800 Sarah was able to spend a few months with relatives in Princeton but then returned to Philadelphia to live with her stepmother, her older brother, and three stepsiblings.

In a remarkable document reminiscent of Puritan autobiographical accounts of an earlier period, Sarah Miller recorded her religious struggles as she experienced them in the earlier part of her life, up until 1807. This was fortunately preserved by her son and printed in part in the first volume of his *The Life of Samuel Miller, D.D., L.L.D.*, which he published following the death of both his father and mother.[4] In this document Sarah speaks of early religious reflections, intimations, and memories, but also of a period of "follies and temptations" that coincided with her boarding school years. The death of her father renewed a serious concern with religious matters, but she

---

3. James W. Alexander, *The Life of Archibald Alexander* (New York: Charles Scribner, 1854), 272–73.

4. The published parts of her memoir, on which the material in this section draws, are found in Samuel Miller, *The Life of Samuel Miller, D.D., L.L.D.*, 2 vols. (Philadelphia: Claxton, Remsen and Haffelfinger, 1869), 1:148–67.

reports that after a bit she was caught up again for a period of about five years when she "lived as if the object of life was self-gratification." She amused herself by going to the theater and attending balls and parties, and she became especially addicted to card playing: "Every evening not thus employed was vacant and tedious." One evening, not realizing the level of the stakes, she ended up losing all the money she had with her. Somewhat embarrassed, she considered applying to a relative for a loan but somehow was able to win back in the second night all she had lost the previous night, and more. "The sum which I had lost," she wrote, "was more than restored, but without a restoration of my tranquility."

Struggling to free herself from some of these habits but time and again falling back into them, Sarah at last began to sink into a depression: "The world rapidly lost all its attractions, and realized to my view the wilderness which the word of truth represents it to be. . . . From this time, for several years afterward, I was like a drowning wretch, ready at every instant to perish." She suggests that she had possibly been prescribed laudanum (a tincture of opium popularly included in patent medicines of the day), but "soon discovered that such stimuli rather increased . . . than relieved my distress."

Sometime around 1800 Sarah began to be courted by an older gentleman who had been a student and friend of her father. She writes,

> He had visited us for some time, and I knew had serious intentions with regard to myself. He had large property, and I had already formed plans of universal benevolence, which were enlarged by becoming connected with a benevolent society in Philadelphia, the first of its kind, and just then formed for the relief of the poor. But besides other objections, this gentleman was probably double my age, and, had I married him, it would have been without any feeling of affection, as I deeply experienced at every interview. In the firm persuasion, however, that this step was duty, I knelt and prayed for direction and aid, not doubting but that both would be given in favor of my plans with regard to this object.[5]

She was convinced that she "had lived to little purpose in the world" and that having a "desire to be useful," she might have more means and opportunity as a married woman.

In the spring of 1801 Sarah had also casually met a young Presbyterian minister from New York named Samuel Miller. Later that same spring Samuel Miller came to Philadelphia as a commissioner for the first time to the General Assembly of the Presbyterian Church. Although taking full part in the deliberations of the General Assembly, he also took the occasion to spend

---

5. Ibid., 1:162.

as much time as possible visiting the Sargeant household. Writing in his diary on the occasion of his forty-fifth wedding anniversary, he reveals his side of the story:

> It was not my own wisdom that selected this precious companion. I was led to make the choice by what we are accustomed to call "pure accident." The circumstances of hearing her strongly recommended to another, in a confidential conversation, not intended to reach my ear, determined me to seek her hand. But for this circumstance, there is no probability that I should have dreamed of the connexion. . . . The Lord chose for me far better than I could have chosen for myself.[6]

Having not yet made any definite commitment to the first gentleman, when Samuel Miller proposed, she felt free to accept, and Sarah Sargeant and Samuel Miller were wed on October 24, 1801.

Even so, the event did not go entirely smoothly. Yellow fever was at the time raging in New York City, and the Health Committee of Philadelphia had put a fifteen-day quarantine into effect for all visitors from New York. Samuel Miller had to obtain a special dispensation to come to Philadelphia and proceed with the marriage. Further, the marriage was to be performed by the Rev. Dr. John Ewing, provost of the University of Pennsylvania and half uncle of Sarah Sargeant by marriage. He was seventy years old and somewhat forgetful in his habits, and his wife did not want him blurting about the arrival of this visitor from New York who would not be undergoing quarantine. Thus his wife did not tell him until the very last minute that he would be performing a marriage that day or whose marriage he would be performing. Arriving at the Sargeant home where the wedding was to take place, he stated that he did not like being kept in the dark about these things and, as it was a Saturday, he would only perform the wedding on condition that Samuel Miller would preach for him the next morning![7]

After many years of marriage, in a long diary entry on October 24, 1847, Samuel Miller reflected on how much Sarah's support had meant to him in his work over the years. He praises her abilities at managing the household, her knowledge of people, her "energy, and physical and moral courage," and her taste and judgment in making household purchases. In one paragraph in particular, he makes note of her skill in ministry and the value he placed on her ministry and the contributions she made to his own ministry:

6. Ibid., 2:481.
7. Ibid., 1:143.

She is really better qualified than many ministers to instruct the inquiring, and to counsel the perplexed and anxious. Hundreds of times have I profited by her remarks on my sermons, and other public performances, more than by the remarks of any other human being.[8]

In addition to raising a large family (the Millers went on to have ten children, though one of them died in infancy), supporting the work of her husband, and entertaining students and guests at the seminary, Sarah Miller gave much time to organizing the women of Princeton for benevolent work. "She was never happy unless she had some schemes for doing good in hand," wrote John Frelinghuysen Hageman, Princeton's nineteenth-century historian.[9] She had a special interest in the education of children. As early as 1816, she had helped form the Female Benevolent Society of Princeton, which she served for many years as its president. Its work included visitation work among the poor, especially those who were sick. It also raised scholarships for poor children to enable them to attend one of Princeton's private schools in the days before public education. She herself organized a school in her home, where she gave daily instruction for children from Princeton's sizable African American community and also ran a weekly Sabbath School for children from her neighborhood.

By 1825 the Female Benevolent Society had opened a school of its own for free instruction for the poor, an institution that continued more than forty years, even after public education became available. Sarah Miller was the chief manager of the school and was often in attendance herself to oversee operations. On other occasions, she would send one or more of her children to assist the teacher in the work of instruction. She also helped establish the Mount Lucas Orphan and Guardian Institute near Princeton and raised a considerable endowment for it. The funds were well managed, and when the Orphan Institute was no longer needed, the endowment she had raised was transferred, with her help, to the new Ashmun Institute in Chester County, Pennsylvania. This was the first institution for higher education established specifically for the education of African Americans, who at that time had limited opportunities for higher education. In 1866, after the assassination of President Lincoln the year before, the Ashmun Institute was renamed for him, and Lincoln University continues its work to this day. Among its many notable graduates are Thurgood Marshall, Langston Hughes, and Kwame Nkrumah.

Despite Sarah's complaints about the various boarding schools she had

8. Ibid., 2:496.
9. John Frelinghuysen Hageman, *History of Princeton and Its Institutions*, 2 vols. (Philadelphia: J. B. Lippincott, 1879), 2:411.

attended, it is clear that she had a sound education, on which she continued to improve throughout her life. According to Hageman, she was

> accustomed to mingle in the society of strong-minded and learned men who partook of the hospitalities of her home. . . . She was, even to the very end of her life, a close student of the Bible, and was accustomed to spend a portion of the day, generally after breakfast, at her table with her Bible and Commentary, in reading and studying the word of God, as though she were a teacher in the seminary; and she was always prepared to take part in the discussion of religious questions that might arise among the clerical guests at her house or among her own children.[10]

In fact, she was particularly concerned in the matter of the education of her own children. She helped found and lead a Maternal Association that met to pray for their children, to encourage one another in their child-raising endeavors, and "to stir each other up to greater parental fidelity." Of her husband she even "once queried whether some of the lectures which he was delivering at the Seminary might not be useful to his own family," and accordingly he began to set aside time to gather the family in his study several times a week "reading to them his Seminary prelections upon Biblical and Ecclesiastical History and Chronology, and examining the older children afterwards upon them, and requiring them often to write out from memory and outline of what they had heard."[11]

Samuel Miller died in 1850, but Sarah Miller went on to survive him another eleven years. Her interest in the education of the young and her other charitable activities continued, though her energy slowly declined with the passing years. "By day, she reclined upon a couch in the family sitting-room," remembered her son, and one day "quietly as an infant drops asleep, she closed her eyes, at length, upon all earthly scenes." The date was February 2, 1861, and she had celebrated her eighty-third birthday just a month before.[12]

Janetta Waddel Alexander and Sarah Sargeant Miller, the first two faculty wives at Princeton Seminary, will have to stand in as representatives of generations of faculty wives to follow. They raised their children, supported their husbands' work, entertained students and visitors to the seminary, and made their contributions to the social, religious, and charitable organizations of Princeton, and often to wider ecclesiastical circles and innumerable good causes.

10. Ibid., 2:411.
11. Miller, *The Life of Samuel Miller*, 2:420–21.
12. Ibid., 2:550.

AFRICAN AMERICAN CHURCH LEADER

A very different story may be told of another woman connected to the early history of Princeton Theological Seminary who went by the name of *Betsey Stockton*. The Stockton family was one of the oldest families of Princeton. Richard Stockton had moved to the area of what is now Princeton in 1696, and in 1701 he purchased over five thousand acres from William Penn. Upon his death, this property was divided among his sons, who married and reared their own children in the Princeton area. Richard Stockton's grandson, also named Richard, was one of the signers of the Declaration of Independence. His cousin, Robert Stockton, served as a quartermaster in the Revolutionary War. Sometime near the end of the eighteenth century, a slave, given the name of Betsey, was born on the family estate of Robert Stockton in Princeton. Robert's daughter Elizabeth had married a Presbyterian clergyman and graduate of Princeton College named Ashbel Green, and he decided to give the young slave girl to his daughter as a present. Thus Betsey, as a small child, came into the home of Ashbel Green.

Ashbel Green, as his father before him, was a strong opponent of slavery. He was the chief author of the 1818 antislavery resolution of the General Assembly of the Presbyterian Church, which stated that the church considered "the voluntary enslaving of one part of the human race by another as a gross violation of the most precious and sacred rights of human nature . . . and as totally irreconcilable with the spirit and principles of the gospel of Christ."[13] Therefore, Ashbel Green raised the young Betsey as a member of the household, tutoring her along with his own children and eventually formally manumitting her when she came of age. For a few years, in her early teens, she went to live with his nephew, who ran a school in South Jersey, but she came back to the Green household again when they moved from Philadelphia to Princeton. In 1812 Ashbel Green had become the president of Princeton College and, in the same year, the first president of the board of directors of the newly formed Princeton Theological Seminary. In the winter of 1814–1815 there was a revival of religious concern that swept through Princeton College and the seminary, and Betsey, who had been attending Sabbath School classes taught by some of the Princeton Seminary students, underwent a religious experience that led her to apply for full membership in the First Presbyterian Church of Princeton. After examination, she was duly baptized and admitted into communicant membership.

13. *Minutes of the General Assembly of the Presbyterian Church in the United States of America from Its Organization A.D. 1789 to A.D. 1820 Inclusive* (Philadelphia: Presbyterian Board of Publication, 1847), 692–94.

Simple membership in the church, however, did not seem to be enough for Betsey. She began to develop a desire to go abroad and serve as a missionary. When she learned that Charles Stewart and his wife, Harriet, had been accepted to serve as missionaries to the Sandwich Islands (as Hawaii was called in those days), she began to dream of going along with them. The Stewarts had been frequent guests in the Green home, and she knew them well. She shared her interest with the Stewarts and with Ashbel Green. The American Board of Commissioners for Foreign Missions had been formed only a few years earlier, in 1810. Ashbel Green had already been helpful in preparing and aiding in the financing of some of the earliest missionaries of that board. The idea of sending a single woman as a missionary, however, especially a single African American woman who had been born into slavery, seemed entirely novel. Nevertheless, Ashbel Green wrote a persuasive letter to the American Board of Commissioners recommending her for missionary service:

> . . . she has been, for a good while, exceedingly desirous to go on a mission and I am willing that she should. I think her, in many respects, well qualified for this. . . . There is no kind of work in a family at which she is not very expert. She is an excellent nurse. But I think her well qualified for higher employment in a mission than domestick [*sic*] drudgery. She reads extremely well; and few of her age and sex have read more books on religion than she; or can give a better account of them. . . . She calls herself Betsey Stockton.[14]

Michael Osborn, one of the Princeton Seminary students who also knew her well, sent along a long additional supporting letter, which gives further insight into her character and the way she impressed people:

> I would say in general, as the result of an intimate acquaintance with her, that I think her pious, intelligent, industrious, skillful in the management of domestic affairs, apt to teach, and endowed with a large portion of the active preserving, self-sacrificing, spirit of a missionary . . . for about a year and a half she has been a member of my class in the Sabbath School at this place. Her recitations have been chiefly from S[*acred*] *Scriptures*, the *Larger Catechism*, *Jewish Antiquities*, and *Sacred Geography*. She has a larger acquaintance with sacred history and Mosaic Institutions than almost any ordinary person, old or young, I have ever known. . . . I recollected a multitude of instances where, for my own information, I have questioned her about some fact in Biblical history, or some minute point in Jewish Antiquities, and have immediately received a correct answer.

---

14. The text of the letter is reproduced in full in Constance K. Escher, "She Calls Herself Betsey Stockton," *Princeton History* 10 (1991): 77–78.

> She has enjoyed unrestrained access to the private library of The Revd. President [i.e., Ashbel Green] of Nassau Hall (in whose family she was raised, with the exception of three or four years, from her infancy) and I am persuaded has improved the privilege. I will mention but one of many instances of her love of study. At the commencement of one of our six week vacations, I lent her a copy of Bishop Horne on the Psalms, intending she should transcribe the table in which he has classed the psalms under their appropriate heads, and read his remarks on a few of them, preparatory to committing them to memory. At the end of the vacations, she had made time to study the whole book, preface and all. That she had studied it thoroughly, I was convinced by her frequent and appropriate references to his remarks. She loves to teach children, and has sometimes during vacation acted as a teacher or superintendent of a sabbath school. During some months she has appropriated a part of every week to the instruction of a number of coloured children. For a considerable time, she has been studying with the ultimate view of taking charge of a day school for coloured children. . . . I am of the opinion that few pious young ladies of her age will be found to equal her in knowledge of the Bible, and general theology.[15]

With these strong testimonies, Betsey was accepted for missionary service and a special contract was drawn up allowing her to accompany the Stewarts as a help especially for the four-month-pregnant Harriet, but also specifying that she was not simply to be regarded as a servant but also employed in the mission as a "teacher of a School, for which it is hoped she will be found qualified."[16]

Betsey Stockton had been saving up the wages that Ashbel Green had been paying for her domestic help in his household, and Green added some additional funds of his own "to prepare her outfit for the mission."[17] She joined the second company of missionaries who were setting out for the Sandwich Islands in the late fall of 1822. In addition to Betsey, at this time about twenty-five years old, and the Stewarts, there were others, including Artemas Bishop, another former Princeton Seminary student, along with his wife, Elizabeth, and several young men who were natives of the Sandwich and Society Islands and who had studied theology at the Mission School in Cornwall, Connecticut. These young men would be able to serve the mission as translators when they reached their home islands. They left from New Haven, Connecticut,

---

15. Ibid., 79–80.
16. Ibid., 81.
17. *The Life of Ashbel Green, V.D.M. Begun to Be Written by Himself in His Eighty-Second Year and Continued to His Eighty-Fourth*, ed. Joseph H. Jones (New York: Robert Carter and Brothers, 1849), 326.

on a whaler, the *Thames*, for a five-month journey with no stopovers around Cape Horn and into the Pacific.

In 1822 Ashbel Green reached the age of sixty and, retiring from Princeton College, moved back to Philadelphia, where he accepted the editorship of a religious newspaper, the *Christian Advocate*. Betsey Stockton kept a journal of her voyage to Hawaii, in which she recounts her experiences aboard the ship, including seasickness; the shipboard ceremonies at the crossing of the equator; her marvel at the beauty of the ocean ("If it were in my power I would like to describe the Phosphorescence of the sea. But to do this would require the pen of a Milton: and he, I think, would fail, were he to attempt it"); the birth of the Stewart baby at sea; and reflections on her own spiritual state and those of the sailors aboard ship. Although her original journal is lost, she sent a copy to Ashbel Green. He in turn printed the text serially in his newspaper.[18] "Some of her letters," he wrote, "were so well written, that, with very few corrections, I inserted them in the *Christian Advocate* . . . and they were greatly admired."[19]

Betsey Stockton remained as a missionary in Hawaii for somewhat over two years. Shortly after landing in Honolulu, she, the Stewarts, and another couple were invited to Lahaina on the island of Maui, at that time the capital of the kingdom of Hawaii. We learn from her journal how she began a school there with ten students, both English and Hawaiian. In a later letter, also published by Ashbel Green in the *Christian Advocate*, she reports, "I have now a fine school of the *Makeainana*, or lower class of people, the first I believe that has ever been established."[20] Charles Stewart, in reporting on the progress of the mission, mentions in particular Betsey's good command of the Hawaiian language. After the birth of their second child, however, Harriet Stewart was increasingly unwell, and it was finally determined that her health required that the Stewarts return to North America. With Betsey's close ties to the family, she decided to go with them to help care for Harriet and the children. The Stewarts returned to upstate New York, the home area of Harriet. Betsey spent time there with the family but also in Philadelphia, where she began a school for young children. She even accepted an invitation to sojourn in Canada for a few months to help organize schools for indigenous people at Grape Island, in today's Ontario province.

In 1830 Harriet Stewart died. In the meantime, Charles Stewart had resigned his missionary position and accepted a post as a chaplain in the Navy,

---

18. "Religious Intelligence. Sandwich Islands," *Christian Advocate* 2 (May 1824): 233–35; *Christian Advocate* 2 (December 1824): 563–66; *Christian Advocate* 3 (January 1825): 36–41.

19. *The Life of Ashbel Green*, 326.

20. "Religious Intelligence. Sandwich Islands," *Christian Advocate* 3 (April 1825): 189.

which kept him away from home for long periods. Betsey became the chief caretaker of the orphaned Stewart children, and in 1833 she decided to move back to Princeton, bringing the children with her. Although Ashbel Green had moved back to Philadelphia, one of the Green children with whom Betsey had grown up, James Green, had married and settled down in Princeton. When Charles Stewart remarried in 1835, he was able to take the children back again, and Betsey decided to remain in Princeton.

Over the next years of her life, Betsey Stockton became a leading figure in the Princeton African American community. In 1836 a fire destroyed the sanctuary of the First Presbyterian Church. The congregation decided to meet temporarily in the Princeton Seminary chapel, which had been constructed only a few years before, but it was not large enough for the entire congregation and had only a small gallery. Free and slave African Americans had traditionally sat in the much larger gallery of the old church building. The African Americans began worshiping separately in a building in their neighborhood on Witherspoon Street. They eventually incorporated as The First Presbyterian Church of Colour of Princeton, which became the Witherspoon Street Church in 1848. Betsey Stockton became one of the most prominent leaders of the new African American congregation, and both a plaque and a window were later dedicated there to her memory.

She also put her educational skills to use, founding a Sabbath School for children and youth in the African American community. The superintendents of the school were usually students at the seminary, who would take up their duties for two or three years at a time while pursuing their studies. But the long-term teachers were literate African Americans, many of whom had been trained by Betsey Stockton and who then went on to teach others, just as Betsey had trained native Hawaiian teachers to spread learning in their communities on the mission field. She also helped found and run a "common," or district, school for Princeton African Americans and an evening class for young working adults, for which she enlisted the help of Princeton College and Princeton Seminary teachers and students.

The younger Charles Stewart, the child Betsey had helped raise when he was young, eventually grew to manhood. He attended West Point, graduating first in his class of 1846, which included such other future luminaries as George McClellan, Stonewall Jackson, and George Pickett. An officer in the Corps of U.S. Engineers, he was able to purchase a house for Betsey in Princeton in the vicinity of the Witherspoon Church. At one point during the Civil War, sick from the battlefield, he retreated there to recover and wrote, "[Betsey] cared for me as she had done when I was a child."[21] In 1865, a few

---

21. Escher, "She Calls Herself Betsey Stockton," 96.

months after the assassination of Lincoln, Betsey herself died. Her obituary was printed in both the *Freeman's Journal* and the *New York Observor*, recounting her many accomplishments. It records that at her funeral, in addition to "a highly respectable congregation of her own colour," were found representatives of the leading families of Princeton's white community and clergymen and friends from as far away as New York and Philadelphia. The service was conducted by John McLean, president of Princeton College, who preached the sermon, assisted by Charles Hodge from the seminary and Professor John Duffield of Nassau Hall.[22]

CIVIL WAR NURSE

Still another woman of the first part of the nineteenth century whose life was closely intertwined with Princeton Seminary, the wider Princeton community, and the great events of her day was *Margaret Elizabeth Breckinridge*.[23] She was born in Philadelphia on March 24, 1832. On her father's side she was related to the Breckinridge family of Kentucky. Her paternal grandfather, John Breckinridge, had served in the Senate and as attorney general of the United States under Thomas Jefferson. His second son, also named John Breckinridge, was Margaret's father. He had come to New Jersey to study at Princeton College. While a student, he became caught up in the religious revivals of 1815 that had swept through the college and seminary, and although originally intending to study law and follow in his father's footsteps, he changed his plans and decided after graduation to enter the seminary and study for a career in the ministry. He also met and asked for the hand of the eldest daughter, Margaret, of Princeton Seminary's second professor, Samuel Miller. They married in 1823. Elected and serving for a short time as chaplain of the House of Representatives, John Breckinridge resigned the position to return to his native Kentucky and serve as a pastor in Lexington. A few years later he was called to Baltimore for a second successful pastorate. In 1831 he was called to Philadelphia as the corresponding secretary of the board of education of the Presbyterian Church, and it was there that Margaret Elizabeth Breckinridge was born. In 1836 her father was elected to the faculty of Princeton Seminary to teach pastoral theology and missions, which brought the family back to the seminary campus again.

22. Transcription of obituary from *The New York Observor* 43 (Nov. 9, 1865): 355, in "Betsey Stockton" files, Women's History Project, Special Collections, Princeton Theological Seminary Library.
23. The biographical material in this section is taken from *Memorial of Margaret E. Breckinridge* (Philadelphia: J. B. Lippincott, 1865).

Margaret Miller Breckinridge, however, had long been suffering from ill health, and when young Margaret Elizabeth was just six years old, her mother died. Margaret Elizabeth was left in the care of her grandparents, Samuel and Sarah Miller, while her father undertook a fundraising tour on behalf of the Board of Foreign Missions. Just three years later her father died as well, at the age of forty-four, leaving behind Margaret, her brother, and two sisters. Margaret developed a penchant for reading and study, and she was a good letter writer and conversationalist. From her grandmother, Sarah Miller, she learned the habit of a regular time set apart each day for prayer and the devotional reading of Scripture. As her grandfather, Samuel Miller, lay dying in early 1850, the seventeen-year-old Margaret read to him from the Bible each day and listened to his words of religious reflection and instruction. It was that same year that she decided to join the local Presbyterian church.

When the Civil War broke out in 1861, Margaret decided to do what she could. She organized her Princeton friends into a Soldiers' Aid Society, which met regularly to knit and sew clothing items and gather various articles of food, such as pickles, dried fruit, and jellies, to send to the soldiers at the front and in hospitals. But eventually she wanted to do more, and in April 1862 she left home for the west, via Baltimore, where she went to learn the needed nursing skills. She began her work in the hospitals of Lexington, Kentucky. Toward the middle of July, the war reached her directly when a Confederate cavalry began raiding the Lexington area, followed by the invasion of a Confederate army, which held Lexington until early fall. When Lexington was finally freed from Confederate control, she was able to travel on to spend the winter with her brother, Samuel Miller Breckinridge, who had moved to Missouri, served in the Missouri legislature, and now was a circuit judge based in St. Louis. There she again took up her hospital work among the sick and wounded.

As demanding as her hospital work was, the most trying work she undertook was her service on the hospital boats that were sent down the Mississippi to bring up the sick and wounded from the various battlefields farther south. Together with a few other women volunteers, she made two such voyages, lasting about a month each. The boats went down the river empty or carrying soldiers rejoining their units, but on the return trip every corner was filled with the sick and dying, even the cabin floors and decks. Nursing care on these voyages was a twenty-four-hour-a-day job. Here is how she wrote about the situation in a letter home to her friends in Princeton:

> It would be impossible to describe the scene which presented itself to me as I stood in the door of the cabin. Lying on the floor with nothing under them but a tarpaulin and their blankets, were crowded fifty

men, many of them with death written on their faces; and looking through the half-open doors of the state-rooms we saw that they contained many more. Young, boyish faces, old and thin from suffering, great restless eyes that were fixed on nothing, incoherent ravings of those who were wild with fever, and hollow coughs on every side,— this and much more that I do not want to recall, was our welcome to our new work. . . . We asked each other, not in words, but in those fine electric thrills by which one soul questions another, "Can we bring strength and hope and comfort to these poor suffering men?" and the answer was, "Yes, by God's help we will."[24]

Contagious diseases threatened to spread to the whole boat. Typhoid fever was rampant. The intense cold weather was another trial for the men. On a second trip, in late winter, the problem was heavy rain. "The rain dashed through the roof and kept the beds so wet I was in despair," she wrote. The nurses improvised some "India-rubber cloth," which they cut into strips and spread over the men, moving it from place to place continually "to meet the new streams which trickled down in fresh places every moment." When the rain finally stopped, the nurses were exhausted and went back to their staterooms, only to find their own rooms full of water as well. Seventeen of their patients died on the first trip up the river, and twenty-one, on the second. Yet not every story was a sad one. "It was a happy thing to see many of those who seemed so wretched at first, reviving gradually under a little care and nursing." She informed her friends about how moved she was by the gratitude she had received from the men for her services, about the ministry she was able to accomplish as she prayed with the men and sang the familiar hymns for them that she had sung at home in Princeton, and how glad she was to be able to bring some comfort to friends and relatives of those who had died by telling them about "the last sad hours of those they love" and passing on to them the dying messages of love with which she had been entrusted.[25]

In March Margaret hoped to make a third voyage down the river, but her health was no longer up to it. She spent her time in the St. Louis hospitals, looked after a family of refugees, and helped organize sewing and knitting for the soldiers. Finally, with her strength failing and struggling with complications of the typhoid fever she had picked up in the course of her work in the army camps on the lower Mississippi, she determined to return east for a period of rest and recuperation. Over the next year she struggled to regain her health, and by the spring of 1864 was hoping to respond to a call for experienced nurses to attend to the casualties resulting from the battles in

24. Ibid., 67–68.
25. Ibid., 80, 61–62, 70–71, 74.

the Fredericksburg area. However, it was not to be. She experienced another relapse, and the final blow came when she learned of the death of her beloved brother-in-law, Colonel Peter A. Porter of Niagara Falls. Porter had died in the battle of Cold Harbor on the outskirts of Richmond. The last words heard from him were "Boys, follow me" as he led his New York State regiment in a charge against the Confederate entrenchments. Margaret traveled to Baltimore to join the family in accompanying the body home for burial in Niagara Falls, but the excitement over the death of her brother-in-law and the fatigue of the journey proved too much. Arriving in Niagara Falls, she once more became alarmingly ill, and on July 27, 1864, she died. She was buried in Oakwood Cemetery in Niagara, near the spot where the family had so recently buried her brother-in-law.

BENEFACTORS

While the stories told so far dealt with women in the immediate Princeton households of persons connected with the seminary, a very important part in the life of the seminary was played by women who lived some distance away but were interested in its program and success. As Samuel Miller wrote in his 1822 *Brief Account of the Rise, Progress and Present State of the Theological Seminary of the Presbyterian Church in the United States at Princeton,*

> The greater part . . . of the support which has been hitherto furnished to indigent Students, in this Institution, has been derived from the contributions of Female Cent Societies, in different parts of our Church. . . . A few pious females, by associating, and contributing annually two or three dollars each, may become the happy instruments of furnishing funds which will nearly, if not entirely, carry through the Seminary, a youth, who may be long an eminent herald of the cross, and a means of blessing to thousands.[26]

In addition to scholarship funds, these churchwomen's groups also donated articles of clothing, such as shirts and hand-knitted socks. In later years they would also sometimes furnish a dorm room.

There were also individuals who could individually contribute much more.

---

26. Samuel Miller, *A Brief Account of the Rise, Progress and Present State of the Theological Seminary of the Presbyterian Church in the United States at Princeton* (Philadelphia: A. Finley, 1822), 57. For further information about these Cent Societies and other early Presbyterian women's benevolence work, see Lois A. Boyd and R. Douglas Brackenridge, *Presbyterian Women in America: Two Centuries of a Quest for Status*, 2nd ed. (Westport, CT: Greenwood, 1996), 1–7.

Some of these were wealthy women. The first and second fully endowed scholarships set up for deserving students at Princeton Seminary were made possible by *Martha Banyar LeRoy* of New York City, a widow whose father and deceased husband had been prominent New York merchants and bankers. Another important woman donor of the nineteenth century was *Isabella Brown*. Her husband was the son of the founder of the first investment banking firm in the United States and was himself one of the founders and the treasurer of the Baltimore and Ohio Railroad. Following his death in 1859, Isabella donated the funds to build a much-needed new dormitory, Brown Hall, in the 1860s. It was the only building of significant size to be constructed in Princeton during the Civil War.

Mary McCrae Stuart was the wife of Robert Leighton Stuart and the sister-in-law of Alexander Stuart. The Stuarts were consistently among the most generous donors to Princeton Seminary throughout the nineteenth century, making substantial gifts for the general endowment, for operating expenses, for faculty housing, and for the establishment of the Stuart Chair in Philosophy. They also contributed books to the library and paid for the erection of the seminary's major classroom building, Stuart Hall. For twenty years Mary Stuart personally funded a faculty position in biblical theology. She was also active with a women's group at the Fifth Avenue Presbyterian Church in New York City, the Princeton Seminary Association of Ladies. They regularly raised funds for seminary needs (including a new reading room stocked with current periodicals for the parlor of Alexander Hall one year) and, for graduating students who could not afford it, provided cloth to have a proper suit made for preaching the gospel. When Mary McCrae Stuart died in 1891, her entire estate, valued at $5,000,000 at that time, was given almost entirely to charitable, educational, and religious institutions, many connected with the Presbyterian Church. The very first bequest in her will was a portrait of her husband, painted by Raimundo de Madrazo y Garreta (1841–1920), one of the foremost portrait artists of his day, whose paintings now hang in some of the finest art galleries in the world. "It is given," she wrote in her will, "to the Princeton Theological Seminary, to be kept and preserved in perpetuity in some place in the seminary."[27] It now hangs on the landing of Stuart Hall, matched with a portrait of Mary McCrae Stuart herself on the opposite wall. She also left to the seminary the funds for constructing Hodge Hall.

27. Photocopy of an undated newspaper article describing the will of Mary McCrae Stuart. "Mary McCrae Stuart" file, Women's History Project, Special Collections, Princeton Theological Seminary Library.

ADMINISTRATORS AND PROVIDERS OF HOSPITALITY

While some women wove their stories into the larger story of Princeton Seminary because of their connection to seminary-related households in Princeton, and others did so through their care and interest in the seminary from afar, still another set of women made themselves a part of the seminary story through seeing to students' needs on an everyday, practical basis. Unfortunately, of these women we often have scant knowledge. In 1847 the seminary constructed a refectory for student dining on its campus. A steward and his wife served this facility. Along with an apartment for the steward's family, the basement of this building also housed the seminary's infirmary, where sick students could be looked after by the steward's wife. As the century wore on and the refectory became less popular and eventually closed, students organized eating clubs. The very first of these was the Benham Club, founded in October 1879. It was named for *Anna Amelia Benham*, a Princeton widow who was glad to be asked to make regular meals by a small group of six Princeton Seminary students who had gotten tired of the refectory food. When news got out about what great meals she was preparing, the club expanded rapidly and soon other such eating clubs were formed as well. By 1881 Anna Amelia Benham had to move to a larger house to accommodate the students, and in 1894 even that house had to be expanded to seat everyone who had joined the club. She is remembered fondly in the official Benham Club history:

> She was an excellent housekeeper and business woman, with unusual commonsense and rarely devoted to her "boys" as she called them. She seldom saw them indeed, being occupied in the kitchen at meal times, but she knew them all and followed their course both in the Seminary and later with a genuine sympathy and pride that was almost motherly . . . all who were in the Club during her lifetime remember not only the overabundant supply of things she provided three times each day, unfailingly, year after year, and the unwearying patience that must have been sorely tried sometimes, but also the numberless little additions that showed she was mindful of the weather, the classroom, a holiday, a birthday, an examination or anything else that might affect the mood of the Club.[28]

At her death she bequeathed to the "Benham Club of Princeton" a sum of $500 and all the dining room furniture, dishes, table linen, silverware, sideboard, kitchen utensils, club pictures, "and my portrait in the parlor," and she expressed the hope "that the said Club may always continue in spirit and

---

28. *The Benham Club of Princeton, New Jersey* (Princeton, NJ: Club House, 95 Mercer Street, 1912), 23.

name as they are now."[29] Other club histories are not so extensive, but the Friars Club histories mention a Mrs. Vreeland from the 1890s and a Mrs. Johnson from the 1920s, the latter of whom the students of that generation remembered especially as "cook, boss, and mother."[30]

The first woman administrator at Princeton Theological Seminary was *Edna Hatfield*. Her career at the seminary spanned forty-five years. From 1914 until 1930 she served as the secretary to President Stevenson, the second president of Princeton Seminary (the office of president of the seminary was not established until 1902, when Francis Landey Patton was invited to become Princeton Seminary's first president). In 1930 Edna became the assistant registrar, serving until 1937 in that position, at which time she was then appointed assistant to the dean of students. In 1945 she was appointed registrar and continued in that position until her retirement in 1959. In addition to her regular duties, Edna Hatfield also served as private secretary to Professor Charles Erdman, helping him prepare his books for publication and providing any other assistance he required. The local newspaper, *Town Topics*, featured her as "Princeton's Woman of the Week" in their October 12, 1952, issue. After her death, a former doctoral student and later faculty member arranged to commission a portrait of her in memory of her devotion to the seminary and its work. He remembered especially how students would come to her for counsel and advice, and the long hours she gave preparing the seminary catalog for many years.[31] By the twentieth century other women support staff begin to be mentioned in the seminary records, particularly a series of single women who came to work in the library. The longest lasting of these was *Isabelle Stauffer*, who came as a temporary hire to do some special cataloging in the mid-1930s and ended up staying for over forty years.[32]

TWENTIETH-CENTURY FACULTY WIVES, STUDENTS, AND FACULTY

Faculty Wives

A highly revealing exploration of the rather heavy ministry expectations for pastors' wives in mid-twentieth-century American Protestant churches may

29. Ibid., 4.

30. *Musings from a Monastery: The Story of the Friars* (Princeton, NJ: The Friar Club, Twenty-Two Dickinson Street, 1952), 23.

31. Unpublished memoir by Daniel J. Theron. "Edna Hatfield" file, Women's History Project, Special Collections, Princeton Theological Seminary Library.

32. "I Was in the Brewery," *Alumni News* 18 (Autumn 1977): 25–26.

be found in a book published by *Carolyn Philips Blackwood*, the wife of Princeton Seminary's professor of homiletics, Andrew Blackwood. Written as a kind of guidebook for future ministers' wives and based on her own years of experience, *The Pastor's Wife* was published in 1951. Wives who were here in the late 1940s recall presentations concerning proper dress when answering the manse doorbell and reasons for avoiding sex on Saturday nights.[33] Carolyn Blackwood followed this work with an even broader set of reflections on the role of unordained women in the church in her 1955 volume *How to Be an Effective Church Woman*.[34] In the days of President Stevenson (1914–1936), a few student wives (there were very few) met with his wife, *Florence Day Stevenson*, and the wives of faculty members for socializing and prayer. When John Mackay came to Princeton Seminary as president in 1936, his wife, *Jane Wells Mackay*, organized this group into a formal Student Wives Fellowship, with just seven women. By the time John Mackay retired in 1959, the Student Wives Fellowship had approximately two hundred members.[35] They met for social occasions but also for Bible studies and for lectures on topics chosen by the wives and delivered by members of the seminary faculty or visiting missionaries and guest speakers. In 1953 a study group was established to look at the role of women in the church. Seminary wives joined with interested female students from the School of Christian Education to explore this topic.

Students

While women were a part of the seminary story to some extent in a variety of ways from the very beginning, there were no women students formally

33. Carolyn Philips Blackwood, *The Pastor's Wife* (Philadelphia: Westminster Press, 1951). This book touches on a wide range of social expectations of a minister's wife in a Protestant church at mid-twentieth century and makes clear how much real work of ministry a pastor's wife was doing and was expected to do in that period. Among the topics treated are homemaking, hostessing (complete with recipes), presiding at meetings, counseling, taking care of finances, offering "kindly criticism" to her husband, and dealing with criticism directed at her. In a subsection under the title "She fills many gaps," the prospective pastor's wife is told to be prepared to "attend all board meetings; lead many devotionals; help train the junior choir; sing occasionally in the adult choir; serve as a substitute teacher; play the organ when needed; teach mission study classes; organize cradle roll and church nursery; assist at bake sales and suppers; help with the husband's correspondence; run off the bulletins on duplicating machine; mail out notices of meetings, and so on. . . . "

34. Carolyn Philips Blackwood, *How to Be an Effective Church Woman* (Philadelphia: Westminster, 1955).

35. "Letters and Reflections from the Student Wives Fellowship, May 1959," John A. Mackay Collection, Special Collections, Princeton Theological Seminary Library, series 9, box 14.

enrolled in the first one hundred years. Beginning in the early teens of the twentieth century, the seminary catalog starts to occasionally list women as "partial" (or as we would say today, "part-time") students. Usually they were the wives of students or missionaries on furlough who had signed up for a course or two of special interest. In one case it was the daughter of a faculty member. It was understood that sometimes, beyond these officially recognized students, other wives would audit courses or attend a few lectures that interested them while their husbands were there for formal studies, even if they did not specifically enroll as part-time students. This would particularly be the case if they did not have the requisite college degree. We have informal accounts of women who would start to attend a course at the beginning of a term but then drop out for some reason, such as becoming pregnant or finding too many other things they wanted to do.

That changed in 1928, when *Muriel Van Orden* applied to come to the seminary with the intention of earning a degree.[36] At Radcliffe College she had been impressed with several teachers in women's colleges who had responsibility for teaching courses in history and Bible. She herself was a history major and had a strong interest in Bible study, and she desired to prepare herself for a similar position. Upon graduating from Radcliffe, she wrote to various schools and seminaries, trying to find a school that taught Hebrew and would accept her. Her search was fruitless until she drove down with her mother from their home in North Jersey to inquire about the program at Princeton Seminary. Her original interview with the male registrar was discouraging, but she then was invited to talk with J. Ross Stevenson, president of the seminary. He, in contrast to the registrar, was very welcoming. He explained that she should not expect to get a degree but that she would be welcome to audit courses. Muriel insisted that she did not simply want to audit courses but wished to take exams and work toward a degree. President Stevenson told her that he would have to take the matter up with the board of directors of the seminary.

Two weeks later she got a phone call to return to Princeton. The board had granted permission for her to enter in the regular program with the possibility of earning a degree, provided that several conditions were met. First, she was "not allowed to disturb the gentlemen taking classes." Second, she was expected to complete the full program of courses that the male students took, keeping up with them academically. Third, when it came time to graduate, all of the faculty would need to agree that she deserved a degree. Quite content

36. The biographical material in this section draws on several unpublished oral history transcripts in the "Muriel Van Orden Jennings" file, Women's History Project, Special Collections, Princeton Theological Seminary Library.

with these conditions, Muriel showed up at Princeton Seminary in the fall of 1928. By all reports her reception at the seminary was excellent. "Everyone was kind to me. Everyone was like a big brother to me," she later remembered. Of course housing was a problem, as there were only male dormitories. The first year she rented a small room with the family of the Scotsman who had charge of the seminary grounds. The second year she and another young woman shared a room over the old Princeton post office, where they could look outside their window and see Charles Lindbergh come in to pick up his mail each morning. At the end of her second year, President Stevenson arranged for her to rent an apartment with his Scottish secretary. There was also no common dining room for meals. Thursday was "Ladies Night" at the seminary eating clubs, and she could always count on an invitation to eat at one club or another. Faculty also would invite her for a meal from time to time. Otherwise, she purchased a meal ticket to eat at one of the local Princeton hotels five nights a week until, sharing the apartment in her last two years, she could prepare her own meals there. As there were no facilities in the classroom building for women at the time, President Stevenson gave her a key to his own washroom.

Faculty also tried to help her out in other ways. In those days classes were either Monday–Wednesday–Friday or Tuesday–Thursday–Saturday. Although tuition was free, she still had to meet her other expenses and had accepted a job at a Presbyterian church in Newark, teaching religious education classes, doing youth ministry, and holding special services at a home for unwed mothers, at the city jail, at a county hospital, and at the Newark "Home for Incurables," a residence for women who needed ongoing medical care. This meant taking a 3:00 p.m. train on Friday up to Newark and a return train that reached Princeton at 2:00 a.m. on Monday morning. As a result she missed an hour of Hebrew on Friday afternoon and all of her Saturday classes. The Hebrew professor, George Wailes, gave her extra help with her Hebrew studies and was so fond of her that he remained in touch with her regularly even after she graduated until shortly before he died. Professor Caspar Wistar Hodge, who taught systematic theology, told her, "Muriel, you have so much to do that you just take this book and read it and when you are finished I will give you an examination and this way you can make up for the year of systematic theology that you missed." President Stevenson also arranged for her to earn some extra money by teaching released-time religious education classes at the First Presbyterian Church in Trenton. This was a class of forty-eight seventh-graders who were being given time out of the regular school day to attend classes in religious instruction once a week. While the students enjoyed being free from their regular classroom, they were a bit on the rambunctious side. "They had no more interest in studying their Bible than they had in fleas," Muriel later remembered. "I think they would have liked fleas better. They came in tossing their hats in the air, just having a high old time." For the first three weeks of the class the church had tried three different male seminarians, none of whom was able to keep discipline. When they approached President Stevenson for "another man," the president recommended Muriel instead. By her own report, she quickly established order and then strove to present the material in a way that was appropriate to their grade level and caught their interest. She got to keep the job.

Muriel also tried to stir up social life at the seminary. She began to befriend two single young women who worked in the library, some faculty daughters, and other available young women. They organized a monthly hike on full-moon nights to which they would invite seminarians and especially some of the foreign students, and they would head up into the hills north of Princeton, where they would build a fire, roast marshmallows, and sing. Over three years she estimates that some ten couples found each other on these hikes and ended up marrying.

In her first year at the seminary, for about six months she dated a young seminarian named Carl McIntire, who would go on to become a well-known, fiery, fundamentalist radio preacher. "He was so opinionated, terribly so, but he was a marvelous ice skater, and I would put up with anything to go ice skating," she remembered. "He was the only person I ever knew who could walk with a girl around a lake on a moonlight night and fight the whole way. He would still be arguing when he said, 'Goodnight. I will see you in class tomorrow.' He was a real nice fellow but he sure had ideas of his own." Finding Princeton Seminary not fundamentalist enough, young McIntire left with a number of his classmates and Greek professor J. Gresham Machen at the end of his first year to found Westminster Seminary in Philadelphia, but he soon quarreled with that group as well and eventually founded his own separatist fundamentalist denomination and seminary.

In her second year Muriel was invited by Mrs. Stevenson to help out at receptions by pouring punch. One young man kept coming back for glass after glass at one of the receptions. "Who is this person?" she thought. "Doesn't he do anything besides drink punch? He has already had fifteen glasses." The young man was a new seminarian by the name of Harvey Jennings. She later discovered that he was also very eager to gather sticks for everyone for her marshmallow-roast outings and that his interest was not so much in the punch as in her. Over the course of the next few years, Muriel and Harvey got to know each other better and planned to marry after Harvey's graduation.

Muriel did outstandingly well in her studies at Princeton Seminary, and when she had completed the three-year program, the faculty was polled on whether she should be awarded a degree. All the faculty were in favor with the exception of one—in fact, the youngest of the faculty members—who had strong reservations about women receiving a theological degree.[37] As a result, she was not able to receive a degree with the rest of her class. However, since her fiancé Harvey Jennings had still one more year to complete before finishing his program, she decided to stay on for additional coursework. When she showed up to register for that final additional year, she was ushered into President Stevenson's office. Asking her to sit down, he explained that the objecting faculty member had resigned his position for health reasons. As a result, when Muriel Van Orden graduated from Princeton Seminary in 1932, she was not only the first woman graduate but the first person to take two degrees at the same time. She received both a bachelor's and a master's degree in theology that year, and a few weeks later she and Harvey Jennings were married.

Harvey and Muriel went on to a fruitful life of ministry together. In addition to serving congregations, they had a long-term connection with the Montrose Bible Conference in Pennsylvania. Regularly bringing young people to Montrose for youth gatherings, in 1940 they were named codirectors of the youth conference, positions that they held until 1966. In 1948 Muriel began a children's camp at Montrose as well, and by the 1950s scholarship funds were being raised to offer the camp experience for needy children from New York City. This allowed them to integrate the camp with children from various national and racial backgrounds and provided an opportunity for promoting greater interracial understanding. She and her husband also taught evening Bible classes for adults at the Hyde Park (Scranton) Bible Institute for many years.

An indication of how much Muriel had impressed her teachers at Princeton Seminary came when the seminary began its doctoral program in the early 1940s. They made a special effort to invite her to come and be one of the first students in this program. Although appreciating the offer, she felt that she had to turn the opportunity down. The Second World War was on, which meant that gas was rationed. Her husband needed the limited gas available to do parish and hospital visiting, making it difficult for her to commute to the seminary for classes. But a second reason, she felt, was even more compelling. She already had two degrees while her husband had only one. If anyone in the family should have the opportunity for further studies, she thought that it should be her husband. "I just did not feel that it was the right thing to do, so I did not accept the invitation. I did appreciate the offer very much,

37. Finley D. Jenkins outlined his arguments against the movement to license and ordain women in "The Self-Destruction of the Movement to License and Ordain Women," *The Presbyterian* (March 27, 1930).

however," she remembered. In 1981 she was honored with a special Service of Recognition for fifty years of children's and youth work at the Montrose Bible Conference.[38] In 1982 she received the Distinguished Alumni/ae Award from Princeton Theological Seminary.[39]

After Muriel Van Orden had opened the way, it would be another ten years before a second woman would apply to take the full degree program. *Eileen Bergsten Remington* graduated with a Princeton Seminary degree in the class of 1945. By the time she graduated, however, a major change had taken place regarding women at the seminary. This change involved the Tennent School of Christian Education, which moved from Philadelphia to the Princeton campus in 1944, offering a three-year Master of Religious Education degree. In 1947 the first class of six students graduated from the School of Christian Education at Princeton Seminary. Out of this first group of six, four eventually went into the mission field, serving in Japan, Brazil, Korea, and Cameroun. *Anna Jane Molden*, who received her MRE in 1952, was Princeton Seminary's first African American female student. Altogether, about 180 female students earned an MRE degree at Princeton Seminary between 1947 and 1970.

In 1956 the General Assembly of the Presbyterian Church U.S.A. opened the path for women to become ordained ministers, and slowly the number of women students coming to Princeton Seminary for full training as pastors would increase. Clearly, the "bastion of male dominance" was giving way to a new, more inclusive social form. But not until the 1970s would more women come for the BD (MDiv) degree than those coming for the more traditional women's degree in Christian education.

FACULTY

With the arrival of women students in the new MRE program in 1944, the seminary seems to have felt the need to include female instructors in Christian education on an adjunct or short-term basis. Over the years from 1946 through 1960, these included *Jessie Dell Crawford, Bertha Paulssen, Dorothy Fritz, Jean Boleyn Cassat, Dorothy Faye Kirkwood*, and *Harriet Prichard* (see appendix C for dates). Each of these women made important contributions beyond the seminary. Harriet Prichard, for example, founded the nonprofit

38. A brochure commemorating this event can be found in the "Muriel Van Orden Jennings" file, Women's History Project, Special Collections, Princeton Theological Seminary Library.

39. "on&off Campus," *inSpire* 5 (Summer/Fall 2000): 7.

organization Alternative Gifts International; in her twenty-three years as president, the organization raised over $424 million in support of more than one hundred nonprofit organizations in dozens of countries. *Freda Gardner,* who joined the faculty in 1962, would become the first long-term woman faculty member, but not until the 1970s would women faculty members be hired in areas beyond practical theology.

2

Princeton Theological Seminary Women Trailblazers

The ministries of the pioneering women of PTS described in the previous chapter have helped us to see a broader and deeper understanding of what constitutes ministry. We move now to contemporary trailblazers. They are lighting the way for the next generation of women struggling to lead the church into the future with renewed vigor and vision. This chapter consists of snapshots of ten women associated in different ways with Princeton Seminary.

Our resources for writing about these women included in most cases personal interviews, their books and articles, autobiographical materials, other published documents, and oral histories from their colleagues. Much more material could have been included on each person; we hope that these brief pieces will pique readers' interest to find out more about them. Nominations were gathered from PTS women networks, past and present longtime faculty and staff, contacts with professional organizations, judicatories, and publications. We learned of so many women associated with PTS who could qualify as trailblazers that it was difficult to select just ten individuals.

If you know of other women who are deserving of this designation, their stories and materials could be included in the PTS women's archives. Nominees must have some association with PTS, as alumnae, part of the staff or faculty, members of the board of trustees, service and support to the seminary, or other relationship to the seminary. You are invited to send these names to womeninministry@ptsem.edu for consideration for inclusion.

Our hope is that the recognition of these women's outstanding contributions in the church and the world will provide further occasions to celebrate and support women in ministry, broadly defined. The goal is that one day women will be praised not just for being the first woman in a given position but rather recognized as who they are apart from their gender.

THELMA DAVIDSON ADAIR

Village Mother of Harlem

Educator, Church Leader, Activist, Mother, Grandmother, Great-Grandmother

Dr. Thelma Adair's life has been marked by leadership in every endeavor during her long and fruitful life. This has included her work as a top-flight educator, including three decades as a professor at the City University of New York and service as a visiting professor at Princeton Seminary; a world-renowned church leader, especially in the Presbyterian Church; an advocate for human rights, peace, and justice issues; a writer; and a civil rights activist. She was described by one person as a "towering presence for so many African American women (and men)" and "what a preacher!!"[1]

No doubt Adair's passions for civil rights were born through her living in Harlem for most of her life. Through the decades she worked in the civil rights movement with political leaders such as Rev. Dr. Martin Luther King Jr. and Presidents John F. Kennedy, Lyndon B. Johnson, and Jimmy Carter "to bring about social justice and economic empowerment."

1. Absent firsthand information about Adair, the following were used: (1) "A Celebration of 90 Years of the Life, Legacy, Leadership and Love of Dr. Thelma Davidson Adair," Congressional Record vol. 157, no. 50 (April 7, 2011), E659–E660 (www.gpo .gov/fdsys/pkg/CREC-2011-04-07/html/CREC-2011-04-07-pt1-PgE659-5.htm); (2) "Thelma Adair," Board of National Missions, United Presbyterian Church, U.S.A., and the Presbyterian Board of Christian Education fact sheet, 1968; (3) perspectives from Peter Paris, professor emeritus, Princeton Theological Seminary; and from Michael Livingston, executive pastor, Riverside Church, New York City.

She was a part of President Bill Clinton's delegation that attended the historic inauguration of South African President Nelson Mandela. Her indomitable involvement in these issues is illustrated by the fact that in March 2015, at age ninety-six, she was invited to join in the fiftieth anniversary of the Selma March with President Obama and other national figures.

She was also active in the church and the community. Thelma, with her husband, the Rev. Dr. Arthur Eugene Adair, the founder and senior pastor (1943–1979) of Mount Morris Ascension Presbyterian Church in New York City, became leaders in Harlem during its renaissance. They became a crucial focal point of African American leadership in the empowerment and liberation movements, and they founded the Arthur Eugene and Thelma Adair Community Life Center, Inc. Their Head Start initiative served over 250 children and families annually in five Head Start centers in Harlem. As the church prepares now for the thirty-fifth anniversary of its latest incarnation (it has experienced at least three mergers since its founding in 1905–1906), the Adairs are still fondly remembered. Eugene Adair died in 1979, but Thelma still lives in the community. She played an active role in the Council on Church and Race (COCAR), which was the vanguard for racial justice in the Presbyterian Church (U.S.A.) for a quarter of a century, as well in the creation of the Self-Development of People's program. In addition, she served on the Presbyterian Board of Christian Education in 1964–1965 and on the boards of trustees of the Interdenominational Theological Center and Johnson C. Smith Theological Seminary. In 1976 she became the first African American woman to be elected moderator of the UPCUSA, at its 188th Assembly.

Her leadership was so outstanding that she was asked to write the introduction to the 1987 special edition of *Church and Society*, dedicated to the memory of Edler G. Hawkins, the first African American moderator of the Presbyterian Church (U.S.A.).

For her future teaching and scholarship, Adair was equipped by her education, holding MEd and DEd degrees from Teacher's College, Columbia University, and undergraduate degrees from Barber-Scotia Junior College and Bennett College in the Carolinas. Her specialty was childhood education, but she also trained members of the U.S. Peace Corps for service in Africa, South America, and the Caribbean. She was a professor at the City University of New York's Queens College (thirty-one years of teaching); an instructor in religious education at Union Theological Seminary, the University of Ghana, and Columbia University; and a visiting professor at Princeton Theological Seminary in Christian education from 1974 to 1978.

SANG CHANG

Born a Feminist in Male-Dominated Korea

Transforming Education, Church, and Politics

The Rev. Dr. Sang Chang has worked tirelessly to empower women in Korea, serving as president of Ewha Womans University, acting prime minister of South Korea, and founding member of the Korean Association of Women Theologians. She received the PTS Distinguished Alumni/ae Award in 2003. From 2010 to 2015 she served on the PTS board of trustees, becoming the first non–North American trustee, and in 2013 she was elected president for Asia of the World Council of Churches.

Born to a Christian family in North Korea, church was central to daily life. Political pressures caused her widowed mother to flee to South Korea when Sang was in grammar school, and the subsequent outbreak of the Korean War meant extreme poverty and hunger for them. Her mother recognized her daughter's academic potential and insisted on educating her beyond the primary-school level typical for most girls at the time. Already as a child, she was outspoken and showed a feminist spirit. She was easily the smartest in her elementary class and also tall and strong, so she expected to be chosen "class leader"; she objected when her teacher chose a boy instead of her. The teacher told her to "lead the boy," and Sang figured out how to become the de facto leader.

She showed exceptional talent in mathematics and matriculated at the prestigious Ewha Womans University in Seoul with a full scholarship. Once there, she felt an inner calling to study theology, but the university administration insisted that she complete her mathematics degree. After graduation, she worked in evangelism in poor neighborhoods and taught mathematics at Ewha. Yet her desire to study theology persisted. After graduate work in theology at Yonsei University, she came to the United States for further study at Yale and then entered the New Testament doctoral program at Princeton Seminary. At PTS she continued to speak her mind. Her dissertation proposal was not immediately accepted because the review committee did not grasp her use of a mathematical term; she went to the dean, insisting that the term was appropriate for her project and suggesting that her idea would have been taken more seriously if it had come from a white man instead of a Korean woman. The proposal was reconsidered and approved. Her husband (Dr. Joon Suhr Park) was a PhD student in Old Testament at the same time, and their older son was born during their studies; having a pregnant Korean woman serving as a teaching fellow was certainly a "first" for PTS in the 1970s!

After graduating from PTS in 1977, she returned to Korea and joined the faculty in religious studies (New Testament) at her alma mater Ewha (the largest university for women in the world), where her administrative abilities were soon noticed. She served in six senior administrative posts before becoming president of the university in 1996.

Over the years, her leadership in academia, church, and society extended far beyond Ewha. She served as chair of the Korean Council for Presidents of Private Universities. Ordained in 1988 by the Presbyterian Church in the Republic of Korea, she was a founding member of the Korean Association of Women Theologians. She advocated for the rights of Korean sex workers and served as a vice president of the National Council of Churches in Korea. She became active in Korean politics and was elected leader of her party. In 2002 President Dae Jung Kim appointed her as acting prime minister. Political controversy over the appointment was heightened because of her gender, and eventually her nomination was not confirmed; but her courageous acceptance of the appointment paved the way for other women.

JANE DEMPSEY DOUGLASS

Repeatedly Surprised by New Opportunities to Work for Justice

Church historian and global ecumenist Dr. Jane Dempsey Douglass has advocated for justice throughout her life, especially for gender justice. Discouraged by segregationist attitudes in the congregation of her youth, she briefly gave up on the church until she discovered antiracism Christian activists in her college community. She fell in love with history when she realized that "real history writing was about solving mysteries."

While a senior and exploring future options, she was surprised to receive a letter inviting her to do a Presbyterian internship year in Geneva, Switzerland. There she took her first church history course, and in Coudekerque-Branche, France, a gritty industrial suburb of Dunkerque on the North Sea, she had her first encounter with a Christian social service organization witnessing to the gospel in the midst of abject poverty. Toward the end of that year, again with no next step in place, she was surprised by another letter, this one inviting her to become associate director in a Presbyterian student center at the University of Missouri. She arrived as a twenty-two-year-old with no experience, only to discover that the senior chaplain had resigned and that she was in charge of the entire program! The program thrived. She led World Council of Churches (WCC) work camps in a black sharecropper village and a gun-infested urban neighborhood. Although not seeking ordination to Word and Sacrament herself, she spoke courageously on behalf of women's ordination in a presbytery that then voted unanimously against her views.

Eventually, her love of history led her to graduate study in church history at Harvard. In an unhappy surprise, the professor with whom she had thought to study never managed to distinguish her from the secretaries, so she sought out a more supportive adviser. She became the first woman ever to serve as a teaching fellow at Harvard Divinity School, and in 1963 she was the first woman to receive a Harvard University doctorate in religion.

She joined the faculty of Claremont School of Theology and Claremont Graduate University and became active in a local Presbyterian congregation, where she met her economist husband, who was also a professor. Soon the family included three small children. Fortunately, Claremont's flexible class hours allowed her to teach while the children were sleeping. Surprised by questions about the history of women in the church and about the global church, she said, "Let's learn together," and the curriculum changed. As the first woman president of the American Society of Church History, she gave her inaugural lecture on the then virtually unknown Genevan reformer Marie Dentiere. After the lecture a surprised colleague said to her, "What happened? You used to do real history." But she was of course doing real history: Dentiere's name is now engraved on the famous Wall of the Reformers in Geneva.

In 1983 Douglass gave the Warfield Lectures at Princeton Seminary and shortly thereafter received yet a third unexpected letter, this one inviting her to join the PTS faculty. She was appointed as the first female full professor and immediately joined with others to press issues of importance to women on campus.

After many years of global ecumenical work, she was elected in 1989 as one of three vice presidents of the World Alliance of Reformed Churches. A year later the president unexpectedly resigned, and to her astonishment Douglass, a woman from North America, was chosen to preside over this predominantly male organization in which three-quarters of the member churches were in the global South. In this and subsequent posts she worked tirelessly on behalf of women, initiating women's conferences across the globe that considered issues not just of women's ordination but also of women's health, safety, and rights in family and workplace. Women at Princeton and throughout the world have been blessed by her leadership.

FREDA GARDNER

Advocate for Early Women Students at PTS

Dr. Freda Gardner was the first woman to hold a long-term appointment to the Princeton Seminary faculty (1961–1992). She has been a tireless advocate for Christian education in the church, and her support was central to the survival of women students at PTS from the 1960s onward.

Gardner grew up in a small town in upstate New York, daughter of an elementary school principal and a night duty nurse, attending a tiny church. Not liking needles, she chose teaching and taught sixth grade in public schools for several years. Although she had never heard of a Christian educator or a church that had one, when she learned of the Presbyterian School of Christian Education (PSCE, at that time called the Assembly School for Lay Workers), she felt God's nudge and enrolled. She was one of only two "Yankees" in the school where everyone was part of the interconnected old southern Presbyterian "cousin system" tradition. Although it was a difficult adjustment, she knew that she had found her life calling.

After graduation she became the director of Christian education in a Presbyterian church in Plainfield, New Jersey. When the church was without ordained clergy, interim preachers from the PTS faculty filled the pulpit. Thus PTS came to know her work and in 1961 invited her to join the faculty in Christian education.

For the next nine years she was the only woman on the faculty. Her apartment was in Tennent Hall, then the only dormitory for female students. She and the graduating women played late evening hide-and-seek in their caps and gowns on the Princeton Battlefield. She faced down male students who spoke in class of church women's organizations as "the stitch and bitch club" (those men later apologized and became lifelong friends); she laughed to herself when the faculty retreat sign-up sheet asked her to choose a preferred faculty roommate; she was less happy when she arrived for her assignment to serve Communion in Miller Chapel, only to be told that she was not needed because the other woman invited to serve could not make it. She does not recall whether she only thought or said aloud, "Do they think the chapel will tip over if only one side is served by a woman?"

She arranged gatherings for entering MDiv women to share their stories in the era when most of them had never heard a woman preach or met a female pastor. She supported the women students when they organized the Women's Center in the early 1970s and insisted that it needed a physical space. She persuaded the seminary president to establish a faculty committee on Women in Church and Ministry and also to establish the annual Women in Church and Ministry Lectureship. With Professor Katharine Sakenfeld she established the first PTS course in women's studies in 1976. She cared about justice in every venue, not just for women. The seminary president once spoke of her (to her embarrassment) as "the conscience of the faculty."

Her influence extended far beyond the seminary. An ordained Presbyterian ruling elder, she was active in her local congregation, gave workshops nationwide, and served multiple terms on the board of PSCE. In 1981 she was chosen Educator of the Year by the Association of Presbyterian Church Educators. In 1999 she was elected moderator of the PC(USA). Known as a personal supporter of gay and lesbian ordination, she graciously balanced her own views with the official nonaffirming stance of the denomination as she visited countless congregations. Now living again in upstate New York, she has been instrumental in establishing the Capital Region Theological Center, an interdenominational organization bringing high-quality continuing education events to an underserved area.

PATRICIA BUDD KEPLER

Pioneer Pastor, Champion for Inclusive Theology

The Rev. Patricia Kepler has managed to achieve what few have, that is, to pastor churches and work in education in the same geographic area for over forty years. She is an active member of the Boston Presbytery, living in Arlington, Massachusetts, with her husband. She was one of three women to graduate with a BD from Princeton Seminary in 1958, and later a ThM in 1967.

She has been a tireless champion for the recognition and empowerment of women in all spheres. She answered God's clarion call to proclaim the importance of feminist theological reflection within the framework of a broader inclusive theology. She embraced diversity and pursued justice throughout her ministry, for women and men seeking wholeness, minorities struggling against prejudice, Palestinians fighting oppression, middle-class Americans one job away from economic disaster, and peacemakers working to prevent pain, poverty, and destruction. In the midst of her pastorates she published several books, so she is both a scholar and pastor.

She was licensed to preach in 1958 by the Philadelphia Presbytery. Her ministry began as pastor of an African American church, Westminster Presbyterian of Manalapan, New Jersey, in 1961, and in 1964 she was ordained by the Monmouth Presbytery. She and her husband Thomas were the first clergy couple to graduate from PTS. Together they have three grown sons.

In 1968 she was called to serve as director of the Women's Program in the Board of Christian Education of the United Presbyterian Church U.S.A., and later was staff to United Presbyterian Women and then to the Task Force on Women. Her work nationally for the Presbyterian Church included establishing regional task forces on women and working with Church-Employed Women and the Women in Leadership Initiative. These were trailblazing years, as women worked for acceptance at all levels of church and society, a struggle not for the faint-hearted.

Kepler's next ministry was in the prestigious and challenging position as the first director of ministerial studies at Harvard University Divinity School in 1973. After five years of strengthening that program, serving students of many different Christian traditions, and teaching courses in the field of practical ministry, she returned to her first love—parish work.

Kepler served the Presbyterian Church of Sudbury as an interim pastor and then was pastor of Clarendon Hill Presbyterian Church in Somerville, Massachusetts, for twenty years. In the 1980s, through the Clarendon Hill church she reached out to Palestinian and Lebanese communities, which led to advocacy and leadership through the Synod of the Northeast. The church extended its international ministry to include people from Africa as well as becoming a More Light congregation that advocated for LGBT rights and a more inclusive ethic of sexuality.

Her last years of ministry have been as the interim university chaplain at Tufts University and the copastor at Good Shepherd Presbyterian Church and First Presbyterian Church of Waltham, Massachusetts.

Over the years came a growing concern for liberal churches' waning membership and a need for a theology capable of reclaiming the Christian church from its right-wing captivity and image. The justice causes that she supported seemed by necessity to be driven more by social/ethical concerns than by doctrinal shifts in theological perspectives.

During these past decades she navigated the controversial issues that have challenged the Presbyterian Church and society by connecting and engaging with the gifts and vision of many others, having a compassionate pastoral ministry, paying attention to wise administration, and above all, being supported by God's grace and persistent prodding and guidance.

When asked what advice she would give to future women pastors, she responded, "Be true to yourself and open to the Spirit"—certainly the leitmotif of her life.

INN SOOK LEE

*Crossing Gender
and Cultural Barriers*

To understand why Dr. Inn Sook Lee became a trailblazer, one must know the story of her family. She grew up in South Korea in a home of devout Christian parents. Her father was a Presbyterian minister, chaplain, and teacher at Taegu High School. Her mother, the daughter of a Presbyterian minister, wanted to attend the Taegu mission school because she heard women speaking from the pulpit. She was highly educated and became a teacher and church worker. They founded an orphanage for two hundred children, ages ten to seventeen, and twenty staff, who were displaced by the war from North Korea. The family lived in Taegu, but more accurately she and her five brothers lived in the church, as weekend all-day services began at 4:30 a.m. Because her parents followed God's leading in their lives, they encouraged her to follow God's call wherever it might lead.

Beginning as a sixth-grader, Inn Sook assisted her parents in both the orphanage and the church. She directed the annual Christmas pageant and taught music from different countries with dance movements, as well as performing in dance competitions. She is truly a daughter of the church. As she stated, "God was preparing me from the beginning."

What God was preparing her for was a series of firsts. This was possible because she followed her own advice, which she offers to Korean women who want to work in the church. To the church she says, "Give them a chance," and to the women she says, "When the opportunity comes, just take and work it." Her career is an inspiration to many who want to follow God's leading. Her soft-spoken and gentle demeanor belies her resolve to break down all the gender and cultural barriers that a person of lesser resolve might not have had the courage to do. She graduated from Yonsei University in 1960, one of the few women (one hundred versus seven thousand men)—though the women won all the top honors!

Upon graduation, she came to the United States for further education and married Sang Lee after a five-year international correspondence. They are a couple who supported each other's educational and career pursuits. Sang Hyun Lee was the Kyung-Chik Han Professor of Systematic Theology at Princeton Theological Seminary, and Inn Sook became the first Asian woman professor and the director of the Master of Arts in Pastoral Care and Counseling Program at New York Theological Seminary (NYTS, 1986–1991) and was then a professor at New Brunswick Theological Seminary (1991–1997) and an adjunct professor of Christian education at Princeton Theological Seminary (1989–2011).

It was her work at NYTS that was groundbreaking, as she launched the first bilingual Korean/English MDiv program. The students were predominantly first-generation Korean male pastors, and it was the first time that they had been taught by a woman. But the pastors wanted an American MDiv degree, so they accepted her because of all her educational credentials (MA and EdD, Columbia University, and MS, University of Michigan) and her multiple scholarly publications. In addition, her standing in the Korean American community was stellar. She was the president of a number of organizations, including the National Korean American Presbyterian Women and the National Korean American Church Women United, an elder in the Princeton Korean Presbyterian Church, and the founder of the Korean School of Princeton. And, as she adds with a smile, "Being the wife of Sang Lee was an assurance to these male pastors." In short, she was a woman working in a man's world, crossing two cultures with grace and assurance, and always true to God's call in her life.

MERCY AMBA ODUYOYE

Mother of African Women's Theology: "The Circle"

In the 1994–1995 academic year, Princeton Seminary was blessed to have Dr. Mercy Amba Oduyoye serving as the John A. Mackay Visiting Professor of World Christianity, teaching courses on African culture, missions, theology, and literature, including the course Women, Religion, and Culture in Africa, based on the writings of African women theologians. It is our honor to count this legendary African leader among our PTS women and to include her among our trailblazers.

Born in Ghana in 1934, thus in the era of British rule, she experienced firsthand the pain and pressures, joys and tragedies, of the transition to independence in her country and in sub-Saharan Africa generally. She helped to raise her younger siblings before entering university herself in Ghana and then doing postgraduate work in theology at Cambridge University. A lifelong Methodist, she has an ecumenical focus and a heart for women and their place in church and society in African cultures.

Her ecumenical involvement has been wide-ranging, serving a term as chair of the World Student Christian Federation (1973–1977), as youth secretary for the All Africa Conference of Churches (1970–1974), and over the years holding various posts with the WCC. With the WCC she worked with Paulo Freire in the Education Department, then as deputy general secretary for Programme Planning and Coordination (1987–1994), the first woman from sub-Saharan Africa to hold this high position.

As African Christian theologies were emerging in the 1970s, Oduyoye recognized early on that the male theologians were not taking account of the patriarchal aspects of African cultural traditions. So she began to dream of an organization of African women theologians. Of her many achievements, perhaps the most significant is the bringing to fruition of this dream. After fifteen years of conversations with women across Africa, in 1988 she convened a planning committee. Under her leadership they organized the inaugural session of the Circle of Concerned African Women Theologians (popularly known now as "the Circle") held in Accra in 1989. Seventy women attended and heard her keynote address calling for a women's theology that would be distinctly African while still recognizing enormous diversity of local needs and perspectives. Because of this leadership she has been described as the "mother of African Women's Theology." Begun by Christian women, the Circle today also embraces Muslim and Jewish women and women affiliated with indigenous African religions. As of 2015 it counted a membership of over six hundred. It supports and encourages younger African women theologians and has many regional and local branches. It sponsors both regional and major Africa-wide conferences on topics of concern to women. Following Oduyoye's example, members of the Circle understand themselves to be activist theologians; beyond research, writing, and publishing on women's issues, the members also support one another and their communities of women in active work for social justice.

Oduyoye's work is also significant for its global reach, as she continues to travel and speak internationally. She introduces African women's theology to audiences far beyond Africa, and she graciously helps Western women to recognize ways in which their work may perpetuate inaccurate perceptions of African women. Author of many books and more than eighty articles, she has been awarded ten honorary doctorates from institutions on the continents of Asia, Africa, Europe, and North America, and she received the 2001 Outstanding Service in Mentoring of Women Award from the Society of Biblical Literature.

In her "retirement" she is developing an Institute of Women in Religion and Culture at Trinity Theological Seminary, Legon, Ghana, and establishing major program initiatives concerning gender justice and human rights generally.

ANNA MAY SAY PA

"Ya-bah-deh" (It Is Possible)
in the Face of Repression

Recipient of the Princeton Seminary Distinguished Alumni/ae Award in 2010, Dr. Anna May Say Pa was born into a Christian family in Myanmar (then Burma), where Christians represent less than 10 percent of the population. The family belonged to an ethnic minority group called the Karen. In 1962, just as she was completing her university education, a military coup gained power and drove all foreigners, especially Christian missionaries, out of the country and also prohibited the study of English. Fortunately, she had already studied in English and was able to pursue her dream of becoming a church leader by immediately enrolling in a two-year master's degree program in religious education at the Myanmar Institute of Theology (MIT), a Baptist institution on the outskirts of Yangon, where 40 percent of the faculty had been foreign missionaries expelled by the military government.

Say Pa's remarkable ability was noticed; new local faculty were needed; and immediately upon graduation she began a fifteen-year stint as lecturer in biblical studies, serving also for five years as dean. In 1979 she arrived at Princeton Seminary, having incredibly been able to obtain a passport from the military dictatorship that allowed her to exit Myanmar. She earned her PhD in Old Testament in 1989 with a dissertation on Second Isaiah's view of Israel's relation to other nations and their gods, a topic of direct relevance to her future work in a predominantly Buddhist country.

She returned home to MIT, now her country's premier theological school, and immediately became vice principal while also resuming her teaching in Old Testament. She served as principal (president) from 1998 until her retirement in 2006. During those years she led the way to establish four new degree programs. She guided the school toward a new perspective on Christian mission, stepping back from denigrating Buddhist and other religious traditions while giving more attention to interreligious dialogue. At the same time, she became a tireless advocate for feminism within a very traditional patriarchal culture and church. Courses in all aspects of feminist interpretation were introduced for all degree programs. As early as 1997 three of the senior officers of the school were women, as were half of the faculty and nearly 45 percent of the students.

Her oft-stated determination in the face of great odds, "Ya-bah-deh" (It IS possible), enabled MIT to survive and even thrive through the post-1988 era of severe repression under the dictatorship's State Law and Order Restoration Committee (SLORC), walking a fine line of resistance under the radar. Government personnel regularly listened in on lectures and sermons. Once she was detained for a terrifying interrogation by a military intelligence officer because of a "subversive" sermon she preached on Genesis 1:27–28 titled "In God's Image." Her "error" was her suggestion that people should be free to fulfill God's plan for their lives.

Say Pa held leadership posts in many national and international Baptist and ecumenical organizations, among them World Vision Myanmar, the Central Committee of the Christian Conference of Asia, and the World Council of Churches, and in particular led numerous women's advocacy commissions. She served as editor of several theological journals in Myanmar and founded a feminist journal, *Dee Hline Than* (*Sound of Waves*), now published in both Burmese and English. Each issue takes on challenges facing women in Myanmar, such as health, education, work, environment, or violence in the home. Now retired from MIT, she is based in the United States to provide academic leadership for Burmese immigrant religious education programs sponsored by the American Baptist Churches U.S.A. and the Karen Baptist Convention, U.S.A.

ANSLEY COE THROCKMORTON

Overcoming Naysayers on the Journey to Many Firsts in the Church and Seminary

Rev. Dr. Ansley Coe Throckmorton followed God's call to become a director of Christian education, pastor, seminary president, and the vice president of the

World Alliance of Reformed Churches. She also initiated the first inclusive-language hymnal.[2]

Born into a long line of ministers that included her father, she grew up loving the church. Drawn to Scripture at an early age, she majored in biblical studies and religion at Wellesley. She matriculated at PTS in 1952 while her husband, New Testament scholar Burton Throckmorton, was teaching at Princeton University. She experienced PTS as academically superb in theology, biblical studies, and ethics. The Throckmortons moved to Maine in 1954 when he was offered a professorship at Bangor Theological Seminary (BTS). When their children were seven and five years old, she completed her theological degree at BTS in 1964.

Throckmorton fell in love with the idea of becoming a pastor before fully realizing "how impossible that was." Her deep hunger to become ordained was met with a rejection that was all too common in the church at the time. The 1970s, however, became a decade of explosive change for women, a time when "all of us were trailblazers." Heroic men emerged, working at making room for women in the ordination circle, men such as Peter Mercer, senior minister of the Hammond Street Congregational Church in Bangor, who faithfully encouraged her ministry. As the first director of education in that congregation, she was subsequently ordained as associate minister. Eventually she became its senior pastor; hence she was the first woman in the United Church of Christ to lead a multiple-staff church. As the congregational vote was not unanimous, her first pastoral visits were to the naysayers. She promised them that she would be the best minister she could be. A note followed from a disgruntled church member, announcing the withdrawal of his financial pledge. Throckmorton discovered that the hastily withdrawn pledge amounted to one dollar per week, hardly a budget-breaking loss. She never held a grudge, however, and was clear throughout her ministry that in the heart of a pastor, there is no room for resentment.

While serving the church in Bangor, in 1982 she became the vice president of the World Alliance of Reformed Churches, the only woman serving on the alliance at the time. In this role, she became the first woman to visit the head of the Eastern Orthodox Church, who did not before that moment allow women in his presence. She then became the general secretary of the Division of Education and Publication for the United Church of Christ, and during that time she took the lead in the creation of the first fully inclusive-language hymnal, the *New Century Hymnal*. While the creation of this controversial

---

2. This account is based on a personal interview of Throckmorton conducted and written by Sarah Foulger, pastor of Congregational Church of Boothbay Harbor, Maine.

hymnal was a scarring experience, she considers it to be her greatest accomplishment. In 1995 Throckmorton became the first female president of Bangor Theological Seminary (founded in 1814), where for five years she offered leadership that was both powerful and pastoral.

Throckmorton attributes her successes, in part, to timing—that is, being part of the explosive 1970s—and to her husband, an ardent feminist known for his work on inclusive language. She is grateful as well to all those heroes who made room for women, who took a stand for women in ministry, whether in seminary, in the church, or in their own families. Her advice for women preparing for a career in ministry was "Be the best possible minister you can be. If you do this, the backbone of the church will stand with you."

RENITA J. WEEMS

Womanist Scholar and
"Midwife of the Inner Wisdom"

Completing her PhD degree at Princeton Seminary in 1989, Rev. Dr. Renita J. Weems became the first African American woman anywhere to earn a doctorate in Old Testament studies. Having received her MDiv from Princeton Seminary in 1983, she has been an ordained elder in the African American Episcopal Church since 1984. First in her family to graduate from college, an avid quilter and bicyclist, Weems has had a distinguished career as professor, administrator, pastor, and author that continues to offer encouragement and empowerment to women of all backgrounds, especially to women of color. Her biography appears in *Black Stars: African-American Religious Leaders,*[3] alongside such impressive figures as Adam Clayton Powell, Elijah Muhammad, Sojourner Truth, Howard Thurman, and Dr. Martin Luther King Jr.

Her groundbreaking PhD dissertation took on a "women's issue" when most women students were advised not to do so and many male faculty were

---

3. Jim Haskins and Kathleen Benson, *Black Stars: African-American Religious Leaders* (San Francisco: Jossey-Bass, 2008).

uncertain or uncomfortable advising such topics. She analyzed marriage imagery in the Hebrew prophets, developing challenging and often painful insights into the use of this metaphor. Her research moved beyond traditional scholarship, which looked only at the "love" side of the marriage metaphor, to point out the violence associated with this biblical imagery. Her volume *Battered Love: Marriage, Sex, and Violence in the Hebrew Prophets*[4] brought this important work to a wide audience, with powerful hermeneutical reflection on implications for contemporary understandings of God and of marriage.

Her outstanding scholarship enriched her career of teaching and other service. First teaching at Vanderbilt, then at Spelman College, she is currently vice president of academic affairs and professor of biblical studies at American Baptist College, in Nashville, Tennessee. This historically black college continues to prepare a predominantly African American student population for leadership, service, and social justice in the world. In addition to her academic leadership, she ministers along with her husband at the Ray of Hope Community Church in Nashville. Widely sought out as inspirational speaker and academic lecturer, she was the first African American woman to give Yale University's prestigious Beecher lectures in 2008.

While still writing her dissertation, she published *Just a Sister Away: A Womanist Vision of Women's Relationships in the Bible.*[5] Her chapter on Hagar and Sarah, highlighting the contexts of slavery and of contemporary relations between black and white women, has become a classic that has been assigned to generations of seminary students. Women and men of all races and ethnicities have been awakened through her work to see Hagar the Egyptian slave as a full human being to whom God spoke directly.

This book inaugurated a second major trajectory of her work, in which she movingly "midwifes" her readers' birthing of their own inner wisdom. Her writing, lecturing, and preaching continue to focus on spirituality, especially women's spirituality. She draws deeply on resources from Scripture and literature, but most strikingly, she generously shares with her readers her own intimate personal stories of faith and doubt, acceptance and rejection, growing up, marriage, and motherhood. Among her publications, *Listening for God: A Minister's Journey through Silence and Doubt*[6] won the Wilbur Award, and her bestselling *Showing Mary: How Women Can Share Prayers, Wisdom, and*

---

4. Renita J. Weems, *Battered Love: Marriage, Sex, and Violence in the Hebrew Prophets* (Minneapolis: Fortress Press, 1995).

5. Renita J. Weems, *Just a Sister Away: A Womanist Vision of Women's Relationships in the Bible* (San Diego, CA: LuraMedia, 1988).

6. Renita J. Weems, *Listening for God: A Minister's Journey through Silence and Doubt* (New York: Touchstone, 1999).

the Blessings of God[7] received the Best Inspirational Book of 2004 Award from *Black Issues Book Review*. Whether in academia or in the pulpit, whether in public speaking or in writing, her beautifully crafted and compelling words invite and strengthen audiences to explore their own hopes and fears, call upon women to support and empower one another, and show them pathways to do so.

7. Renita J. Weems, *Showing Mary: How Women Can Share Prayers, Wisdom, and the Blessings of God* (New York: Warner Books, 2002).

PART II

One Ministry, Many Forms: Women's Voices

INTRODUCTION

"God does not call the qualified but qualifies the called."

This quote from one of our first-person stories of ministry sets the tone for this section of our book.[1] Through their accounts of call, spiritual journey, and ministry, it is clear how God has equipped these women for the many challenges faced and the varieties of vocation, under the banner of Christ's leading. It is inspiring to read of the rocky roads of some, the relatively smooth sailing of others, the tenacity of all those who in the face of doors closed to women found a window to new and unexpected avenues of service.

These PTS women were selected to tell their stories not because they are famous or are personally known to the authors. Instead, through extensive research we identified a cross section of women from the seminary's database of over three thousand alumnae and other women associated with PTS and targeted twenty different categories of ministry. We then, with the expert help of several PTS student research assistants, located more detailed information on many individuals, finally creating a list of seventy-five candidates from whom a small advisory committee helped us to select twenty-eight to tell their stories. They are diverse in many respects: Black, Anglo, Latina, Native American, and Asian; ages ranging from the early thirties to mid-sixties; numerous denominations in addition to PC(USA); and involvement in

1. Charlotte Ruth Mallory, "Surrounded by a Cloud of Witnesses while Preaching Release to the Captives," p. 83 below.

many kinds of ministry. These ministries are organized into six chapters: Pastoral Leadership and Christian Formation; Chaplaincy; Higher Education: College, Seminary, Mission Field; Church and Seminary Administration; Creative Expression; and Innovative Ministries. In the invitational letters, we asked if each considers her work as ministry, based on our definition that ministry is the work of all baptized Christians who understand themselves to be called by God to serve God and others, not just the work of those who are ordained. Because we were inviting women both inside and outside the parish and church, our purpose was to reflect this broad understanding of ministry. We also included six suggested questions to frame their stories. We did light editing but essentially left these stories in the voices of the authors in order to celebrate their variety of writing styles and ministries. They write from their experience and their passion.

These women have shared the threshold moments of their lives; we trust that through their stories our readers will find encouragement to overcome obstacles in their own lives. These stories, like those of the earlier pioneers and trailblazers, reflect the amazing acts of God and the hope for years to come.

3

Pastoral Leadership and Christian Formation

THE PATCHWORK QUILT: A PARADIGM FOR MINISTRY

Sonja Gall Pancoast

On the day of my ordination, my mom handed me a small pile of six-inch-by-six-inch white fabric squares. On each square someone had created something beautiful. My mom had mailed the fabric squares to my family and friends, who had supported and encouraged my faith and especially my journey to ordination in the Evangelical Lutheran Church in America. There was one from my grandmother, Betty Iverson, representing the faith of our ancestors who came from Norway bringing only the clothes on their backs and their faith across the ocean; another one was from Pastor Marc Miller, my pastor when I was in high school, who planted the seed that ordained ministry could be a wonderful use of my gifts; another from Pastor Ron Letnes, the Director of Sky Ranch Lutheran Camp, a place that allowed me to dive deep into the questions of faith. Another from my parents, who had faithfully taken me to worship and who encouraged me to be whatever I wanted to be; and another from my husband, who had loved and supported me in my seminary studies. The others were from other friends and family who had loved, cared, and prayed for me along the way and who I knew would continue to support me in life and ministry. They each decorated these squares with a variety of mediums, including embroidery, iron-on transfers, permanent markers, or paint—just to name a few.

I treasured these squares, not only because they came from special people in my life but also because I have quilted since I was ten years old. I took each of those precious squares and quilted them together into a wall hanging with the words "Cloud of Witnesses" embroidered by my mother-in-law across the top. This was to remind me of the Scriptures used at my ordination from Hebrews 12:1–2a, "Therefore, since we are surrounded by so great a cloud of witnesses, let us also lay aside every weight and the sin that clings so closely, and let us run with perseverance the race that is set before us, looking to Jesus the pioneer and perfecter of our faith." Each of these quilt squares represented someone who was part of my personal cloud of witnesses. These squares were pieced and patched together just as the pieces and parts of my life had helped create the woman I had become.

I love quilting because each fabric is unique—colors, patterns, textures. When I create a quilt, I choose the amount of fabric I use: a lot or a little. Every piece is important. Two different patterns can come together to make something even more beautiful than each pattern on its own. I access my creative being when I quilt. From fabric scraps, I make something beautiful. I connect with my generosity by creating pillows, blankets, table runners, baby blankets, and wall hangings for others, and I rarely keep what I quilt. Quilting allows me to see a project to completion. So often in life and ministry, I feel that much is left unfinished or that I may not see or know the results of my work. Quilting allows me to create a finished product.

Quilts are identified by the variety of fabrics and colors used to create them. If there is too much of just one fabric, then it's really more like a blanket than a quilt. My life before entering seminary was much like a blanket with the same colored materials. I was baptized at Our Savior's Lutheran Church in Denver, attended Sky Ranch Lutheran Camp for a week or more every summer since fourth grade, was confirmed at Augustana Lutheran Church in Denver, and graduated from Pacific Lutheran University in Tacoma, Washington. So many Lutheran faith experiences. So many of the same color fabric. As I looked toward seminary, I wanted diversity. I wanted a quilt, not a blanket. I was drawn to Princeton Theological Seminary because of the diversity of the student body. Half the students were Presbyterian, and the other half were from a variety of other denominations and faith expressions. Princeton also attracted me because it was a seminary rather than a divinity school. It was an institution of the broader church, and it had historically trained pastors and academics for the church. I realized that due to my exclusive Lutheran background, I thought my worldview was the view of most people. I used lots of Lutheran language that others outside of my tradition didn't understand. I wanted to attend a seminary that would honor my Lutheran theology and heritage while challenging me to think critically about why I was Lutheran, what I love about being Lutheran, and then would also teach me an appreciation of the many gifts that other Christian denominations bring to the table.

The patchwork quilt has been both a literal means to draw people together and an image of those people drawn together for support and prayer in ministry. The first time I drove up to Alexander Hall, one of the dormitories at Princeton Theological Seminary, all of my belongings fit into my small four-door Subaru Legacy. There in the midst of the clothes and books and other belongings was, of course, my sewing machine. I began classes at Princeton and was immersed in learning, with an abundance of reading, reading, and more reading. I wasn't sure any human could actually read everything that was assigned, but I sure tried. Yet with all the rigorous studies, I still found that I needed something more to fill my soul. The quilt of my life and ministry needed more pieces. One piece that took my mind off my studies was my quilting work. Another invaluable piece of that quilt was a patchwork of women that surrounded me with love and prayer. Quilting also became a gift that I shared with others. One day, one of the women in my prayer group asked me why I kept a sewing machine in my very small dorm room. I showed them some of my quilting projects. A few of them wanted to learn, so I taught them the basics, and they were off creating beautiful quilts, pillows, and even a queen-sized bedspread. Quilting had touched a chord with them as well.

As I finished up my seminary education and started into parish ministry as a solo pastor at St. Bartholomew Lutheran Church in Trenton, New Jersey, I prominently displayed my "cloud of witnesses" quilt on the wall of my office. I knew that there would be days in ministry when I would need a reminder of my cloud of witnesses who were still praying for me and supporting me on my journey of faith. I also came to realize that there were many people not represented on that quilt who were part of my cloud of witnesses as well. One key person was the Reverend Doctor Patricia Medley, who graduated from Princeton Seminary in 1976 and was the first woman pastor at St. Bartholomew Lutheran Church. She had paved the way for my ministry in Trenton twenty-five years before I got there. The path continued from there with two more women pastors, the Reverend Cynthia Krommes and the Reverend Beth Schlagel, who followed Pastor Medley. I was the fourth woman pastor to serve St. Bartholomew. For twenty-five years, this congregation had only had women pastors. It was such an integrated part of their patchwork quilt of ministry that a nine-year-old boy in my congregation was quite confused to hear that my husband was also in seminary and would one day be a pastor. He said, "I never knew that a man could be a pastor." What a reversal from what so many other women have heard for so long!

As I began my ministry, I wanted the care and support of a local cloud of witnesses, so I began to piece together a patchwork of colleagues around me. I helped start a weekly Bible study of pastors in our area, and reached out to a few women pastors who were also in their first call. This group of "first call" women were blessed to meet monthly for a number of months with Dr. Geddes Hanson, who shared vital information with us about congregational systems, congregational health, and how to prevent congregational conflict. I was also fortunate to be able to audit classes at Princeton Theological Seminary because my husband was still a student there. Now that I was actively serving in a congregation, I was amazed at how much more interesting and informational the Congregational Ministries classes were, and how vital that opportunity for learning was to my ministry. I soaked up every word, and this time you can believe I read every word that was assigned! It took actually being in the parish to realize what I didn't know and still needed to know.

As I have continued in ministry over the years, my method of quilting has changed. I no longer have time (or maybe more honestly, I no longer choose to make the time) to create fabric quilts. Instead, I quilt through my ministry. There are many people who each have a unique combination of gifts from God: callings and passions as well as brokenness and longing. My calling is to help people discover the gifts they have been given by God and connect them with ways to share those gifts to help change the world. My calling is bringing together these patchwork pieces of various individuals and to help sew them together into something greater. In the larger quilt of ministry, people often find that while they are individual colors or kinds of fabric, they become so much more together than they ever were alone.

In both congregations I have served, ministries around quilting, crocheting, and knitting have emerged. At St. Bartholomew they developed a "Crafting through God's Love" group that meets regularly to make prayer shawls, chemo hats for breast cancer patients, and baby blankets for single mothers. At my current call at Zion Lutheran Church in Loveland, Colorado, a prayer shawl ministry emerged that meets once a month for devotions and fellowship and makes hundreds of prayers shawls each year. In 2015 they branched out with a "Crocheting through Lent" small group. Each week throughout Lent the members came together to learn how to make a different granny square and together worked through a daily devotional. At the end of the Lenten season, all of these squares were pieced together to make a beautiful crochet quilt for each small group member. The most amazing part of each of these ministries is that they emerged simply by people from the congregation stepping forward with the gifts God had given them and seeking to share these gifts to change the world. I, as the quilter/pastor, help to connect the gifts and the needs while witnessing a beautiful quilt blossoming in the congregation.

The quilt of my life and ministry no longer hangs on the wall like a beautiful work of art to be admired from a distance. It is a living, breathing, growing quilt made up of the patchwork pieces that God brings into my life to help sew together. I help to fit them together, but only God knows how the quilt will look in the end. Sometimes I'm so distracted by the small pieces, I struggle to see the larger creative work as a whole. Other times all I see are the knots on the back and not the beautiful work of the front. In those times, I look to Jesus as the pioneer and perfecter of our faith to direct and lead how the pieces come together, knowing that I am helping to sew these people together as I used to sew pieces of fabric together. My quilt is no longer my own but God's quilt, and I am one of many quilters.

MY "I MUST":
PREACHING THE GOSPEL

Pam Driesell

Even in my mind's eye the tattered photograph is fading, but it remains a definitive image of my childhood. I am barely four weeks old, and someone is holding me up next to the newspaper. The paper and I are about the same size. The December 1960 headline declares, "Davidson Upset Wake Forest" in my father's first game as a college basketball coach. For better or worse, my childhood was defined by my father's vocation as a coach. His devotion to and passion for his calling left indelible marks on my soul. With his life, my father exhorted me to do what Rainer Maria Rilke so eloquently exhorted his young poet correspondent to do: "Dig deep to find a strong, simple, 'I MUST,' then build your life in accordance with it; your whole life, even its humblest most indifferent hour, must become a sign and witness to this impulse."[1] I discovered that impulse, that divine imperative, at age sixteen. While at a summer youth camp, I was seized by the power of a great life-affirming affection. Although my theology has evolved significantly since that experience, its core affirmation remains at the heart of my faith, my identity, and my calling: God's love has a claim on me and compels me to love and serve others. I knew then that I would build my life around the call to share, in Word and deed, the transforming love of God revealed in Jesus Christ. Proclaiming the gospel is, quite simply, my "I must!" The shape and form of that call has changed significantly over time.

In 1979, in the Maryland suburbs of Washington, DC, I was one of four seniors from every high school in the county chosen to participate in an internship program for one semester of my senior year. The student participants would shadow a mentor in a career of interest to them and participate in leadership training. My interview with the placement team left them dumbfounded: I wanted to shadow a minister. There were none on the list.

1. Rainer Maria Rilke, *Letters to a Young Poet*, trans. Stephen Mitchell (New York: Modern Library, 2001), 6.

There were politicians and doctors and business people and scientists, but there were no ministers. Eventually, I was assigned to an associate pastor at a Presbyterian church in Bethesda. I was not aware until I arrived there that the congregation was preparing to break from the PCUS, largely over the issue of women's ordination. It was there I learned that "the Bible forbids a woman to preach." I was seventeen. I trusted my spiritual mentors. I didn't miss a beat: God must be calling me to be a volunteer youth leader. I was pretty sure the Bible didn't forbid that. I still look back on that time with embarrassment and shame at not having been more discerning. Why didn't I ask more questions? Why did I simply accept the assertion that the closest I would ever come to being a minister would be to marry one? I wish that I could say that it kept me up at night, but it didn't. I drank the Kool-Aid. Gulped it all down and didn't give it another thought. I made another plan. If God didn't want me to be a minister, then I would major in communications and work in public relations. And my "I must" would be satisfied by working with youth in a volunteer capacity.

When I moved to Roanoke, Virginia, I sought out the local Young Life area director to tell him that I was interested in serving as a volunteer. Bob Bingham had barely known me a month when he spoke into my soul, affirming my "I must." "Pam," he insisted, "you have gifts for ministry. Have you ever thought about ministry as a vocation?" I was confused. "Well, I thought women were not supposed to take on leadership positions in ministry, so I figured that meant I should just be a volunteer." He laughed, and next thing I knew, I was working for Bob and leading a youth ministry at Salem (Virginia) High School. A few years later, I was serving as the area director and was invited to be the first woman camp manager and speaker for a five-week assignment at a camp in upstate New York. When word got out that a woman was going to be speaking, some of the area directors around the country refused to bring their youth to the camp. I could not have been more confused. I went to my regional director, Chuck Reinhold, and confessed that I was really uncomfortable being at the center of a controversy that was dividing the organization. I pleaded with him, "Could I please just serve as the work crew boss?" He laughed. "Look, Pam," he said. "God used Deborah to lead a nation. God can use you to lead this camp for five weeks. I am confident of that. Just do your job." During my time on the Young Life staff, I met people of various theological persuasions. I began to experience increased confusion about a number of nagging theological questions, including the nature of biblical authority and issues of ecclesiology. In 1995 I sensed God calling me to take an educational leave of absence from Young Life ministry in order to study these issues in more depth and to seek ordination so that my ministry would come under the blessing of the institutional church. At the time, I was a member of an Episcopalian congregation, and I began the process of discernment. I chose Princeton Theological Seminary because of their outstanding faculty, the community life for families (I had two children), and their commitment to preparing students for ministry.

During my time at Princeton, I discovered a language that expressed my evolving faith: the language of Reformed theology. I discovered a way of being Christian community that resonated with my own convictions: I am Presbyterian (U.S.A.) not by default but by prayerful discernment and the strong call of God. Conversations with Dr. Tom Gillespie helped me look back and see how the seeds of my faith were planted well before that conversion experience at age sixteen through the ministries of Presbyterian congregations in Davidson, North Carolina, and Silver Spring, Maryland. I began to feel God's thumb in my back, nudging me into ministry in the local congregation and into the pulpit to preach the Good News. Those nudges came through the faculty at PTS, who always had time for my questions about discerning call. Jim Loder, Bruce McCormack, Jack Stewart, and David Willis all spent countless hours with me sorting through my theological, vocational, and personal conundrums.

As a mother of young children, I observed Nancy Duff with great admiration. She was "doing it all" with such grace and authority. I invited her to lunch so that I could inquire about the "secret to her success." She laughed when I told her my impression of her as someone holding it all together so effortlessly. Her honesty about how hard—and exhausting—it all was, and how often she questioned herself and her vocation, were a source of great comfort and inspiration for me in years to come when I would struggle and question my own capacity to live into my vocation fully.

My senior year, as most seniors do, I accepted the daunting invitation to preach in Miller Chapel one morning. That afternoon I walked into my Preaching in the African American Tradition class with Cleo LaRue. The class settled down, and Dr. LaRue was perched on his stool in front of the class. "Brothers and sisters," he began in his powerful Dr. LaRue way, "this morning we witnessed a gift. And with that gift comes a responsibility." He looked straight at me. Why, I wondered? *Wait . . . was he referring to my sermon that morning in chapel?* It took a moment for that to sink in. I was overwhelmed. It was a transformative moment. For days I struggled with the question "Was my call to preach?" Up to that point, I had still envisioned myself leaving seminary and going back into youth ministry. I realized that the internalized voices of those who were so sure that a woman should NOT be in the pulpit were still haunting me. Dr. LaRue's exhortation that I had a responsibility to use my gift and the culmination of all the encouragement and affirmation that my other professors had bestowed upon me at Princeton led me to the absolute conviction of the "I must" to which I somehow knew I was called as a high school senior. My call was to pastor and preach. I was never surer about anything.

After learning that I fit the personality profile of someone who might be a successful church planter (and that only 6 percent of seminary graduates fit such a profile), I sensed the Spirit compelling me to use my gifts in a new-church-development venture. In many ways I was not "qualified" for such a call. I had never been an adult Presbyterian. I had never been in parish ministry. Still, the Northeast Georgia Presbytery search committee for an organizing pastor for a new church in Oconee County decided to give me what I call "transfer credit" for my experience leading a parachurch ministry. They took a chance on me. In the early days I would often call Jack Stewart, David Willis, and Cleo LaRue for advice. They were always available, offering insight and encouragement and practical wisdom. This particular new-church-development model was called the "pastor as evangelist," which meant that I started with no members—just a charge from the presbytery to plant a church within a particular geographical location. Starting with no members was frightening in so many ways. One conversation I had with Cleo LaRue ended with this sage piece of advice, which has become a mantra for me: "Pam, you just love the people and preach the gospel . . . the Lord will bring the increase." And so the Lord did. My call to organize and pastor the Oconee Presbyterian Church was the source of unspeakable joy and immeasurable spiritual growth for me. It remains a thriving congregation and a beacon of light in Oconee County. I think of her as my third child, whom I will always love and in whose growth I will always rejoice.

When Trinity Presbyterian Church in Atlanta, a congregation of 2,200 members and a staff of nearly thirty, including five clergy, called me in 2010, I was initially not interested in pastoring a large church. I had planned on doing another church plant at some point. This was another position for which I was not really "qualified." How could I be senior pastor and head of staff at a large congregation when I had never even served as an associate on the staff of a large congregation? As my conversations with the search committee grew more serious, we became convinced that the Spirit was at work and that one's basic instincts about leadership and ministry are transferable from one setting to another. Relying on God's grace, I joyfully and humbly accepted the call to Trinity Atlanta almost five years ago. I have faced leadership challenges here that have stretched me beyond anything I could have imagined. While Trinity has a long history of affirming lay and clergy women in ministry and there are no issues around women holding positions of senior leadership, what I discovered in myself and in the culture was that there can be subtle biases favoring "masculine" ways of leading and resisting more "feminine" ways of leading. There is no doubt that this is a reflection of our larger culture, but when I bumped up against it in my role at Trinity, I had to confront the ways that I myself had internalized these values. It cut both ways. When I felt the pressure to exercise leadership in more masculine ways that were simply not resonating with my sense of what I needed to do, I had to find the strength to lead in intuitive and nurturing ways even when that caused anxiety in others. On the other hand, leading such a large community through crises and change sometimes required me to access my own more archetypally masculine energies, leading with decisiveness, clarity, and firmness.

Through it all, I have sought to "love the people and preach the gospel" faithfully. My mentors at Princeton have been my companions all along the way, a resounding chorus of voices in my heart and soul, always reminding me to be true to my "I must."

Thanks be to God.

A NEWYORRICAN CALLED
TO MULTICULTURAL MINISTRY

Karen Hernández-Granzen

I am a "Newyorrican," a Puerto Rican born in New York City, and a "PK," a.k.a. pastor's kid. When I was born in the early 1960s, my father, the Rev. Jose Belen Hernández, was the pastor of Templo Emanuel Pentecostal of Brooklyn, New York. I am the *penultima*, second to last in a family of twelve children. As the youngest daughter of my clan, I enjoyed the blessings of being cuddled and spoiled by the members of my father's congregation. The church became a place where I sensed God's unconditional love.

In one of my early childhood memories, at the age of 3½, I remember waking up in a crib in the church nursery and not feeling fear. I could hear my father's voice from his church office across the hall. I didn't cry out to him because I was content quietly waiting for him to come and pick me up when he was ready because I felt totally safe. This internalized positive image of the church has helped me remain passionately committed to its reforming whenever it fails to actually be a Beloved Community sent out to create God's reign of loving justice and mercy throughout the world.

My father died of a heart attack soon after that early childhood experience. He was only forty-four years old. My mother, Margarita Hernández, became widowed at the age of thirty-two, having just given birth to my youngest brother five months prior. I felt as though we had lost both our father and our mother when she became emotionally withdrawn due to her profound grief. These tragedies led me at a very young age to desperately seek an intimately personal relationship with God. God responded by graciously gifting me with a deep awareness and assurance that I was a beloved and protected child of God. God became my father and filled the void that my father's death created. Although on the surface my faith journey may sound typically patriarchal and traditional, I can boldly confess that my faith deepened in its core knowing that God was watching over me like a parent. For several years during my early adolescence, when instead of going to church I chose to hang out with friends on the corner adjacent to the church, I imagined God patiently awaiting God's prodigal daughter's return home. Even though I still didn't know that God would call me to become an ordained clergywoman, I remember at the age of sixteen telling my friends that not going to church was just a phase in my life because I knew that I would return to serve God. They all just laughed at me, and one friend said, "Yeah right, we'll see you back here in just a few months."

What brought me back to the church fold, at the age of fourteen, was the First Hispanic Reformed Church of Brooklyn's after-school program. The pastor, the Rev. Efrain Felix, and his leaders administered many desperately needed crucial community programs within their small storefront church. Felix hired me to work as a tutor and then expanded my role over the years to serve as his administrative assistant. Felix's model of ministry attracted a lot of former churchgoers who felt disillusioned by the institutional church yet still felt very passionately committed to serving our urban community. I appreciated and adopted his approach to working with key leaders throughout the community without regard to their religious or nonreligious background. By the age of eighteen I was an ordained elder in the Reformed Church of America and the youth director of our local church and the former Classis of Brooklyn. I served in those capacities until I moved to California at the age of twenty-one.

In 1983 a friend who was visiting me in California met the Rev. Hector Delgado, a former new-church-development pastor of the Los Ranchos Presbytery. Hector was seeking to hire a youth director. Through the $10,000,000 Mission on Your Doorstep funds raised by one of my mentors, the Rev. Tim Hart-Anderson, a new model of hiring two full-time staff members was being implemented for PC(USA) Hispanic/Latin@ new church developments in Los Angeles and Orange counties. When my friend referred me for the position, Hector said, "Karen Hernández from New York? Is she Jose Belen Hernández's daughter? If she is anything like her father, we want her here!" Glory to God that almost twenty years after my father's death, his legacy opened the door for me to begin my ministry within the Presbyterian Church (U.S.A.). Several months after I was hired, Hector suddenly looked up from his desk and said, *"Karen, tu has pensado en el ministerio de ordinación?"* (Karen, have you thought of ordained ministry?) I immediately responded, "No," as my mind became flooded with many reasons: I had never met an ordained female minister. I was socialized within a Hispanic/Latin@ culture that preferred male leadership, and last, who was I to follow in my father's footsteps? Yet it was precisely at that very moment, when Hector asked that question, that I then knew without a doubt that God was clearly revealing God's call for me to become an ordained clergywoman! Needless to say, the very next moment I was also fully aware that the journey toward ordination would be long and demanding.

Little did I know that while I was still in my mother's womb, God was calling me and preparing me for multiracial, multicultural, and racial reconciliation ministry. As a Newyorrican, I am a descendant of Puerto Rico's indigenous Tainos, white European Spaniards, and black Africans. I have always incorporated the gifts of my richly diverse heritage within my worship leadership. I'll never forget the culture shock that I experienced while worshiping for the first time at a Presbyterian church in Los Angeles. Except for the Spanish language spoken, sung, and preached, every other aspect of worship was Eurocentric, i.e., traditional hymns played exclusively with a pipe organ. Rev. Hector Delgado and Los Ranchos Presbytery became very supportive of my efforts to include Hispanic/Latin@ cultural hymns, praise songs, rhythms, and instruments within our worship when they witnessed a significant increase in the number of worshipers and members. No longer were worshipers expected to leave their Hispanic/Latin@ culture at the doors of our sanctuary.

My call to multiracial, multicultural, and racial reconciliation ministries within an urban context led me to pursue a Master of Divinity degree at McCormick Theological Seminary. Their former Hispanic program was the first one founded in the United States, and many Hispanic/Latin@ students were enrolled. Its founder, the Rev. Ruben Armendariz, and Professor Lois Livezey, a former Princeton Theological Seminary professor, became my mentors. Ruben modeled a healthy, balanced respect and appreciation for Hispanic/Latin@ and Eurocentric cultures. Lois modeled an authentic commitment to nurturing future female clergy and church leaders. Throughout those years of study and intentional praxis, I was privileged to take multiple courses taught by Dr. Justo González, in Spanish, on the theology and practice of multicultural worshiping congregations; completed a full-time academic-year internship at Fourth Presbyterian Church in Chicago, a Eurocentric "high church" worshiping congregation; and completed a summer internship at Old First Presbyterian Church in San Francisco, a More Light congregation.

Those experiences that happened over twenty years ago helped to prepare me to become the pastor of Westminster Presbyterian Church, an urban church in Trenton, New Jersey, that in 1995 was expected to close within five years. With God's faithfulness and wisdom, the leaders and I have worked together to radically transform our congregation from a predominantly white, homogeneous, Eurocentric worshiping congregation into A House of Prayer and Praise for People of All Nations. Westminster's mission statement is inspired by Genesis's affirmation that women and men are created equally in God's image, Pentecost's declaration that the body of Christ is called to be united by the Holy Spirit in the midst of its rich diversity, and Revelation's image of the City of God where all tribes, nations, peoples, and languages will worship God.

Mentoring, and not merely supervising, over forty Princeton Theological Seminary field education students has been a revitalizing part of my call. I intentionally invite students to look with fresh eyes at what Westminster has been doing and then openly share their probing questions and honest reflections in order to help improve our effectiveness and deepen our praxis. Westminster makes room for students to enhance and expand our ministry by incorporating their unique gifts. Students are expected to adopt Westminster's two norms: "care-fronting," that is, caring enough about relationships so that conflicts are never avoided but rather dealt with loving with truth-telling;[2] and *Hablar sin pelos en la boca* (Take the hair out of your mouth; do not swallow your voice). Given the fact that the vast majority of field education students have never worshiped in multiracial and multicultural worshiping congregations, my call to help equip culturally proficient church leaders to serve the larger church and society continues to be reaffirmed and appreciated.

Although the term "missional" had not been coined when I attended seminary, my understanding of ministry within an urban setting has been and remains missional. Westminster "sends out" its leaders and members to seek the shalom of the city of Trenton throughout every aspect of their lives. We partner with ecumenical churches, interfaith communities, and government and civic leaders to address low-quality public school education, a fast-growing population of non-English-speaking immigrants, a lack of employment opportunities, overpolicing in racially diverse urban areas, high rates of broken families, high rates of incarceration, and multiple obstacles to becoming ex-offenders (i.e., "returning citizens") due to mass incarceration and unjust policies.[3] Michelle Alexander's book *The New Jim Crow: Mass Incarceration in the Age of Colorblindness* crystalized my call to missional urban ministry and has become a required read for all my field education students.[4]

My father has been a strong role model in my urban ministry. His congregation and colleagues kept this legacy alive by sharing their memories with me. In the early 1960s, even before such terms as holistic ministry, social ministry, cooperative buying, and microbusiness loans became nomenclature in urban ministries, my father had already implemented these effective

---

2. David Augsburger, *Caring Enough to Confront: How to Understand and Express Your Deepest Feelings toward Others* (Ventura, CA: Regal, 1981), 10.

3. W. Wilson Goode Sr., Charles E. Lewis Jr., and Harold Dean Trulear, *Ministry with Prisoners & Families: The Way Forward* (Valley Forge, PA: Judson, 2011), 8.

4. Michelle Alexander, *The New Jim Crow: Mass Incarceration in the Age of Colorblindness* (New York: New Press, 2012).

church strategies. Although as a modern-day woman who is married with two children, I have never been able to pray three hours daily like my father, I am committed to praying constantly in order to seek God's wisdom and not merely to rely on my seminary training. When I have felt unworthy and intimidated by God's prophetic call in my life to boldly speak truth to power within and outside of the church, I have been empowered and encouraged by Micah 6:8, "And what does the LORD require of you but to do justice, and to love kindness, and to walk humbly with your God." I have learned to live out the Hispanic/Latin@ idiom: *Con temor hacia delante!* (Go forth despite fear!)

I am truly grateful that the use of inclusive language for God is a mandatory requirement for all the PC(USA)-affiliated seminaries. This discipline became pivotal in broadening my own intimate experience of God, helping me to see and value the feminine image of God within me and other women, and helping me to overcome internal messages that unconsciously undermined my sense of call to ordained ministry. Unfortunately, none of my field education sites provided me with trained female mentors. I believe that seminaries would greatly improve their ability to better equip women for ministry by recruiting women practitioners in ministry in order to train them to become effective mentors and then pairing them with individual female students and/or small groups. Mentoring during all three years of seminary will have the greatest impact because it ensures a disciplined, ongoing dialogue regarding the contextualization of theological studies and the praxis of ministry. My hope is that female graduates, upon receiving their first call, will seek an experienced mentor within their presbytery, and that they will themselves eventually become trained and committed to mentoring other women in ministry.

**BECOMING VALUED
AS A CHRISTIAN EDUCATOR**

Gail McArthur Moody

My faith journey has been gradual yet constant. As a child, I attended a Presbyterian church in a suburb of Pittsburgh, Pennsylvania. My early memories are of going to church with my family; however, I also have a strong memory of my first-grade Sunday school teacher picking me up on Sunday mornings and taking me to Sunday school. I cannot remember why she picked me up, but I do know that it made an impact on me, and I enjoyed being part of the class. I continued to be active in my church as a teenager and participated regularly in youth group activities, confirmation class, and worship. I remember playing volleyball on summer evenings, participating in Wednesday evening programs as a youth, and going on youth outings and retreats.

Upon entering college my intent was to major in psychology; however, I found the classes to be too scientific for my liking. For two summers while in college, I worked as summer staff at two different Presbyterian churches in my hometown. I discovered that I enjoyed working in a church setting and developed a good relationship with the minister of Christian education at my home church, my first mentor in the area of ministry. As a result of my summer experiences, I decided that rather than major in psychology, I would instead create an interdisciplinary major. Since you could not actually major in Christian education at my college, I majored in religious studies with minors in both education and sociology. I had no intention of becoming a teacher but rather began thinking that I might want to go on and pursue a seminary education, specifically with a concentration in Christian education. Through my experiences with my education courses I discovered that I enjoyed working with children, and I felt that I had gifts and talents in that area.

My senior year in college I became serious about attending seminary. I began to explore the possibilities. I narrowed my search to Pittsburgh Theological Seminary and Princeton Theological Seminary. The primary person I turned to for guidance was the minister of Christian education at my home church, who had been my mentor. I respected his opinion because Christian education was his area of specialization. Although he had attended Pittsburgh Theological Seminary, he recommended Princeton because he felt that Princeton had a stronger Christian education program. The senior pastor at my church also encouraged me to attend Princeton. He had graduated from Princeton and felt that it would be a good choice. At that point in my life, my only mentors in ministry were men. I had not really been exposed to women who had chosen to go into ministry. Although I was accepted at both seminaries, I chose to attend Princeton.

I spent the summer before I entered seminary in Orlando, Florida, living with my sister and her family. Although I worked as a waitress part-time, my sister connected me with the director of Christian education at the Presbyterian church in Winter Park, and I was also able to work part-time at the church. I would consider Pat, the director of Christian education, to be my first female ministry mentor. She allowed me to create a one-day-a-week program for elementary children. It was my first experience to actually create something of my own, and I learned a great deal from that experience.

Because my interest was primarily in Christian education, I entered the Master of Arts program in Christian education. When I entered seminary in the fall of 1975, it was at a time when women were offered more opportunities in ministry. More and more women were being ordained. The question I received the most from other seminary students, both men and women, was "Why don't you want to be ordained?" Their assumption was that since women could now be ordained, I should want to choose this opportunity for myself. The problem was that I didn't feel that I was being called to be an ordained pastor. I tried to explain this to people, but they still didn't seem to understand. The very people who were answering their own call didn't seem able to recognize that my call to ministry might be different than theirs. I spent the majority of my two years in seminary explaining to people why I chose my particular path.

Having been a religious studies major in college, I was able to waive some of the introductory courses and instead take some of the upper-level courses in New Testament and theology. Although my emphasis was Christian education, I was still required to take a certain number of Old Testament, New Testament, theology, and church history classes. My favorite classes, however, were the ones I had with Freda Gardner. I felt very fortunate to have her for so many classes. Freda not only was excellent at teaching content, but you also learned by the way she taught the class. She was a wonderful role model, and I have carried much of what I learned from her throughout my ministry.

Although Dr. Campbell Wyckoff was on sabbatical my first year of seminary, he did return for my last year in the program, and I was blessed as well to learn from him. Because there was just a small group of us going through the program together, we were able to build relationships with one another and with our professors.

The next challenge I encountered as I pursued my call was that when I graduated from seminary, there was no classification for me in the Presbyterian Church. In previous years there had been commissioned church workers, which included individuals in the field of Christian education. By the time I graduated, however, this category no longer existed and there was a void for people working as church educators. After I had been working in the field for about five years, the northern and southern Presbyterian churches united, and the opportunity to become a certified Christian educator became a possibility. I immediately took advantage of this and went through the process to become certified. Because I had already received a master's degree in Christian education, my primary requirement was to take the exam, which was quite comprehensive. In the fall of 1983 I was recognized by the Presbytery of New Brunswick as a certified Christian educator. Although I now felt that I had a place in the Presbyterian Church, there was a new challenge. The presbytery did not seem to know what to do with this new classification.

Following graduation I worked in two different churches as a director of Christian education. Some of my responsibilities were to recruit and train teachers, choose Sunday school curriculum, coordinate a Wednesday afternoon program for middle school youth, and plan adult education programming. My most unique experience was when Dr. Wyckoff, a member of one of the churches where I was working, became the chair of the Christian education committee. Although I found it a bit intimidating to work so closely with the chair of the Christian education department at Princeton Seminary, I must say that he was very supportive. My last major project was to design a comprehensive elementary Sunday school curriculum for the church.

In 1984 we moved because my husband, an ordained Presbyterian pastor, received a call to a church in California. Our daughters were young, so I did not immediately seek a position in a church. The New Brunswick Presbytery, however, did communicate with the San Fernando Presbytery to let them know that a certified Christian educator was now a part of their presbytery. Although they had no idea what to do with such a communication, it did help to increase my visibility. About a year after we moved, I was contacted by a minister in the presbytery who was seeking a part-time Christian educator for his church. The position was to start at ten hours per week, with the possibility of increasing hours in the future. Thus began a new chapter in my life and ministry. I stayed at St. Stephen Presbyterian Church for almost eleven years and finished my time there working thirty hours a week.

My years at St. Stephen were positive ones. I felt respected by the congregation and the staff. During my years there my responsibilities increased, and I was able to build the ministry to both children and adults. I also became involved in the presbytery and served on several committees, including the search committee for the associate executive presbyter and a special committee called the Blue Ribbon Committee. I felt that my talents and abilities were valued and that I was able to contribute to the life of the presbytery, even though my status as certified educator did not allow me to hold certain positions that required ordination as a pastor or elder.

In January of 1996 my husband received a call to a new church, this time in Salem, Oregon. Although my goal was to find a church that was seeking a church educator, during my first nine months in Salem I was unemployed. I did a slight amount of consulting at a small church in the Salem area but was hoping to find a more permanent position, preferably in a Presbyterian church. Finally two opportunities emerged, one at a Baptist church and one at Westminster, the Presbyterian church where my husband was pastor. Although my husband and I had always served in different churches, our ministries were now established enough that we felt that it would work to serve together. My husband's church dragged their feet. Some were uncertain if we should work together on the same staff, while others were excited about the possibility. I finally ended up interviewing for the position at the Baptist church and was offered the job; however, in my heart I knew that I really preferred staying in the Presbyterian tradition. Westminster eventually interviewed me and after checking my references also offered me the position of director of Christian education. My prayers were answered, and my husband and I were now serving the same church, he as senior pastor and I as director of Christian education. Thus began what has now been a nineteen-year ministry.

I started out with a focus on children's ministries and adult education, but over the years my responsibilities expanded and grew, adding family ministries, an after-school midweek program, and Sunday evening adult programming. When I began my ministry in Salem, my focus was definitely on programs for children, for families, and for adults. But as the years have passed, I have found that relationships and hospitality are more important than programs. Serving in the same church for nineteen years has allowed me to form deeper relationships, and I have come to understand how important these relationships are. It has changed my style of recruitment, and it has changed my priorities on a Sunday morning. I have discovered that I possess a gift for hospitality and for welcoming those who come to Westminster. Scriptures that have been most influential in my ministry are Deuteronomy 6:4–9 and Ephesians 4:15–16.

No matter which presbytery I have been a part of, my journey as a Christian educator has encountered similar roadblocks. My decision not to seek ordination has resulted in my inability to be a full-fledged member of presbytery.

My most recent reminder of this was when I was asked to serve on the presbytery's personnel committee. Once they discovered that I was not ordained as either a pastor or an elder, I was informed that I was not eligible to serve in this capacity after all. My years as serving as a certified educator did not qualify me to serve on this committee.

Despite the challenges I have encountered over the years, I do not regret my decision to follow my call. For the most part, my ministry has been rewarding and has allowed me to encounter many people who have impacted my life in a positive fashion. I continue to look for ways to be creative and to make an impact on today's church.

RESILIENCE, A MINISTRY MUST-HAVE

Cecelia Evelyn GreeneBarr

Before accepting the call of God for ordained ministry, I was not your average church member, even though I thought myself to be. In fact, I was a preacher in training but didn't know it. I worked in my academic field of training, mostly with men, and I didn't segregate the gospel from my secular employment life. I went to work during weekdays and found no professional or personal conflict in expressing my faith and devotion to Jesus. My behavior was not limited to bowing my head and praying over my meal in the company lunch facility. I freely exclaimed, "Thank you, Jesus" whenever I could see the hand of God active in my mind through insight and creative ideas. There was a Bible on my desk, and not a tiny New Testament well hidden under a scarf or any such thing. I wore my gold cross daily around my neck, long before the ungodly began to don them as costume jewelry. Breaks and discussions with coworkers about how their weekends were spent, or about personal situations they faced, included me interjecting viewpoints nonreflective of the current culture. My life recommendations were not of the norm. I did not presume to have a scholar's understanding of theology. My input was molded by what I had come to learn from Scripture and revelation by the Holy Spirit. Although I spent very little time in the company of nonchurchgoers, it surprised me when my spiritual posture made my professing Christian coworkers, fellow choir members, young adult group members, and college classmates uncomfortable. I wasn't "preachy"; I was just present in their midst with a convicting worldview. I would later learn in seminary that I was functioning in the ministry of presence.

Here is an example of one of many occurrences that arose as I followed the leading of God in my life. One day I was in a Christian bookstore looking at random titles. I saw a book that caught my attention, and I knew that one of my coworkers would be blessed to read it. The topic dealt with theodicy, why bad things happen to good people. Because this was preseminary days, I certainly didn't know the word *theodicy* at the time. But my coworker had been sharing about hardships he and his wife had been experiencing. When he told me about these hardships, it wasn't with an attitude to solicit prayer from me. Instead it was more to mock my faith in God for confident living. I wanted to buy this book for him. There was a very strong urge from within to buy this book for him, yet I resisted. I knew that when I presented it, my actions would be met with hostility. And God knows I didn't want to go through the anger, criticism, and whatever else would surface. I stood in front of the display of books with a perplexed countenance, a deep sense of dread in the pit of my stomach, and a profound knowing that the Spirit of God was using me to meet a spiritual need in the life of my coworker. It was not going to be pretty. It had to be done, and I was the vessel God was using to bring change in the life of this family. I purchased the book, wrote a simple line of explanation on the inside, and presented it to him. I'd like to tell you that my coworker surprised me and received it with gladness. He didn't. He was offended that I would give him a book with a title that implied anything about the condition of his soul. My coworker stopped speaking to me for a while. As a woman academically trained to work in a male-dominated industry, I was accustomed to the subtle realities of workplace isolation. As an African American woman, however, I did value the work-based fellowship with African American brothers, including my coworker to whom this book was given. There were very few minorities working for the company, so the few to whom he vented his frustrations also distanced themselves from me for a season. It was a lonely time, but I was at peace in my spirit because I had obeyed God. Before I left the company for a better job, relations with my coworker improved as he began to read the book and the Holy Spirit ministered to the needs in his family. He finally expressed thanks for the book; but for some reason, his expression of thanks did little to ease the experience of his disdain at my obedience to be a blessing in his life. This would only be one of many occurrences as I followed the leading of God in my life of ordained ministry.

After accepting the call of God for ordained ministry and completing my theological education at Princeton, I've spent my life in the presence of preachers, pastors, evangelists, and bishops. I work among those who read and preach the biblical message of God's sovereignty and the compelling call to live out great exploits of faith for the kingdom of our Christ. Yet I've found that my experiences even among this group of Christians are still very similar to my "preacher in training" years. I've come to understand that bold confidence in God is rarely celebrated in the moment of execution. Martin Luther King Jr. is an example, because when he walked in God's calling to address American injustice, much of the clergy community disdained him and his message. King's experience is well known and even portrayed in cinematic form. But it is Jarena Lee whom I think about more often, especially as I've answered God's call for me to serve the African Methodist Episcopal Church as a bishop.

The history of Jarena Lee's ministry tells of the initial and subsequent times that she approached the founder of our church, the Rev. Richard Allen, and communicated that God had called her to preach the gospel. In her autobiography Lee records Allen's response that another woman had previously approached him with a similar testimony, but that the Methodist Episcopal discipline did not have accommodations for women to preach the gospel.[5] Those few words of spiritual and physiological dismissal obviously do not adequately convey the atmosphere, attitude, and animosity resulting from her confident declaration of God's call. When cutting through tense spiritual atmospheres to bring forth what Jesus calls new wine in new wineskins, it is never that cut and dried.

In my ministerial years as an ordained preacher and pastor, I've often had that same deep sense of dread in the pit of my stomach because I heard God's instructions. Like that long-ago experience with my coworker, I knew the execution of them would not be pretty. There would be ridicule. There would be backlash. There would be criticism and conspiracy to silence my prophetic voice and presence. Even as I pen this account of my ministerial journey, I am less than ten months away from the Bicentennial General Conference of the African Methodist Episcopal Church. On July 11, 2016, I will be on Ballot 411 for the office of bishop. There is a sense of spiritual turbulence in the atmosphere as I present God's agenda, otherwise known as my bishop candidacy campaign platform. When I approach tense moments and deal with extensive travel, I think to myself, "Is this how Jarena Lee felt when she announced to the Rev. Allen that God's intention for her life was not in sync with his and the denomination's view of her personhood?" I wonder about her sense of isolation as God's group of reverends shared their thoughts about her bold confidence in God as she traveled and preached without the full acceptance or support of the bishop.

Jarena Lee is now a celebrated figure in the history of the African Methodist Episcopal Church. She remained faithful to the call of God upon her life. Her travels took her to several states and across many miles as she proclaimed the gospel. Throughout these next ten months, from the time of writing this story until the election, I will remain steadfast to the divine call of God upon me to serve as a bishop in my denomination. I've traveled at least 90,000 miles thus far to reach voting delegates. I've stood before many annual conferences, district planning meetings, and various gatherings of African Methodists to press my case that God has called me to be a bishop in our church. My claim is clearly articulated; I am a relevant and authentic ambassador for the next level.

5. William L. Andrews, ed., *Sisters of the Spirit: Three Black Women's Autobiographies of the Nineteenth Century* (Bloomington: Indiana University Press, 1986), 36.

Jesus was accurate when explaining how a prophet is without honor at home. My experiences of dishonor and attempted humiliation by colleagues in the Fourth Episcopal District have proven to be very biblical. Yet throughout my travels beyond my home district, I've largely been received with honor and gladness as I stand to proclaim this dimension of call upon my life. I speculate that the gifts and graces required to serve as a bishop are not identical to those necessary to become a bishop. Leaving my husband to care for our two young children as I travel throughout the country, weeks at a time, is a ministry unto itself. I'm often quizzed by curious persons who wonder how I find the ability to campaign. I expect curious inquisitors. I even navigate around the downturned expressions from contentious detractors. Encouragers are present along the trial, but even their words are not the pure fuel that keeps me pressing my case. That pure fuel comes from the conversation I had with the Lord at my initial calling. The Lord spoke to me from Jeremiah 1:4–10, 17, where the call and warning were given should Jeremiah shrink from his prophetic assignment because the countenance of his audience would be disapproving. I'm convinced that the wrath and sordidness of humanity pales in comparison to being confounded or broken to pieces by God. My history with God has proven that the Lord will fight for me. I do not give my time or energy to wrestle with flesh and blood. Instead, I do all that is within me to press past opposition and remain faithful to the call. My ultimate goal in all that I do for God is to eventually hear the Lord say to me, "Well done, Cecelia; you've been a good and faithful servant."

4

Chaplaincy

JOURNEY FROM CONGREGATIONAL PASTOR TO DEPLOYED CHAPLAIN

Barbara K. Sherer

When I felt that tug from God saying, "Stop what you are doing right now, and prepare to be a minister to my people," I thought that I understood where this was leading. I grew up in a Presbyterian church and was even elected an elder in my home congregation while still in high school. I was fairly close to the pastor who led my home congregation, and my best friend's father was a Baptist minister. I think that I had a pretty good feel for the life of a traditional pastor in a local church. So this was now to be *my* call: to attend seminary, then work in a Presbyterian church or a union congregation of some sort associated with the polity and theology with which I was familiar.

So naturally, when selecting a seminary to attend, I wanted to find a PC(USA)-sponsored seminary that had a reputation for producing pastors well rounded in a wide variety of ministerial areas.[1] This was why I chose

---

1. At the time I [Barbara Sherer] entered seminary, the uniting of the UPCUSA and PCUS churches to create the PC(USA) had not yet occurred. However, my home church was in a "union" presbytery, where both these denominations worked together.

Princeton Theological Seminary (PTS) for my studies. It had precisely such a reputation. I was not disappointed. In the three short years I attended PTS, we touched on almost every important subject for a PC(USA) pastor. From biblical studies, homiletics, and counseling to evangelism, history, polity, and worship, we covered it all. This very broad-based course of study equipped me to follow my expected career path: serve a couple years as an associate pastor, maybe followed by a stint as a solo pastor of a small church, and if lucky, move up the ladder to even larger congregations. This was my plan, and Princeton Seminary prepared me for it.

I graduated and was called by a church in Stillwater, Oklahoma, to serve as their assistant pastor. Soon after, I was advanced to associate pastor. The plan was unfolding as expected. Then things changed. With some urging from an elder in my congregation, I joined the U.S. Army Reserves (USAR) as a chaplain. With the blessing of my church, I now wore an Army uniform one weekend a month and for two weeks each summer.

After ten years in Stillwater, which included eight years with my USAR unit, I was encouraged to enter the Army full time as a chaplain. I took the challenge, and for the last twenty-plus years this has been my ministry. I am endorsed by the PC(USA) to serve on active duty as an Army chaplain. I have served with military units ranging from medical to armor (tanks), at locations like the Pentagon and near the DMZ in Korea, and I have deployed to combat four times. These experiences have radically changed my concept of ministry.

It would be impossible in the short span of this work to cover all the ways my views have changed. Instead, I will focus on two of the areas where I have had to make the greatest adjustments; these are my "congregation" and my work environment.

Princeton prepared me to serve as a pastor for a congregation of Presbyterians. My flock would certainly all be Christian; that was a given. As to other social dynamics, it has been my personal observation that a typical PC(USA) congregation tends to be middle to upper middle class, theologically open-minded, and politically centric to somewhat liberal. Pertaining to race and ethnicity, most congregations are fairly homogenous.

My military flock, on the other hand, is quite diverse: African American, Asian, Latino, Caucasian. Socioeconomically, they are all over the map. And as far as faith background, they might be Baptist (any one of the many varieties), Roman Catholic, Christian nondenominational, Jewish, Muslim, Wiccan, atheist, and maybe, just maybe, a couple of Presbyterians.

Why do I call them my "flock" if they are not from my denomination or

---

Rather than complicate the article, I will use PC(USA) as a generic term to refer to the church I have belonged to since I was a child.

even my faith group? This is the unique ministry of the military chaplain. When I took my oath of office, I swore to support and defend the Constitution of the United States of America. For a chaplain, this is especially highlighted by the First Amendment, "Congress shall make no law respecting an establishment of religion, or prohibiting the free exercise thereof. . . ."[2] This is what we chaplains call the "free exercise clause"; it is the mantra for the Army chaplaincy. A chaplain ensures that every soldier in the unit has the opportunity to practice his or her chosen religion or is allowed to choose to practice none at all.

My ministry as a chaplain involves *performing* those religious acts when I am able and *providing* an alternative when I am not able. I will offer a few examples. I perform ministry by planning and leading Protestant worship services and also offering Communion for any confessing Christians. I perform adult and infant baptisms and celebrate marriage rites for those who meet the requirements of local laws. I offer pastoral counseling for soldiers or family members who are troubled, and I have been honored to assist families in grief by presiding at funerals or memorial ceremonies for their loved ones.

These are examples of how I perform ministry. And they would all sound very familiar to anyone serving as a pastor of a civilian congregation. It is in the act of *providing* for my soldiers that my ministry becomes unique. Mass offered by a priest is very important to Roman Catholic soldiers, especially when they are deployed to dangerous areas of the world. I cannot pretend to perform Mass myself; that would be highly inappropriate. So when I have Catholic soldiers who are stuck on an isolated post, I arrange for a helicopter or convoy to take a priest to visit them.

Providing for my Catholics is one of the more straightforward missions I might undertake. Sometimes the religious requirements of my soldiers have called for some very creative problem solving. While deployed to Somalia, I had two Muslim soldiers who needed a place to pray. After an unsuccessful attempt to work things out with leaders in my task force, I found myself negotiating with the Pakistani liaison officer. He offered my soldiers the opportunity to join his unit for *jumu'ah* prayer on Fridays. I have also asked for Jewish soldiers to be released from duty to attend Passover services and explained to leaders at West Point why a Zoroastrian cadet needed a room where he could burn a candle. These few examples just scratch the surface of the many ways I provide ministry for my soldiers.

I was never trained to do this in seminary. Nothing prepared me to provide support for a Muslim or a Roman Catholic, let alone a Wiccan member of

2. U.S. Constitution, Amendment 1.

my "congregation." I was prepared to minister to Presbyterians or to people interested in learning about what it means to be a Presbyterian.

What about my work environment? When I was in seminary, where did I expect that I would work each day of my pastoral career? Most churches have an office for the pastor (or pastors), which might include a full- or part-time secretary. The church office is where members drop by for a cup of coffee or for counseling, and to attend committee meetings. As a local pastor, I might leave the office to visit a church member in the hospital or to call on a visitor who left contact information in worship the previous Sunday. Community gatherings and funerals might also pull me away from the church building, but most of my activities would revolve around the church structure, with the key focus being worship in the sanctuary on Sunday mornings and other appointed times.

The military has hard-standing chapels, but an Army chaplain who makes his or her ministry revolve around that structure will quickly lose contact with the soldiers. Army chaplains are embedded with units, going where they go, living and working in the midst of their congregations. We call this "a ministry of presence." When the soldiers meet early in the morning to run five miles for physical training, we are with them. (We are required to meet the same height and weight standards and pass the same physical training tests that every other soldier must complete.) If they jump out of airplanes or road march twelve miles, we are there. When the unit is out in the heat, rain, and mud, away from family, so are we. And when our units deploy to a combat zone halfway around the world, we go with them.

During the first month of Operation Iraqi Freedom, I lived out of my Humvee. That was my "office," and the soldiers knew how to find me because of the camouflage flag hanging on my antenna. I would drive to the location of a platoon or company, set up for worship, and the hood of my vehicle would become the Communion table.

While I usually have a traditional office in the unit headquarters, my "work environment" is with my soldiers and their families. Since I work in the same place, wear the same uniform, and stand in the same "hurry up and wait" lines, I understand the pressures they face. This creates a very special bond with them, and they share things with me that members of my civilian congregation would never dream of sharing. I understand more about their lives than I do when making an occasional visit to the lawyer or the auto mechanic or the schoolteacher in my civilian congregation.

The one difference between myself and my soldiers is that I do not carry a weapon. In fact, it is currently against Army policy for me to even train or familiarize with weapons, so there will be no confusion about my role on the battlefield. But teamed with me is a noncommissioned officer who has a variety of administrative and planning skills to assist in the mission of providing religious support. And this soldier *is* armed and provides security for the team when we are in dangerous places. So my "secretary/receptionist" goes where I go and carries a weapon!

There are many more ways the application of ministry varies between a civilian and military parish. Other matters like evangelism and stewardship have their own sets of challenges when one wears an Army uniform. This is certainly a unique type of ministry, and one not meant for everyone. After more than thirty years wearing the uniform, I hear the term "ministry" and no longer picture interacting with a group of Christians who all believe as I do. And my image of where that ministry occurs now includes dining facilities and gyms, dusty roadsides, and leaky tents.

My studies at Princeton Theological Seminary did not prepare me specifically for this unique ministry. However, they did teach me about taking care of people. That is the key to ministry for our service members: recognizing that they are all God's children and taking care of them. When you internalize that, you can figure out the rest.

SURROUNDED BY A CLOUD OF WITNESSES WHILE PREACHING RELEASE TO THE CAPTIVES

Charlotte Ruth Mallory

I am the namesake of Charlotte Garrett Scott, my beloved paternal grand-mother. She was virtually unknown to my father, Robert Henry Scott, the youngest and only boy of the four children she gave birth to. My father was only nine years old when his mother died in the Greystone Psychiatric Hospital at thirty-six years of age. The shame and stigma attached to mental illness kept me from knowing anything more than her name and birthplace until only recently. However, I know that it is no coincidence that I found my paternal grandmother this late in life. I am sure that I am here because of her *faith living still.* My grandmother, Charlotte, affirms that I am surrounded by *so great a cloud of witnesses.* As I have been blessed to work as a ministry intern, not only in a psychiatric care facility but also in a major teaching hospital and youth correctional facility, I am grateful that her life and legacy informs my ministry *for such a time as this.*

My upbringing was in the loving proximity and nurture of both my moth-er's and my father's families. Yet for me there remained a gaping hole in the family history, as I sought to know the woman for whom I was named. Ironi-cally, a death certificate obtained in 2014 provided much more insight into her life. She was born to Mary Williams Garrett and Henry Garrett on June 5, 1899. By age twenty-four, my grandmother had given birth to four chil-dren. It was sometime not long after the birth of my father that the family was forced off their land in Dawson, Georgia, and fled to Newark, New Jersey. This sudden change in the circumstances of her life must have taken its toll, as some time shortly afterward she was admitted to Greystone Psychiatric Hospital in Morris Plains, New Jersey. She remained there until her death in 1936. My great-grandmother, Mary Williams Garrett, survived her daughter. Perhaps then it was the "faith of *her mother, living still*" that sustained Char-lotte during the difficult years of psychiatric hospitalization. Certainly it is not by coincidence that my experiences in field education and clinical pastoral education provided significant, firsthand, ministerial encounters not only in the state psychiatric hospital in Trenton but also the state youth correctional facility in Bordentown, New Jersey.

I believe that finding my grandmother at this late stage of my life has given her a voice—a voice that she may never have had during her short and tumultuous life—a voice that was missing in my own life and only more fully comprehended as I discerned my "call" to the gospel ministry.

As a child, my faith was nurtured at home and at the Mt. Olive Baptist Church in my hometown of East Orange, New Jersey. I attended Sunday school classes followed by morning worship services along with my maternal grandparents, Lois and Whittier Collins. Papa and Mama, as I affectionately called them, were doting grandparents who provided the means for us to receive a Christian education. However, it was not until moving into adulthood that I began to feel a yearning to draw closer to God. I desired an understanding of what our Lord meant when He said, "I am come that they might have life, and that they might have it more abundantly" (John 10:10 KJV). Thus my religious experience and development brought me to the point of believing that I should study theology as an academic discipline. As I was led to begin scholarly study of the Holy Scriptures, I was also led to search out the opportunities that were available in order to prepare to devote my life's work to the Lord. Through the work I engaged in at my home church, Fountain Baptist, in the areas of HIV/AIDS ministry, teaching, and mission trips to Kenya and South Africa, and after conferring with my pastor, Reverend J. Michael Sanders, I came to discern a call to seminary education.

Whether my gifts and work were recognized early on, I cannot say. What I am certain of is that I have had the phenomenal support of my pastor from the instant that I discerned my call unto this very day. I must confess that I did not perceive to have an actual "call" experience, but rather felt a very definite "ordering of my steps" as I followed a "call" to study theology in the academy. I remember one significant experience, as I worked at the Samaritan Baptist Church in Trenton as part of my student ministry experience. The pastor of Samaritan was the Reverend Joseph Ravenell, a PTS graduate and now a bishop, who had a significant impact upon my theological education. During one of our weekly theological reflections, Pastor Ravenell, having listened to my protestations about being prepared for "preaching," freed me with these words: "Charlotte, right now the Lord has called you to be a student. So be a student." Truly, everything fell into place after I rested in the knowledge that by studying and continuing as a student at the seminary, I was answering the "call" that the Lord had placed on my life at that time.

As a member of a Baptist church, I consider myself to be part of the whole Christian family who stress the experience of personal salvation through faith in Jesus Christ, symbolized both in baptism and the Lord's Supper. I continue to believe that my faith in God, through God's revelation in Jesus Christ, forms the basis of my faith. My faith in God continues to permeate every aspect of my life. This is the knowledge that informs my ministry of pastoral care. I stand firm in this belief even as I minister to those for whom Jesus Christ is not the way.

My understanding of ministry has evolved and developed as I have experienced chaplaincy. Through the PTS field education and clinical pastoral education programs, I interned at Albert C. Wagner Youth Correctional Facility in Bordentown, New Jersey; at the State Psychiatric Hospital in Trenton; and later as a resident chaplain at the Robert Wood Johnson University Hospital. These opportunities allowed me to offer pastoral care in the form of emotional and spiritual support to patients, inmates, and their families, as well as the staff of both the hospitals and prisons. This work served to provide the basis for my ministry to the inmates, custody officers, and staff of the Edna Mahan Correctional Facility, where I have served as a full-time chaplain since 2008. As were my previous internships, my work at the prison involves serving a multifaith population that continually calls me to theological reflection.

My role as full-time chaplain to the women of Edna Mahan has been at the same time one of the most challenging experiences and one of the greatest blessings I have ever had in my life. Because this is the state's only prison for women, I minister to women whose sentences range from a few months to life in prison. I am there to minister not only to the inmates but also to staff and custody officers. It is a blessing to spend my life's work "standing in the gap" for the people I serve. I do not represent administration, custody, or staff. I make myself available to serve anyone and everyone who would seek my spiritual presence and guidance. As with any position within a department of the state, there is a lot of paperwork that must be tended to. However, as a minister, I have the privilege and blessing of being able to drop everything to go to anyone in need. One can only imagine the trauma of receiving a death notice of a family member, or a notice of serious, life-threatening circumstances of a close family member, while being "locked up."

My responsibilities include the coordination of religious services that take place almost every day of the month in both maximum- and minimum-security areas. It involves paperwork that must be submitted daily so that our volunteers can enter the institution and so that our inmates are allowed to attend. Almost 95 percent of those serving prison sentences will at some time leave to return to the community. Helping inmates to return to the community has necessitated the development of a mentoring program. We, as chaplains, coordinate the role of mentors who come into the prison and begin meeting with the women when they are within nine months of leaving the institution. Developing our mentoring program to help the women return to the community has also necessitated the training of churches to be open, receptive, and nurturing to these "returning citizens" who will come back to their churches. Churches that have allowed us to come inside and offer the training to members of their congregations receive certification as a "Station of Hope," as sponsored by the American Baptist Home and Mission Society.

My calling to seminary studies followed many years in various leadership positions in both the public and private sectors. It was in this capacity that I found myself yearning for more. When I began to hear and understand the call to seminary, there were those who warned that such pursuit could threaten my faith. Although I did find my studies to be tremendously challenging, my faith only grew stronger. It was also the *faith of my mother, living still* that helped me stay the course. My mother, Myrna Scott Chapman, has always been my rock of support and fortification. She is also my biggest cheerleader in achieving higher educational pursuits and she, most of all, lives out the call to *love one another* . . .

Being Baptist and studying in a predominantly Presbyterian seminary allowed me the freedom to fully explore my own tradition from a new and different perspective. I have been enriched because of it.

The Field Education office at PTS, and particularly my advisor, the Reverend Chester Polk, were significant in my formation in specialized ministry. Reverend Polk listened carefully as I expressed my hesitations and reticence about my "call." With his help and advisement, I was able to take part in field education experiences that changed my life forever. It prepared me for the blessing of the ministry in which I serve today. All of this leads me to believe that it was God's perfect plan that has chosen me. I remain so very grateful that God does not call the qualified but qualifies the called. I am able to say without hesitation that I am exactly where God would have me to be.

Chaplaincy presents the opportunity to consider the abilities and interests that God has given me while I wrestle with the issues of daily life, theological perspectives, and questions about my own inner urgencies. My growing edge continues to require me to examine the strengths and weaknesses I bring to ministry. I must look at and consider how my relationships at work and at home reveal my character and personality. I must acknowledge that this life continues to be a journey of exploration. I should always be changing, evolving, and growing. It is an ongoing discernment of my call to pastoral care. I have made the decision that where God leads me in this journey, I will follow.

I am forever grateful that I have been "compassed about with so great a cloud of witnesses" (Heb 12:1 KJV). These witnesses include not only the help of present family, friends, and associates who impact my life, but also those who have gone on before. They include my grandmother, Charlotte, whom I desire to give a voice to even now, as well as my maternal great-grandmother and great-grandfather, Jessie and Birdie Collins, ministers in the Methodist Church and Holiness movement, respectively. There are countless others who, by the record of their lives, reassure me that endurance is possible, that hardship is temporary, that the grace of God does and will sustain, and that the joys of faith's rewards are enduring.

Finally, with respect to theological education in the future, I believe that there must be a greater effort to recruit a more diverse female faculty. The seminary faculty in particular needs to be more representative of the diversity of race, background, and culture of the many women who are now called to the ministry. In addition, I believe that clinical pastoral education should be a core requirement of the seminary as opposed to being a requirement of the denomination or faith tradition that students follow. When these things take place, they not only benefit our churches and faith-based associations but also our society as a whole.

EVANGELICAL ROOTS, LIBERAL COLLEGE CHAPLAIN

Taryn Mattice

Someone needs to study this fact: many of us—could it be a majority?—who become clergy in the mainline church begin our faith lives in the evangelical world. Why is this? Is faith more likely to "take" in that world and to become the searing, compelling force that leads to a vocation? I am still that fourteen-year-old girl who walked forward at a Young Life meeting and gave her life to Jesus decades ago. I've just changed my mind about a few things.

I grew up in the San Francisco Bay Area, and my family can't remember the last generation who regularly attended church. And I don't recall any family in my midcentury suburban neighborhood piling into their station wagon on Sunday mornings to head to a place of worship. So in that sense, I was living in a world of "nones" long ago. It was California, and Americans had left plenty behind in the mass migration west.

There is a piece of mystery to my story and a piece of happenstance. The mystery is this: from an early age, I did everything I could to get into one of those churches. On Easter Sundays I'd beg my parents to take me, promising to clean the garage in the afternoon. Once, I convinced my parents to drop me off every week at a Sunday school at the closest church to our home, which happened to be Presbyterian. We were in the middle of a project, making a construction-paper "library" of all the books of the Bible, when the Presbyterian church offered a loan to the Angela Davis Defense Fund and my father announced, "No daughter of mine is going to a church that would give money to that woman." So ended my Sunday school career but not my desire to be among people who sang and spoke about goodness and love. I think that's all I really understood about what went on in those buildings. But I knew I wanted it.

My spiritual awakening coincided with a similar awakening in my community. The Billy Graham Crusade came to the Bay Area one summer, and not a few adults in my town got religion. One of them was a handsome and charismatic orthodontist, and he and a few others began a Young Life club for the high school, attracting hundreds of young people each week. I was offered a ride to a "club meeting" the first day of school. The adults were utterly devoted to high school students, spent countless hours at their kitchen tables with us, and took us to church on Sundays. My parents worried that I was "too religious" in those years, and we fought about it constantly. Some people's adolescent rebellion is easy; all I had to do was go to church to really piss off my parents.

I bought most of what I was told in those evangelical circles. That my parents were probably headed to hell, that God didn't make men and women equal, and that the Bible was factual in all it said. But it chafed. The way I understood faith then was that in order to get the good parts, I'd have to swallow the bad parts. This has given me patience and compassion for the fundamentalist college students I've met over the years. If we give them too much challenge or correction too fast, it feels like asking them to leave behind whatever they've learned of goodness and grace.

College was a frustrating time for me, religiously. I didn't belong with the charismatic fundamentalists who prayed in tongues, and I simply didn't understand the mainline crowd who were using feminine imagery for God.

But other parts of life opened up. I took classes with Dennis Brutus, the South African poet. I had a Russian literature professor who spoke so movingly of his own Jewish faith that any lingering idea that he and others like him might be destined for hell faded entirely. Northwestern did for me what college should do; it opened me to both the pain of the world and its beauty. And while it wasn't worked out perfectly, I hung on to my faith while giving up the desire to become a female C. S. Lewis, an Oxford Don with elbow patches—though I did major in English. I volunteered in inner-city tutoring programs and came to believe that urban education would provide me a way to serve God. "Social justice" was not yet a term in common usage, but it was beginning to dawn on me that faith might lead in this direction.

I moved to New York City after college and got a job teaching middle school in East Harlem. What could be a more faithful way to spend one's life than teaching children in a struggling school at the height of the crack epidemic? But I hadn't realized that the proper talents were necessary. I was befriended by a brilliant young teacher in the classroom next to mine (Lisa Damon, the daughter of Virginia Damon, the longtime speech instructor at the seminary). You could walk by her room any moment of the day, and fantastic learning was on display. Not in my classroom; I was drowning and I realized I had to leave. But to what?

Someone said to me, "You like church; why don't you go to seminary?" Becoming a minister was not even a flicker of a dream. I'd never even seen a woman minister, but when he added, "Princeton has a lot of money; you might not have to pay anything," the idea stuck. Three years to lie in the grass reading theology while the clouds rolled by the leafy environs of Princeton sounded like heaven. And it sounded like a way out of New York.

Still, I thought the decision to go to seminary should be more serious, more responsible. So I got a friend to take me to the Red Roof Inn in Parsippany, New Jersey, for a self-designed weekend retreat, an opportunity to discern God's will.

Among the pile of books I took with me was Robert Farrar Capon's *Hunting the Divine Fox*, which includes a chapter titled "Knowing the Will of God."[3] Perfect, I thought, this will have my answer. Capon was an Episcopal priest who also wrote a cooking column in the *New York Times*. He was a terrific writer, playful and big-hearted.

In that chapter he says that when most of us conjure an image of God and ourselves, the image is likely that of a parent and child. A portrait of hierarchy. Discerning the will of God under this construct means figuring out what God in God's wisdom would have us do. But that is not the only image of relationship with the divine in Scripture, he says. There are many, including the one that the rabbis found in the Song of Solomon. Lover and beloved. And what a lover wants of a beloved, Capon says, is for her to be what she most wants to be. To do what she longs to do. I sat bolt-upright and thought, "So merely wanting to go to a seminary to study, that might be enough?" And so I packed off to Princeton, more or less because I wanted to. That, I concluded, was my call story. Become a minister? No. But study, and figure out the next steps later—that was what I wanted, so that is what I did. And I am dearly grateful to the seminary for taking a chance on something as flimsy as that.

For the most part, I thrilled to the place. I was not a member of that first group of women who blazed trails in seminary education but a member of the first group of women who were No Big Deal. We were there, a third of the class, and we were hearing about women who were thriving in the world of ministry. I remember an early day when all of us women were invited to a room where Katharine Sakenfeld, Freda Gardner, Betty Edwards, and Lois Livezey each told their story. It felt wonderfully heady, and I knew I was lucky to be there. These were incredible women, and if they blazed trails, one imagined that they would stay blazed.

First semester I was given a field education assignment in a small town. Since I hadn't thought I'd become a pastor, I wasn't deeply invested, but I did what was asked of me. The first time I preached, the pastor said, "You cannot do that again; you simply can't preach." Fortunately, I didn't care. But I did have to go back to the seminary and tell Kathy Nelson, the field education supervisor, and I will never forget her response. She picked up the phone that moment and called the pastor. "Rev. So-and-So, I understand there was a

3. Robert Farrar Capon, *Hunting the Divine Fox: Images and Mystery in Christian Faith* (New York: Seabury, 1974).

problem last week with Taryn's sermon. Oh, you couldn't hear her. Her voice is too quiet? I understand. Do you have a microphone in your church? Wonderful. Take it out of the closet, and let her use it. Thank you. Good day."

Lois Livezey set me straight once, and I've not forgotten that either. During my years at Princeton, the South Africa divestment campaign was gaining ground at campuses across the country, and a number of students at the seminary hoped our institution would do the same. There were conversations within the student government, and not surprisingly, a variety of approaches were argued and executed among the activists. I proposed writing an extensive paper documenting the larger movement and making the case to the trustees. That idea was tabled. But someone, I'm not sure who, disassembled a Volkswagen bug and reassembled it on the third floor of Stuart Hall, with a sign reading, "Divest Now!" Another student stood up at a meeting with a few administrators and said, "I am prouder to be a citizen of New Jersey (which had already divested its pension plan) than a student at this seminary." I cringed and went off to complain to Dr. Livezey about what I imagined was the exact wrong approach thus far. "Taryn, social movements have many parts," she said. "Don't resent the people who want the same thing you want. Play your own part."

My friend Susan Schilperoort and I became codirectors of the Women's Center our middler year, soon after the seminary announced that Stuart Hall was to be redesigned and the Women's Center was to be closed. We thought that the Women's Center, with its own space, was still needed but were unable to convince the seminary's administration. So we planned a reception and sent invitations to alumni to come and celebrate the Women's Center's last day. I understand that the seminary received lots of alumni feedback, and on the night of the celebration it was announced that a new location was found in Roberts Hall. It was to be temporary, but there was also a promise of a permanent future home.

My ministry has been in higher education for the past twenty-seven years, at three different institutions. Currently my ministry at Cornell University includes a Sunday morning worship service with a congregation that is entirely students. Its composition is a reflection of the campus as a whole, including students from all over the world. Most have some sort of Protestant background, but some have no religious background. They come, as one student says, "looking for a center in a busy life, full of good things, and yet. . . . " With an office on campus I see the occasional student who drops in with a question, or in pain; and when I can, I try to enlarge my own vision. I organized buses to take students from across campus to the Climate March in the fall of 2014, and now I'm wondering if there isn't something we can do to support the campus Muslim community that hopes to hire a chaplain. Ministry on a campus is like ministry everywhere—improvisational.

I've been glad for those undergraduates I've seen leave Cornell and head to seminary, even though I am sometimes afraid for them. I don't think anyone can be sure what the coming decades will mean for ministry. I'm glad for myself that I was simply invested in the learning those three years and wasn't immediately career oriented. Maybe that's not a bad way for young seminarians to go about learning now, knowing that their careers may or may not be in churches or in professional ministry at all, but believing that a seminary education is its own reward. Years ago the Rockefeller Foundation sent Frederick Buechner, Al Gore, and my own predecessor at Cornell, Sharon Dittman, off to seminary, knowing that they would enrich the institution, and possibly find a vocation.

Last year I asked some undergraduates how they felt about the world of the local church they would soon be entering, away from campus. "Seems like there isn't much learning for adults," one said, and the others quickly agreed. "There are ways to volunteer and serve, in and out of the church," they said, "but we are still learning how to pray, how to think, and we don't want that to end." Perhaps our seminaries might imagine a role educating not just our clergy but also providing the sort of quality education I was able to enjoy for a laity that might welcome it.

THRESHOLD MOMENTS:
MINISTRY AT THE BEDSIDE

Carrie L. Buckner

An Ecumenical Youth. I always loved going to church as a child, and I often went alone, as my parents were recovering Southern Baptists, appropriately skeptical of organized religion and the hypocrisy of the church of their youth. I'd ride my bike or tag along with the family of my churchgoing friends. As a young girl, I blared "He is Jehovah" records and wore my "He Is Risen" Jesus T-shirt until it was, quite literally, ridden with holes and threadbare. I still have my white Bible from the nondenominational church where my brother and I were baptized (full immersion) when I was seven years old. I remember my family (my older brother, mother, and father) staring quizzically at me during this zealous phase of my religious development and wondering, "Where does this girl get all this religion?" I sought comfort in God as an ever-present and loving father, and embracing Christianity provided definitive answers to complex questions of identity and meaning.

My spiritual questioning started at a young age and was strongly influenced by my early Catholic school education and the varied religious affiliations of my peers—Presbyterian, Church of Jesus Christ of Latter-day Saints, Baptist, Episcopal, and so forth. Looking back, I see now how my vocation in chaplaincy reflects the ecumenism of my youth. I attended church services with my friends and enjoyed the messages, music, and mentors I encountered along the way. I found my spiritual home in the PC(USA) during my teen years and officially became a member of the First Presbyterian Church in the small town in northern California where I lived. I loved the democratic polity of the PC(USA) and celebrated that I could bring my deep questions of faith and not receive strictly doctrinal responses. My high school pastor, the Rev. Sandy Brown (whom I was able to reconnect with decades later), encouraged me in exploring a call to ministry. He invited me to lead prayers during worship and also celebrated with me as I went off to college to major in comparative religious studies at the University of California, Berkeley.

Ministry beyond the Walls of the Church. The year 2015 marks twenty years of ordained ministry for me in the Presbyterian Church (U.S.A.). It's hard to imagine that I graduated from Princeton Theological Seminary over twenty years ago, and a meaningful career in hospital chaplaincy and supervision in clinical pastoral education unfolded. Two significant life experiences contributed to my call to this form of specialized ministry. First, when I was eight years old, my father suffered a life-threatening accident, and my family spent much of that year in a San Francisco hospital where he had been airlifted in critical condition. I prayed fervently for God to make my dad whole again, in the quiet of my heart and in my vocal nightly prayers, and I found comfort in the healing stories of the Gospels. Ironically, my father underwent months of surgeries and physical rehabilitation in the same hospital where I would later serve as a chaplain and supervise Association for Clinical Pastoral Education (APCE) students. I also discovered during my CPE training that I was born in that same hospital—I am adopted and searched for my birthmother during my CPE residency. Because of this experience of my dad's accident, I have always felt at home in hospitals and experience a sanctuary and sacred quality in hospitals.

The other significant experience that impacted my vocational discernment was my field education placement during my second year of seminary. I served as a student chaplain at a general hospital and a state psychiatric facility in Trenton. Both of these experiences had a profound impact on my sense of call and discernment of my spiritual gifts. My understanding of ministry had always stretched beyond the walls of the church, but here it definitively extended into hospital rooms and locked psychiatric units, where I accompanied people in sacred and holy moments. I've been honored to accompany people during times of illness, birth, and death; these I call "threshold moments" in life, and they often happen in hospitals. Threshold moments are those liminal times when we experience life events that define us in new ways—the death of my mother, and becoming a mother myself, are such moments for me. My father's accident was also a threshold moment. These events mark our lives in ways that make us reauthor our identities.

In the mid-1990s I worked as a hospice chaplain, serving people dying from AIDS in San Francisco. In my role as chaplain, I represented a loving face of God and offered prayers of grace. I brought Communion, sang hymns, and even colored one man's hair, as he would only allow his dear friends to visit him at home if he had his signature "red." I also loved working as part of an interdisciplinary team—another signature of ministry as a chaplain.

In this role, I witnessed the important work of life review, making amends, embracing self-love, and forgiveness. I was humbled to listen to peoples' stories, and empathic listening led me to shift from the golden rule to the platinum rule: "Do unto others what *they* would have done unto them." Impending death has a way of empowering people to say exactly what they want and need in the precious time they have left to live. I learned the power of asking open-ended questions about meaning and suffering.

Sacred and Holy Moments. I came to Princeton Theological Seminary in the fall of 1991 following a yearlong church internship. I came to seminary unsure of how my vocational call would manifest in the church. I was not drawn to preaching or church history. I came to seminary to explore the intersection of faith and lived experiences, spiritual struggle, deep questioning, and embracing the joys and pains of life in a spirit of wisdom and community. Initially, I felt called to children's and family ministry. As a seminary middler, I served as a chaplain intern for my field education at a community hospital in nearby Trenton. Early in this internship, I was called to accompany a young woman giving birth. She was nineteen years old, just a few years younger than I was at that time, and she was alone and scared. I encouraged her, spoke of God's love and grace, and affirmed her amazing strength. I offered few words, but she squeezed my hand and I served as a conduit for God's presence with her during a day in her life she will likely not forget—a threshold moment.

I experienced tremendous privilege and open doors on my journey through theological education. I was ordained at Old First Presbyterian Church in San Francisco to a validated call in chaplaincy and ACPE supervision. In 2008 I served as moderator of the Presbytery of San Francisco and was privileged to participate in ordination services by asking our denomination's constitutional questions of the newly ordained teaching elders. Reflecting on these questions led me to reclaim my own ordination vows and commitment to being a servant leader. I am grateful for the many ways my theological education expanded my worldview and gave shape and form to my spiritual gifts and call to service. I am also grateful for the spirit instilled in me by my mother, who believed that I could accomplish anything I set my mind to with little hardship. This enduring legacy and gift I hope to instill in my amazing daughter.

I do recall one hardship that was bewildering and painful. As part of my ordination process, I requested a recommendation letter from a renowned Princeton Theological Seminary alumnus who was the senior pastor of my church during my college years (he shall remain nameless in this story). I'd made an appointment to meet with him at the church, and I was expecting him to be supportive and to encourage me in my desire to attend Princeton Theological Seminary. He sat behind his desk and began interrogating me on my faith journey, questioning how many people I'd "brought to Christ" and how I thought I could pastor a church. At the end of our time, he informed me that he would not write a letter of recommendation for me since I had not experienced being "born again" as a young adult. I was initially hurt and confused, and then quickly became angry that this man, who was so respected and admired in the Presbyterian Church (U.S.A.) and Princeton Theological

Seminary communities, wasn't supporting and encouraging me in my call to ministry. I experienced a disconnect between seeing him as a leader of integrity and faith and being a narrow-minded and judgmental jerk.

Texts and Teachers in a Community of Connected Learning and Knowing. Jesus' life and teachings, much more than his death, always intrigued me. He met people where they were, turned tables in the temple, and washed feet in the same day. Jesus modeled humility and prophecy in congruent ways. I saw in the Gospel accounts an authentic life—authentic action and feelings expressed in relationships of mutuality and truth. I saw power and humility. The story of Jesus' encounter with the woman at the well exemplifies the kind of connected knowing and relational ministry Jesus continues to model for me.

The first clergywoman I met was an Episcopal priest (she was a copastor with her husband) in the small, rural town in northern California where I lived from age ten through high school. She was warm, funny, down-to-earth, and very smart. I loved watching her celebrate the Eucharist—I experienced the power of the sacraments spoken in a woman's voice. As a young teenager, seeing a woman in religious leadership had a profound impact on me. Now raising a seven-year-old daughter, I see how in one generation my daughter sees *so* many more women and people of color as role models than I was exposed to as a child. Her pediatrician, dentist, piano teacher, and softball coach alone reflect a more diverse and inclusive community.

I am grateful for the theological education and spiritual grounding I experienced as a young seminarian. When I look back, I realize that my book learning in seminary stretched my theological understanding in ways that continue to support my ministry today. Being exposed to texts and emerging biblical interpretations profoundly expanded my theological reflection and worldview. My education offered critical thinking and reflection, openness and humility, faith seeking understanding—core pedagogical themes that I draw upon today in my work as a chaplain, educator, and administrator.

The friendships I formed during my three years at Princeton Theological Seminary shaped my theological education as much as the coursework. The small group cohorts (Nathan Byrd *still* teases me for bringing French bread and brie cheese to our Theology 101 potluck!) created communities of connected learning and knowing. Studying for ordination exams in small groups helped normalize my anxiety and fears throughout the ordination process. Relationships and collaborative learning remain core to my work in supervision and chaplaincy.

The amazing opportunity to travel to India in the summer of 1993 (I am grateful that Dr. Charles Ryerson made this happen for many years) opened my eyes to the world. That trip was my first trip outside of the United States, and it profoundly shaped my understanding of systems, privilege, power, and oppression. Travel experiences (both domestic and international) have become important educational experiences for me and my family.

Exploring one's social location and identity, though sometimes-painful inner work, is what I value most about clinical pastoral education. Experiential education, powerful pedagogical encounters, and the action/reflection model of CPE have shaped my personhood and ministry in myriad ways, and for that I am grateful, humbled, and empowered.

5

Higher Education

College, Seminary, Mission Field

**TRIPLE JEOPARDY:
PASSING THROUGH
THE WILDERNESS**

Julia M. Robinson

My journey of faith began with images of the sacred that I experienced as a little girl. I can remember sitting on a pew in my home church, St. John's Presbyterian Church of Detroit, Michigan, and wishing that my feet could touch the floor. I can still see the preacher in a black robe with his arms outstretched over the pulpit, telling the people about God. As a child, both of my parents attended their respective churches separately. My mother attended St. John's Presbyterian Church with my grandmother, while my father was a member of Second Baptist Church of Detroit, and I alternated churches on Sunday between the Baptist and Presbyterian faiths. Though the majority of my Sundays were spent at St. John's Presbyterian Church, I enjoyed attending my father's church more, simply because they served real wine during the Communion service (a big thing for a young child like myself), and they occasionally got away from the traditional hymns that were sung at my mother's church. Here again, the image of God and Jesus was white at Second Baptist. In the church vestibule, where every member had to pass by before going into the sanctuary, from the ground floor was a fifteen-foot mural of a white Jesus standing over the city of Detroit. Once inside the sanctuary, church members could look at another beautiful stained-glass image of the face of Jesus with European features. As I grew up attending other churches—Baptist, Methodist, Pentecostal, Holiness—the image of Jesus was always white, yet at times the hair color of my savior would change from brown to blond, depending on what church I attended.

The color of Jesus was an unspoken frame of reference within my world as I grew up in Detroit. As a child, I was born with very fair skin for an African American, and my cousins, friends, and even occasionally my own father would tease me because I was so light. My nickname in my neighborhood was "light-bright almost white," "high yella (yellow)," and, more often than not, "red." This intraracism I experienced among my own people was heightened by my experience of being an African American in a country where black people were historically subjugated, oppressed, and dehumanized by their white counterparts. As a child, I knew black Christians in my community who would put a lot of emphasis on skin color. Many would emphasize the harsh realities of what they called "being black in America." Yet these same people worshiped and relied on a white image of Jesus. This reality intrigued and confused me as I grew up in Detroit and attended two predominantly black churches. The local black church was also an enigma to me, as I heard over and over again how white people did not like black people. Yet this white image of Jesus was, for many African Americans, including myself, the blessed savior.

As a young adult, my parents thought it necessary to teach me more about racism, and so one day my mother sat me down in front of our television set and had me watch the *Eyes on the Prize* documentary series, which exposed the struggles of African Americans during the modern civil rights movement. I remember watching the documentary expose the horrors of the bombing of Sixteenth Street Baptist Church in Birmingham and the murder of Emmett Till. I just couldn't understand why God would let someone kill children sitting in His own church. I was shocked that people with varying shades of brown and black were beaten, murdered, and discriminated against by white people who had the same physical characteristics of the Jesus I worshiped in my own black church. The documentary sparked an ongoing series of questions and explorations on the subject of faith, suffering, the local black church, and the historical experiences of African Americans. I took these intersections of faith and race into my college years, which marked the beginning of my sense of calling to the ministry of the Word and Sacrament.

Though I had been active in both of my parents' churches, I never truly felt a call to serve the Lord in ministry until 1991. That year, I was in my last year of my bachelor's degree at Alma College. I was one of only fifteen African American students in a predominantly white population of fifteen hundred students. My experience with racism was minimal during my time at Alma, and yet I was made keenly aware that many whites still saw black people as inferior. During this period, the Reverend Jesse Perry was the newly hired chaplain of Alma College and was also a member of St. John's Presbyterian Church, my home church. Jesse, as I referred to him, was my first mentor, and he helped me to navigate my faith and the vicissitudes of racism during my college years.

By the end of my senior year, I was torn between wanting to be like Jesse, a college chaplain, or going into the law profession. In my heart, though, all I wanted to do was teach people about Jesus. At both of my home churches, I had offered Sunday sermons during Youth Sundays and Women's Day programs since my teens. As Jesse had witnessed most of my participation in church, he encouraged me to go under the care of the Detroit presbytery. While my mother and grandmother were ecstatic about this decision, my father admitted to me that he was not comfortable with women preachers. Nevertheless, he supported my decision to pursue ordination. By the winter of 1991, I had declared my call to the ministry in the Presbyterian Church (U.S.A.). Yet I still had questions. Questions about racism and black suffering. I was still wrestling with the image of Jesus' whiteness and the reality of white supremacy in America. I had even more questions about how some black folks were able to love this white image of Jesus while openly ridiculing white people. I was also still struggling with the internal racism I was experiencing from my own race because I was so light skinned, and how all of this fit within the love of God.

Although all of these questions plagued my mind, I applied to Princeton Theological Seminary (PTS). In the interim, Jesse had encouraged me to attend a two-day senior visit that the seminary offered to prospective students. I inquired about the two-day senior visit program, was accepted, and visited the PTS campus in the winter semester of my senior year at Alma College. By May of 1991, I had my acceptance letter from PTS, then later moved into Alexander Hall, with a beautiful bird's-eye view of central campus. Within the first few weeks of the semester, I was running up my parents' phone bill with collect calls because of my courses on Old Testament and church history. It wasn't that the course requirements were onerous; it was that the course content was so disturbing. What do you mean that Moses didn't write the first five books of the Old Testament? What did you say about the Red Sea . . . only six inches of water when the Hebrews crossed over? What?! The next semester wasn't any easier, when I had to take a course learning Hebrew! It was then that I recalled the words that seminary President Thomas W.

Gillespie shared during my orientation, "This is a wilderness experience, but God will see you through."

The wilderness experience President Gillespie spoke of had been a part of my life since my childhood. My courses at PTS only added to the questions I already held about race, racism, suffering, and faith.

In response to prayer, the Lord sent mentors to support me along the journey of my seminary experience. Dr. Brian K. Blount was the one of the first mentors to help me make sense of faith, race, and suffering. He was the newly appointed New Testament professor at PTS, and we had numerous conversations about the Gospels and the black experience. My friend and fellow student at PTS, Rev. Evelyn Manson, was also a strong presence during my tenure at the seminary. Rev. Manson, as I called her, was a strong, opinionated, and feisty woman full of love and wisdom, which she freely gave to me during my time at PTS.

By 1994, I found myself walking slowly down the aisle of Princeton University Chapel during my graduation ceremony. That day was one of triumph, faith, and understanding. I knew then that I was on a life journey to spread the good news of Jesus Christ and to confront the ambiguities of racism in America. I had new clarity in my sense of calling, and I knew that God wanted me to teach about race, religion, and even about the places where it looked like He was not present—places of violence. I returned home and entered a doctoral program in comparative black history at Michigan State University. My professors at Michigan State supplied the historical knowledge and background of race and racism in America, but PTS supplied the critical religious and faith perspective I was able to bring to the history of the African American experience.

These skills and perspectives have shaped my vocation and my calling. As an associate professor of African American religion in the Department of Religious Studies at UNC Charlotte, my teaching and scholarship have continually revolved around the subjects of religion and racial violence, which has often positioned me as a consultant and university spokesperson for local and national news media. Alongside my academic position, I also serve the Presbyterian Church as a pulpit supply minister in the Presbytery of Charlotte. My sermons are given in settings where, even today, eleven o'clock is still the most segregated hour for most Presbyterians in the Charlotte area. Though the worship styles may have slight variations between the predominantly white and black congregations I serve, there are seasons of inclusivity between black and white Presbyterians, and both groups celebrate the love of God in Christ Jesus with equal passion and commitment.

As an African American within the Presbyterian faith, I have come to make sense of the perceived "whiteness" of Jesus. I have come to look beyond the limited images of Jesus Christ and see the love of God in His son for all races and all people. While I study race, I do not see it in the reality of God's love in the world. I just see Jesus Christ and His great love for humanity.

In closing, PTS has been a tremendous place for me to grow and prepare for the ministry I have today in the church. However, if theological institutions like PTS are to enhance the educational experiences of their students, the curriculum offered by these institutions needs to address what Theressa Hoover calls the "triple jeopardy" of women in ministry, particularly African American women.[1] While PTS trained me well, there was no training for confronting and overcoming what I term ecclesiastical racism, sexism, and even classism in ministry. Throughout my fifteen years of ministry, I've unfortunately had occasions where I was barred from preaching in the pulpit, kept from performing funeral services, and even sexually harassed by fellow ministers and parishioners alike, simply because of my race and gender. The most scathing forms of racism I've experienced have been from fellow clergymen in the Presbyterian Church, who encouraged me to serve in another denomination because, in their words, the "Baptist" denomination was more suited to my race. Sadly, theological educational centers do not adequately address the "triple jeopardies" of ministry for African American woman, let alone the various forms of discrimination and challenges specifically faced by women in ministry. If there was ever a need to address these issues, it is now, as more and more women are entering the folds of leadership in the church.

Last, I would encourage theological institutions to emphasize the importance of Jesus Christ and His finished work on the cross as a central component in the weekly sermons of the church. Too often, seminarians know more about the historical-critical method and the rubrics of exegesis than they do about the transformative power of Jesus Christ. The calling of a minister to the Word and Sacrament is so much more than the passing of ordination exams. It is a culmination of his or her life experience, the development of skill sets to address the human experience in all of its glories and horrors, and the personal pursuit of an intimacy with Jesus Christ, who loves us all beyond measure.

---

1. Theressa Hoover, "Black Women and the Churches: Triple Jeopardy," in *Black Theology: A Documentary History*, ed. James H. Cone and Gayraud S. Wilmore (Maryknoll, NY: Orbis, 1979), 227–88.

A NEW PERSPECTIVE ON FAITH AND NEIGHBORLY LOVE OUTSIDE THE CHURCH

Kathryn D. Blanchard

If my "faith journey" is interesting at all, it's not because it is unique but because it is symptomatic of cultural trends that are much bigger than my individual life. My journey has led me away from faith and into the wilderness, such that I might now be called a "none"—someone who is unaffiliated with any religion—at least for survey purposes. But before I get to that, it seems necessary to offer some context. So here goes.

These are the states in which I've lived: Virginia, Pennsylvania, New Jersey (four separate times), Kansas, Ohio, Minnesota, North Carolina, Georgia, and my current home, Michigan. When people ask, I say I'm from New Jersey, but this feels less and less true the older I get.

These are the churches of which I've been part: Episcopal (three times), Methodist, Congregational, Presbyterian (three times), and Christian and Missionary Alliance. I married a Presbyterian whom I met at Princeton Theological Seminary and was for a few years a "pastor's wife" in a rural congregation who seemed to think they were Southern Baptist.

These are the academic institutions that have helped shape my intellect: wealthy suburban public primary and secondary schools; Kenyon College, where I majored in religious studies; Princeton Theological Seminary, where I imbibed liberal Reformed Protestantism; and Duke University, where I was schooled in all the Catholic-Mennonite theology, antiliberalism, and virtue ethics that I'd missed at PTS. Teaching multiple religious traditions to undergraduates at Alma College continues to shape me.

These are the demons with which I've struggled over the decades: anger, depression, narcissism, pride, fear, self-loathing, hopelessness, intemperance, and oversharing. I have developed an unfortunately cynical sense of humor as a coping mechanism.

The stable part of my life, such as it is, has been family. Though we are spread across the country, folks on both my mother's and father's sides (northern and southern, respectively) tend to stay married, and they like to get together with extended family whenever possible. I have always been told that you can count on family when everything else goes awry. (You can also count on them to be a little crazy in the way that families often are, but at least you know they're there.) Since getting married by a Lutheran at the seminary chapel in 1998, I have added my spouse's southern family to the list of constants in my often-changing life. Our only child was born in 2004, and we now strive above all things to be there for him. As far as he knows, Alma, Michigan, is the best place in the whole world to live.

All of this information may seem extraneous to the question of faith, but it isn't. My seminomadic existence and my individualistic/narcissistic outlook are not unusual in the United States, where many folks chase jobs around the country, letting economics and career concerns trump stability of community when it comes to deciding where to live or to raise kids. Just as I find it difficult to say where I'm from, I also find it difficult to say what I am in religious terms. I have sometimes envied those people who identified as "cradle-to-grave" members of whichever denomination was theirs or who had clear "conversion" experiences that allowed them to identify unequivocally with a new tradition, leaving an old identity behind. My life has been a smorgasbord of interesting places and people; is it any wonder I'm a bit of a polytheist when it comes to the divine?

My earliest church memories are of singing in the children's choir at a Methodist congregation, where my sister and I attended with my mother (my dad being too busy for church in those days). I loved wearing my red robe, watching the organist, and singing in front of the congregation. I also loved the children's sermons, which always began, "Boys and girls, do you know what's in my brown paper bag this morning?" My mother raised us on Bible stories and hymns and a constant refrain of "Is that what Jesus would do?" decades before WWJD bracelets. We changed churches every time we moved, and mainline churches gradually failed to satisfy my mother's evangelicalism, so as a teenager I found myself in a CMA church where I learned a lot about Paul but felt out of place in the youth group (my parents were college educated and I liked secular music and dancing). I was more comfortable in Campus Life. By college, I identified only as "Christian," not having time for denominational labels. All that mattered, I thought, was my personal relationship with Jesus Christ—summed up by hanging out with Christians, having no sex, and drinking no alcohol. I eschewed church in favor of the student Christian fellowship, loosely connected with Campus Crusade for Christ. I went on mission trips from Daytona Beach to Papua New Guinea, out of a sense of duty to bring the good news to the heathen about how to avoid damnation.

At the same time, I sabotaged my own salvation by majoring in religion.

In my coursework, I began to have the sneaking suspicion that Buddhists, Muslims, even—gasp!—Roman Catholics like Teresa of Avila might have things to teach me. I started asking dangerous questions: *What if non-Christians aren't going to hell? What if mystics are right? What if I don't want to be a missionary? What if I'm only Christian because of where I was born?* I stopped reading my Bible. I alienated my Campus Crusade "discipler" and many of my friends. I got dumped by my Christian boyfriend when everyone else was getting engaged. After commencement, I became a Generation X stereotype, moving in with my parents and working retail. Reality truly did bite.

I'm grateful to my dad, who sensed that I missed studying religion, for being the first person to suggest that I go back to school. He put me in touch with a friend of his, a religion professor, who suggested divinity school as a good option because it would not "prematurely bifurcate" the academic and the spiritual. I planned a road trip to his alma mater, Harvard Divinity School, and on the way I stopped in Princeton to see a college friend of mine at Princeton Theological Seminary. The rest, as they say, is history.

During orientation at PTS in the fall of 1994, the first question most folks asked was, "What denomination are you?" This took me by surprise, having apparently misunderstood the nature of seminary. I started calling myself "denominationally challenged" and avoided chapel, especially on communion Fridays. I resisted prayers at the beginning of classes. Out of fear of disappointing any more American Christians, I did my summer field education placement in Germany and my yearlong placement at a hospital, neither of which required much god-talk.

But over time, hanging around smart, critical, conscious, deliberate Christians made Christianity appealing again. At PTS, I learned church history for the first time; I was appalled by the politics but came to appreciate feeling like one tiny drop in a giant, rushing river. Paul Rorem was especially instrumental in this regard. Christianity wasn't primarily about my personal relationship with Jesus Christ; it was about billions of people over thousands of years trying to figure out how to live in light of his life and teaching. I also gained a new perspective on the Bible, which had been lost to me for a few years. Don Juel, who arrived in 1995, made the Gospel of Mark seem so alive, existing right here and now in the spaces between those of us who read it, even as we also strove to make sense of it in its own historical context.

In addition to offering new perspectives on Scripture and tradition, seminary was instrumental in raising my consciousness about gender, race, and class. Much of this learning happened outside the classroom. Of incalculable importance were the women of Wine & Whine—a third-floor Hodge Hall tradition—where I encountered Christian feminism for the first time. In conjunction with feminist course texts (especially from Katharine Doob

Sakenfeld and Carol Lakey Hess) and through involvement in the Women's Center, I came to see that feminism and Christianity were not mutually exclusive. My only wish is that more of my male colleagues (and some professors) spent as much time learning about gender as I did.

While learning about my oppression as a woman, I simultaneously learned about my privilege as a white person. Not only was I reading African American authors, I also encountered African American students, many of whom were older and braver than me, and who had no compunction about putting me in my place. It was often painful, but also necessary to my education; I had to go through some angry stages to get to a place where I could listen more carefully and think more constructively. Mark Taylor's courses and a semester with Gustavo Gutiérrez were especially crucial to my understanding of how theology, race, and class intertwined in both constructive and insidious ways. Again, I wish that more of my white classmates (and some professors) had come to terms with their privilege.

Upon graduating in 1997, I took a job at the Crisis Ministry of Princeton and Trenton. For the next several years of working and graduate school, I remained well ensconced in the Presbyterian Christian fold. But since coming to Alma in 2006, where I teach multiple religions and where all my time and energy are spent in a liberal arts community, I have not been able to commit myself to church again. For a couple of years, out of guilt, I dragged my husband (no longer serving a congregation) and son on Sundays, but eventually I lost the will to continue. I now get my intellectual religious fix through teaching and, when I can, through meditation with Buddhists.

Does this mean I have lost my "faith"? I confess to being anxious about the word, since it sounds so much like "belief" to most folks. What I believe now certainly looks unlike anything I would have called faith back in the 1990s. But "fidelity" or "faithfulness," including to the teachings of Jesus, is still very much a part of my life. I strive to be faithful to my marriage, my child, my family, my friends, my colleagues, and my students. I cannot save the whole world; it is to my nearest neighbors that I owe the bulk of my finite time and energy. (I fail them time and again, but I keep practicing.) I strive to be faithful to justice, especially for the disenfranchised—the poor, women, racial and religious minorities, migrants, children, animals, and the earth. I practice this in my parenting, my buying habits, my voting, my social media use, my teaching, my research and writing, and my charitable giving. I strive to be faithful to forgiveness over grudges, compassion over hatred or indifference, humility over egoism, and generosity over hoarding. I believe in loving my enemies and dealing with the plank in my own eye, as Jesus taught. I believe in the interconnectedness and emptiness of all beings, as the Buddha taught. My dearest wish is to reduce suffering, both my own and others', through mindful and loving thoughts, words, and actions. I am still very far from this goal.

I know that it saddens my mother that I don't share her evangelical faith. I suspect it saddens our faith mothers and fathers at the seminary to know that some of their alumni do not end up in "the church." But among faith, hope, and love, the greatest is love. Even if my faith journey has led me away from orthodox belief, it has led me imperfectly toward neighbor-love. I am grateful to all of my companions along the way, including those at seminary, some of whom remain faithful to the idea of the one, holy, catholic and apostolic church. Others are Jewish or atheist or Buddhist or "none." But if whoever does the will of God is my brother and sister and mother, then those who are faithful to love, wisdom, and justice in equal measure are teachers to me.

FROM BAKER'S DAUGHTER TO PROTESTANT THEOLOGIAN: MOTIVATED BY THE BIG QUESTIONS

Linda A. Mercadante

None of what I do today was even remotely in my mind growing up. Becoming a Protestant, going to seminary, getting ordained, and becoming a professor of theology were things of which I had no knowledge or aspiration. My father was an Italian Catholic immigrant, and my mother, second-generation Russian-Austrian Jewish. Once they married—defying their families' horror at a "mixed marriage"—they put their religions on a back shelf, opened a bakery in the Italian North Ward of Newark, New Jersey, and kept our home a "no religion" zone. That is, until I came along and ruined everything—because I was very unhappy being "nothing."

I wanted what my Italian cousins took for granted—to go inside the magnificent Sacred Heart Cathedral, to wear a cross, to have my own prayer books. Mostly, I wanted to learn about God. My mother was very upset because, in her mind, I was a little Jewish girl. But no one ever actually told me that, nor did anyone give me any religious instruction. That is, until one day when I was about eight. One of my Italian aunts noticed my interest in a prayer book and said, "Well, Linda, you know, Jesus was Jewish, and *he* became a Catholic." Although people laugh when I tell this story now, at the time it made perfect sense to me. I bonded with Jesus immediately, took matters into my own hands, and became a Catholic. The Baltimore Catechism was my first theology book, helping me start to ponder the "big questions."

All this held me until I graduated from college with a teaching degree. But I wanted a wider world, so I tore up my first teaching contract and joined United Airlines as a flight attendant. While I traveled and gained confidence, my eyes were also opened to sexism in the world as well as in the church, so I quit. Even so, I took a job as a reporter at a diocesan Catholic newspaper. I loved the work, but as it became clear that nuns and priests were ordinary mortals, I suddenly had a "de-conversion" and lost my faith. Next, I became a reporter on a secular newspaper, making my career central. Although I honed my skills with good success, even winning state journalism awards didn't fill my spiritual emptiness. I tried to fill this with all kinds of alternative spiritualities. But I never found anything that could answer the "big questions."

Finally, I quit everything and went hitchhiking in Europe. After some lonely months, I happened upon what I mistook for a hippie commune in the Swiss Alps. By then I was broke and exhausted, so even when I learned that L'Abri was actually a Protestant evangelistic mission, I decided to stay. But the place felt strange to me. Growing up, I had hardly known any Protestants, had never set foot in a Protestant church, and had no idea what Protestants believed. In fact, according to my Jewish and Italian relatives, Protestants had no use for the likes of us.

But the people there welcomed my Jewish background and difficult questions, and even tolerated my feminism. They also introduced me to Reformed theology and gave me a Bible. Suddenly things broke open for me. In the binding of Old and New Testaments, in the story of Jesus, in the ways these people loved God with their minds as well as their hearts, suddenly I felt whole.

I felt the stirrings of a ministerial vocation, but they told me I was wrong. Still, what I read in the Bible, especially Galatians 3:28, spoke to me differently. With the hubris and ignorance of youth, and in my feminist ardor, I figured that if I learned the original languages and retranslated the Bible, I could help these well-meaning people see that their conservative ideas about women were wrong. I enrolled in a somewhat more liberal evangelical school, Regent College in Vancouver, British Columbia. They taught me theology, Hebrew and Greek, and biblical interpretation. But they didn't believe in women's ordination either.

Down the street, in the library of the Vancouver School of Theology I discovered books on Christian feminism and liberation theology that brought biblical themes together with more progressive social views on gender. I was sure that others would be happy to hear about this, so even though I was still only a student, I organized a conference on this theme. People seemed to enjoy my teaching, and I loved doing it. Even so, my professors urged me to go back to journalism rather than earning a PhD. They were especially adamant that seeking ordination would be unbiblical.

Before graduating, I wrote a master's thesis on the history of interpretation of 1 Corinthians 11:2–16. Because the faculty praised it publicly, suddenly I was no longer seen by my fellow students as the scary feminist heretic but a competent scholar. When my oral defense was attended by half the school, my thesis published and used as a resource for church study groups, I knew that I had found my vocation.[2] I began publishing articles on various theological topics and was increasingly invited to speak publicly.

---

2. Linda Mercadante, *From Hierarchy to Equality: A Comparison of Past and Present Interpretations of 1 Cor. 11:2–16 in Relation to the Changing Status of Women in Society*, (Vancouver: GMH, 1978).

I started my PhD at the Graduate Theological Union in Berkeley, California, and searched for a denomination that ordained women. When I spoke with Earl Palmer, pastor at the Presbyterian church in Berkeley, he told me that the PC(USA) believed in an educated ministry and women's ordination, and considered teaching as ministry, so I transferred to Princeton Theological Seminary. I wanted to be at a seminary where both women and men trained for ministry and everyone respected intellectual work.

On my first day there, Prof. Dan Migliore asked me a question no one else had ever asked me: "Do you want to be ordained?" To my great surprise, I answered, "Yes." While ordination had been a central issue in my search for a denomination, it was in the abstract. Now it was personal. Dr. Migliore matter-of-factly assured me that this could be taken care of while I was doing my PhD there.

I majored in historical theology to understand how belief and culture interact. By gaining a deeper knowledge of Christian tradition, I realized that it could be reconstructed with integrity. And although liberation and feminist theology were not yet central in the curriculum, I took these approaches up on my own. In addition, I enjoyed being a preceptor and realized that I loved teaching.

Still, I found PTS culturally difficult. I was used to the warmth and responsiveness of an extended ethnic family, and then of an evangelical community. Here the work ethic was supreme and the cultivation of relationships often seen as a distraction. It was often hard being the only woman in doctoral seminars. Many times my comments seemed to make no impact until a male student repeated them as his own. In addition, I was a young married woman and wanted to have a child. But wouldn't that hurt my career, my male fellow students asked? Yet they were blithely starting families.

My health suffered on account of the stress. I developed infertility problems and had several surgeries to attempt to correct them. Once, I had an adverse reaction to anesthesia and, flat on my back in the hospital, called my professor to explain that I might be a day late in grading student papers. He said I was letting everyone else down. I realized that in order to achieve in this competitive environment, I had to be very circumspect about any problems lest they be seen to detract from my ability.

There were no women faculty in theology, but I found mentors in other departments and among the staff. Although they were very busy, people such as Kathie Sakenfeld, Suzanne Rudiselle, and Kathleen McVey always seemed to have a moment to encourage and advise. At the dissertation stage, I became the first PhD candidate of Dr. Mark Taylor. He supported my questions about gender, doctrine, and culture. He also championed my plan to study female God imagery in the Shakers even though others were writing on more conventional topics. After graduation, I rewrote my dissertation, and it became my second book, *Gender, Doctrine & God: The Shakers and Contemporary Theology*.[3]

I also managed to complete my ordination exams while at PTS. Although I did not technically have a Master of Divinity degree, I was accepted as an "exceptional candidate" by the New Brunswick Presbytery. Once I was offered a position in theology at Methodist Theological School in Ohio (MTSO), it was accepted as my call. Although I had already been serving as an elder at Hopewell Presbyterian Church, now I could be ordained for the ministry of Word and Sacrament.

The faculty and staff at MTSO were very welcoming, grateful to have an ordained Presbyterian woman on the faculty and pleased that I had a strong motivation to write and engage culture. Respected as a full peer, I was given the freedom to follow my theological interests. I found that students' questions inspired me to take on new challenges. I was intrigued that our candidates in the chemical dependency counseling degree challenged some traditional theological concepts and offered a Twelve Step type of theology. So I began to study how our culture was using the addiction concept as a replacement metaphor for the doctrine of sin. This became my third book, *Victims & Sinners: Spiritual Roots of Addiction and Recovery*.[4] I began also writing on theological aspects of film, immigration, trauma, and other topics. I won grants to fund my research and spoke at conferences, universities, secular organizations, and churches.

Soon I became aware that the "spiritual but not religious" (SBNR) population was rapidly growing. I noted how the church stereotyped them and how they likewise stereotyped Christian theology. I wished for them to find a religious tradition that could provide the depth and complexity that a generic spirituality lacked. So in my fourth book, a spiritual memoir, *Bloomfield Avenue: A Jewish-Catholic Jersey Girl's Spiritual Journey*,[5] I shared how I had once been a seeker with serious theological questions and found a home in the church.

This led to my next project, exploring what SBNRs really believed. Thanks to my school's sabbatical policy and being awarded the Henry Luce III Fellowship in Theology, I was able to conduct and theologically analyze interviews around North America. This became my fifth book, *Belief without*

---

3. Linda A. Mercadante, *Gender, Doctrine & God: The Shakers and Contemporary Theology* (Nashville: Abingdon Press, 1990).

4. Linda A. Mercadante, *Victims & Sinners: Spiritual Roots of Addiction and Recovery* (Louisville, KY: Westminster John Knox Press, 1996).

5. Linda Mercadante, *Bloomfield Avenue: A Jewish-Catholic Jersey Girl's Spiritual Journey* (Cambridge, MA: Cowley, 2006).

Borders: Inside the Minds of the Spiritual but not Religious.[6] As a result, I am frequently asked to help diverse religious and secular groups understand this dramatic cultural shift. The book has received excellent reviews, won awards, and I have appeared in the *New York Times*, on NBC's *The Today Show*, on radio programs, and in other media outlets.

It feels like God has brought my questions, life experiences, abilities, and desires together in a way I could never have predicted. While I aim to have a balanced life, I so thoroughly enjoy what I'm doing that I sometimes have to resist saying yes to every new opportunity. I see my ministry as being able to read the signs of the times, absorb difficult concepts, and help others understand them. This is very useful in training ministers, something I love doing, but it also engages those who have little faith in organized religion. My unexpected journey, aided by others in so many surprising ways, has helped me contribute to both academy and church, bringing the nuances and complexity of tradition into an engaged relationship with the culture and its needs and questions.

6. Linda A. Mercadante, *Belief without Borders: Inside the Minds of the Spiritual but not Religious* (New York: Oxford University Press, 2014).

MOVING BEYOND
THE TONGUE-CUT GOD
IN A KOREAN CONTEXT

Hyun-Sook Kim

The Gwangjoo Democratization Movement was stained with blood in the massacre committed in May 1980 by the military government, which seized power through a military coup. Soldiers killed civilians in Gwangjoo City, officially 162 people but unofficially over 300 people. At that time I was a student in junior high school and was not informed of anything about the massacre because the government controlled free speech. I didn't realize that this massacre had happened until my senior year of high school, when my older brother gave me a pamphlet about the Gwangjoo Democratization Movement. As an innocent high school girl, I couldn't believe that my own Korean people had been killed by the Korean government. Moreover, the story of Korean soldiers who obeyed their commanders' orders to kill their own people remained in my mind.

The experience unexpectedly led me to reflect on my faith in God. A song that captured my heart during the time was "Tongue-Cut God." This song was composed by my fellow student, Huengkyum Kim, a theology major at Yonsei University, who also realized then what happened in Gwangjoo. Let me introduce this song:

> Respond to us, tongue-cut God.
> Hear our prayers, deaf God
> Who turns his face away fire-burned,
> Yet the old father dearest to my heart.
> God, are you dead?
> Weeping in a darkening alley?
> Dumped on a trash pit? O poor God![7]

God kept silent and turned away from pain, violence, and injustice; that was the God I experienced. This God even overlapped with the God who

---

7. Huengkyum Kim, "Tongue-Cut God." Song lyric, 1983. Used by permission of Ji Won Han, the wife of the late author.

commanded Abraham to offer Isaac by killing him. I knew the story of Abraham and Isaac by heart, but this story suddenly bothered me so much more seriously. It was difficult for me to accept this story then, in that God commanded such violence of Abraham. Moreover, I had to ask, "Why didn't Abraham question God's command to offer his own son?" This Abraham also overlapped with the Korean soldiers who obeyed their commanders' orders to kill their own people. I couldn't pray to God for a long time.

When I decided to study theology and come to Princeton Theological Seminary for my PhD, that issue was not resolved, and I still struggled with anger and sorrow toward God. I explicitly announced to my friends that I did not believe that God, especially tongue-cut God, existed, and that I was studying theology as an academic discipline. While I was preparing for the comprehensive examinations, I came across a book titled *Obedience to Authority*. This book was written by Stanley Milgram, who examined the problem of obedience to malevolent authority in an experiment conducted in 1963.[8] The important experimental paradigm involved individuals ordered to deliver painful electric shocks to others, especially innocent people. He demonstrated how individuals could be uncritically obedient to the commands of authority. According to Milgram, the main concern of his investigation was to find when and how people would defy "authority" in the face of a clear moral. However, participants obeyed authority to the highest limit, delivering the full 450 volts. Milgram discovered, surprisingly, that in the absence of protest, virtually all participants obeyed authority to the end.

These results from theoretical and experimental study led me to raise several significant questions. Why did the Korean soldiers take part in massive killing they normally would not do? Why did they undo a lifetime's learning of morals, values, and ethics when forced by a powerful command? Might classroom discussions of what one would carry out in a difficult situation be at odds with one's behavior in real-life situations? As a student of Christian education, I wanted to revisit how authority and obedience operate in Christian education, with an interest in these psychological and philosophical concerns as well as in my Korean historical situation. This theoretical and experimental study on authority allowed me to ask how we should teach in a real-life situation in which a teacher exerts some kind of authority, requiring students to obey and play a certain student role.

During my stay at Princeton, I decided to become a pastor and teacher, transitioning from the one who used to denounce God's existence and who used to doubt the role of education to transform people. This happened not

8. Stanley Milgram, *Obedience to Authority: An Experimental View* (New York: Harper & Row, 1974).

only because of Princeton Theological Seminary's theological education but also because of the support of Princeton Seminary women. My fellow female students at the seminary, including Glory, Katie, Jenny, Carolyn, Annari, Marianne, and others, helped me to acknowledge the importance of solidarity against malevolent authority and helped me to enjoy the authority of caring and loving in the educational setting. When I took the comprehensive exams, they walked with me to the exam room and got together in front of the oral defense room, praying for my exams. Praying and playing with them, I learned to assert my opinions in the face of forceful situations and attempted to find the possibility of employing a new kind of authority in the context of teaching and learning. My fellow female students at Princeton enabled me to experience God, who spoke to my anger and sorrow through the authority of caring and loving. This experience encouraged me to move away from the authoritarian model of a teacher as the authority and the students as the obedient, and it challenged me to move away from tongue-cut God.

Now I have become a Christian educator and theologian, namely, the first female professor at the College of Theology, Yonsei University. Society in general, and Korean society in particular, conventionally assigns teachers with the formal position and responsibility to take control in an educational setting. The dilemma inherent in obedience to authority is as old as the story of Abraham and human history, but at the same time, the dilemma and ubiquity of obedience and authority problems still remain and cause concern today. Such violence and injustice that were committed by the military government take place now in every sphere of society, in different forms and on different scales. As a Christian educator and theologian, I have been expected to teach students to listen to God's word and to obey God's authority with faith. However, I have often wondered whether I implicitly teach students to obey authority, even illegitimate authority, by blurring the boundary between illegitimate and legitimate authorities. I have also wondered whether I unconsciously teach them to be silent and turn away from injustice by providing them with the image of tongue-cut God. Moving beyond tongue-cut God toward loving and caring God, I've come to teach in the direction of a shared-authority model based on caring and shared understanding, in which authority is used by endeavoring to share power and in which teachers and students participate in learning as partners, in other words, becoming coauthors of our education.

A CALL TO INTER-AMERICAN SOLIDARITY: INTERNATIONAL MISSION

Karla Ann Koll

For as long as I can remember, I have sensed God's nurturing presence as the Divine One, the weaver of life. I have glimpsed God as weaver in the paintings of Navajo women seated at looms on the walls of galleries in Santa Fe, New Mexico, and in the poems of Guatemalan poet Julia Esquivel, a friend and mentor whom I first met when she was in exile in Nicaragua in the 1980s.[9] I have felt God's fingers, weaving disparate threads together to form the pattern of my calling. Most of the time the weaving is a gentle process, often only discernible by looking back at the pattern that has emerged. Sometimes the process is more painful, a hard tug on a particular strand that makes it impossible to continue to view my own life in the same way, as when I was forced to face the complicity of my own government in the suffering of thousands in Central America. And occasionally, the weaving takes off in a new, unexpected direction.

The church has always been a part of the pattern of my life. As a child, I loved going to worship services in the Presbyterian churches where we lived. I remember a moment on a youth retreat when I realized that my life belonged to Christ. As I learned more about injustices near at hand and far away, the preaching I heard in our white, middle-class church seemed to have very little relationship to the Jesus I encountered in the Gospels. Jesus preached the coming of God's reign as good news for the poor. Why didn't the churches talk about the poor? As my faith deepened, I drifted away from the church.

Central America entered my consciousness while I was studying political economy and environmental sciences at Saint Olaf College. In the late 1970s, military governments supported by the United States in El Salvador, Guatemala, and Nicaragua were murdering thousands to prevent radical social

9. For example, see Julia Esquivel, *"Tejido típico/Indian Tapestry,"* in *Threatened with Resurrection: Prayers and Poems from an Exiled Guatemalan* (Elgin, IL: Brethren Press, 1982), 106–9.

change. I was an exchange student in Germany in July of 1979 when the San-
dinistas overthrew the Somoza dictatorship in Nicaragua. For the first time
I was seeing U.S. foreign policy from the outside, and what I saw caused me
much pain. God was tugging very hard on my life.

At Saint Olaf, the rhythms of the Lutheran liturgy and the support of professors as I strove to understand the systemic causes of the injustices I saw
pulled me back to the church. I began to sense God asking me to serve in
the church. But the church had been complicit in so much suffering in so
many contexts. How would serving in the church further the coming of God's
reign? On a bus riding through the Ecuadorian Andes during my senior year,
I read *A Theology of Liberation* by Gustavo Gutiérrez.[10] Here was a theological
vision asking the same questions I had.

My search for answers drew me to Union Theological Seminary in New
York City, an urban context where my attempts at theological reflection
would have to interact daily with those who were impoverished. At Union,
German feminist Dorothee Sölle showed me that one draws closer to God by
opening oneself to the pain of the world, as she guided my explorations of the
connections between mysticism and revolutionary praxis.

A passage from Paul's second letter to the Christians at Corinth grew to
have more and more meaning for me (2 Cor 5:17–6:2). As one in Christ, I
am part of the new that God is creating. I am not bound by what the pattern
has been, nor am I destined to re-create the status quo. Grace has freed me
and allows me to change my social location. I can be a part of what Paul calls
the ministry of reconciliation, working for more just relationships between
people and between peoples.

Union offered me a chance to do part of my theological studies at the Latin
American Biblical Seminary in San José, Costa Rica. I looked forward to learning from sisters and brothers there how they understood God's presence with
them in their struggles for peace with justice. I went to Costa Rica convinced
that the time for mission workers from outside the region was over. Through
conversations with professors and students at the seminary, the weaving of
my call took off in a surprising new direction as they encouraged me to consider working in Central America. I discerned two tasks that have formed my
ongoing call. On one hand, the growing evangelical or Protestant churches
of Latin America need theological education to prepare leaders. On the other
hand, there was and is a clear need for people who can facilitate relationships
between Christians in Central America and North America, building bridges

---

10. Gustavo Gutiérrez, *A Theology of Liberation: History, Politics, and Salvation*
(Maryknoll, NY: Orbis, 1973).

of understanding and working together toward a more just future for all, reconciliation put into practice.

The session of my home church grudgingly took me under care as a candidate for ministry as, in the words of one of the pastors, "part of their service to the greater church." My gender did not seem to be an issue. The church had already hosted the ordination of a woman as pastor. Much concern, however, was raised over my theological perspective and my work as an organizer for a local ecumenical peace and justice organization that was focusing on the nuclear weapons freeze campaign and on changing U.S. policy toward Central America. When I was ordained as a minister of Word and Sacrament in March of 1986, at the church in which I had been baptized as an infant, I became the only woman minister on the roll of Pueblo Presbytery. Within the broader structures of the Presbyterian Church (U.S.A.), especially the international mission program, I have found continuing support for my call over decades of service in the church.

My call first took me to Managua, where I joined the staff of the Center for Global Education of Augsburg College. With a methodology inspired by Brazilian educator Paulo Freire, we introduced visiting U.S. church groups to the complexities of the region and encouraged them to reflect on God's call for justice in the midst of the low-intensity war that the U.S. government was waging against the revolutionary government in Nicaragua. After two years with the Center for Global Education, I started teaching full-time at the Evangelical Faculty for Theological Studies (FEET), an interdenominational seminary started by Nicaraguan church leaders. At the beginning of 1989, the Presbyterian Church (U.S.A.) appointed me as a mission diaconal worker to serve at the FEET.

Princeton became a stop along my journey. After eight years in Nicaragua, my family and I were ready for a quiet place in which to reflect about the witness of the PC(USA) during the years of war in Central America. My friend and mentor Richard Shaull encouraged me to consider Princeton. My dissertation allowed me to show how the engagement of the Presbyterian Church (U.S.A.) in Central America during the 1980s and our opposition to U.S. foreign policy in the region grew out of both our mission theology and prior mission relationships. As I researched and wrote, I relived the wars in the region over and over again, surrounded by people who didn't remember or who never knew that hundreds of thousands of Central Americans were killed by military forces supported by the United States. In December of 1996, as I was finishing my comprehensive exams, peace accords were finally signed in Guatemala, and Central America officially became a postconflict area.

My primary memories from my first weeks at Princeton were of white men in clerical garb standing in front of us in Miller Chapel proclaiming the importance of upholding the Reformed tradition. I realized pretty quickly that Princeton would not offer many spaces for reimaging my faith from my experiences as a woman. And I was right. The only woman professor with whom I had done coursework during my doctoral studies, Carol Lakey Hess, did not receive tenure. When I defended my dissertation in May of 2003, I was the only woman seated at the table.

Even so, I found a strong community of women at Princeton who supported one another.

During my first year at Princeton, the four women in the Mission, Ecumenics, and the History of Religions doctoral program asked African theologian Mercy Amba Oduyoye, who was a visiting scholar that year, to accompany us in an independent study exploring the ways in which women have appropriated Christianity into different cultural contexts around the world to challenge patriarchal structures. Jane Dempsey Douglass inspired me as a scholar who not only probed the history of the Reformed tradition to ask about the experience of women during the Reformation but also cared deeply about the way women and men were experiencing their faith in Jesus Christ within Reformed churches around the world as she served as the president of the World Alliance of Reformed Churches (WARC).

After I had been in Princeton for six years, the Latin American Biblical University invited me to teach in Guatemala at the Evangelical Center for Pastoral Studies in Central America. Much of my work there was with women, helping them to see themselves as made in the image and likeness of God. My Mayan students allowed me to accompany them as they asked questions about how to be both Mayan and Christian. As their guest at Mayan fire ceremonies, I learned to pray again and found new understandings of God woven into my theological vision.

In Princeton, I was always amused by the Center for Theological Inquiry. In my experience, theological inquiry does not take place in a red-brick building on Mercer Street. Theological inquiry happens in barrios, as women and men read the Bible together and organize to improve their living conditions. It happens as indigenous communities reclaim their millennial spiritualities and seek to follow Christ from within their own cultures and worldviews. It happens when groups of women name their own experience and insist on speaking their own words about God. As a theological educator working in Central America, I am privileged to accompany these processes of theological reflection, offering conceptual tools and encouraging groups to dialogue with the experience of Christian communities in different contexts and different historical moments.

In September of 2013, I moved to Costa Rica, back to the institution where my journey in Central America began. Presbyterian World Mission and the support of many Presbyterian Church (U.S.A.) congregations make it possible for me to serve this part of Christ's church. I am privileged to be part of an international team of educators who believe that theology has a fundamental role in shaping identities and constructing more just societies in Latin America and beyond.

When I feel my life being stretched, as I often do, between multiple contexts, I remind myself that God is the one weaving the web of relationships that sustain me, that hold me up like a hammock suspended between the different geographical and cultural locations that are a part of my life. These relationships have carried me through decades of service in Central America and through unexpected twists, such as an experience with breast cancer. I am grateful for all the gifts I have received at each of the places my call has taken me, including Princeton Theological Seminary. I look to the future, knowing that God continues to weave the new creation through the threads that bind many lives together across multiple contexts.

BACKING IN ALL
THE WAY TO MINISTRY

Julie Neraas

Backing into ministry every step of the way is not a particularly dignified way to live into one's vocation, but it has been my pattern. I have had to say a defiant, yet sincere, "No," and "No" again, before I could say, "Yes." While I was not Jonah exactly, let's just say I resisted the idea mightily and had my foot on the brake the whole way. If you had told me the trajectory of my life and my life's work, I would have been not only incredulous but aghast: Be ordained? By the Presbyterians?! You have got to be kidding. Working for Catholic churches? Becoming a professor (without a PhD)? A spiritual director? Well, the spiritual direction part might have been predicted, but for the most part, each step has been a complete surprise. Yet if you asked me whether what I have done *is* my life, I would say an unqualified and grateful YES.

Ministry came like the confluence of several small streams. A love of big questions, in-depth conversations, ritual, and a hunger for connection with God; these tributaries grew to become a great river I could swim around in. Seminary turned my little boat into a new channel, away from where I was heading: journalism.

One of the obstacles to all this was not knowing what in the world a calling was and how you knew if you had one. I felt completely inadequate on this score. Maybe there was something wrong with me; I had seen no angels with neon signs nor had had any powerful dreams. Now I see that the path to ministry was an intricate series of negotiations and open doors, but I sure could have used a class on discerning one's vocation back then.

I grew up in a very religious Lutheran household, but there was nothing particularly appealing about being part of a church. At the very last minute I decided to go to Whitworth College, a Presbyterian affiliated school. (Backing in, as usual.) I was fortunate; this was a time of great vibrancy in that institution's life. Our president had been a futurist for NASA. He replaced chapel services with something called Forum: Ethical Voices in Conscience. In my first two years alone we heard Buckminster Fuller, Ralph Abernathy,

Cesar Chavez, and Antonia Brico, people with a big vision and the commitment to stand behind it. I saw that a life of faith had to do with taking on big challenges and taking one's place in a centuries-long conversation. I felt myself part of a Larger Story. At the same time I also took classes at two Jesuit universities, out of a deep interest in the monastic tradition and contemplative practices. One of my first college papers was on Thomas Merton. So those seeds were germinating too.

What led me to seminary was a rather pointed, four-word suggestion by our college chaplain, Sharon Parks. "You should consider seminary," she said. Seminary?! "Oh, spare me," was my first thought. Only white men in white shoes do that. (Sharon went on to work with James Fowler in the groundbreaking study of faith development. Her book *Big Questions, Worthy Dreams* has become the seminal text about faith in the young adult years.) But since my other plans were not exactly gelling, and since Sharon had earned an MA degree from PTS, I flew back east to check it out. One night I lay on a terrible bed in Brown Hall, peering up at peeling green paint, saying to myself, "Thank heavens I have decided not to come here." But that is exactly where I did come, six months later. Okay, I will try it for a year, I thought reluctantly.

The turning point came during an internship my middler year at a wretched prison in northeast Philadelphia. The House of Corrections was a colossal misnomer if there ever was one. Nothing got corrected there, as far as I could see. Men hung onto the bars and catcalled like animals when visitors came through. Drugs were prevalent.

For entertainment one night (in lieu of a movie, for those on good behavior), they brought in three erotic dancers. I kid you not. I was a young, naive white kid sitting in a gymnasium next to a skinny, unarmed warden in a sea of sexually deprived men. If I hadn't caught on before this, I knew then that that place was completely nuts. Prison work was also a jolting tutorial in racism, poverty, and corrupt human systems.

Yet something happened there that changed things for me. I got to know an inmate named Russell Williams, a heroin addict who had a profound transformation after surviving a serious heart attack. He found God, learned how to read, discovered self-confidence, and never used drugs again. His openness about his newfound faith encouraged others to open up. Getting people to talk was energizing; I could elicit their hopes and fears quite naturally. Their connection with God in the bleakest of situations caught my imagination.

By my senior year I could imagine myself as a college chaplain, but I went through several job interviews with churches just for the experience. One was hard to forget. An older senior pastor from Colorado asked me, "What will I do if and when you become pregnant?" Really, Reverend? Do you ask male seminarians this question?

After graduation I returned to the Pacific Northwest and was asked to be a part-time college chaplain and a part-time parish minister. I said yes to both.

Role Models. I had never met an ordained woman minister when I entered seminary, nor do I remember hearing anything about women's legacy there. What a loss. As people of color continue to say, it makes all the difference if you have leaders/teachers who actually *look like you*. I had just two women professors (neither one was tenured), and their status at the institution was clearly provisional. Three or four was hardly a critical mass, able to challenge the prevailing culture of the seminary.

Thank heavens for Sharon Parks. I learned from her how powerful conversations could be in the shaping of faith. Sharon says that one of the primary needs of young adults is for a hearth, where they can speak their truth for as long as possible with the freedom and authenticity that can happen around a fire at night in ways it might not in the light of day. Creating environments in which people can speak their deep truths has been at the core of my ministry, and its beginnings were there, in college.

My other role model was Rev. Bertrand Atwood, a distinguished minister from Connecticut who taught preaching. One of my fears was that a parish pastor could not have a rich cultural or social life. But Atwood's disciplined life sprung that trapdoor wide open. His habit was to finish his sermon by Thursday so that he and his wife could enjoy dinner and a movie or the theater almost every week of their marriage. He made it a point to read at least one novel a month, and he subscribed to several literary journals. Here was a man who brought the world of the arts into his life work, and he had at least some command of his time. His life patterns also planted an awareness in me that the arts were the doorway to the sacred for many people.

Women and Theological Education. From the vantage point of forty years, I see that women bring a unique understanding of the sacred to ministry. The male naming of the sacred in patriarchal religion "has given us a strange landscape of the sacred," writes Elizabeth Dodson Gray. Only "a few places, a few people, a few occasions are seen to concentrate and to embody the holy." Cathedrals, temples, priests, rabbis, saints. "'Up, up, and away' is the cry of this religious consciousness."[11] Many activities that women deem sacred happen on the ground, not "up and away": raising children, creating home, gardening, tending the elderly, passing along religious traditions, and healing in its many forms. For women there is less of a distinction between the sacred and the profane. All land is holy land, says American Indian leader Winona LaDuke.

---

11. Elizabeth Dodson Gray, ed., *Sacred Dimensions of Women's Experience* (Wellesley, MA: Roundtable, 1988), 2.

Second, women bring a heightened awareness of our bodies as sacred vessels. This has profound implications. It has been noted that the way we have treated women's physical bodies is akin to the way we have treated the earth. Furthermore, the emphasis in Protestant Christianity on the spoken and written word focuses on only three organs in the body—the ears, eyes, and mouth—although our whole bodies are sacred, as are the body's ways of knowing. Our liturgies ought to reflect this reality.

Third, women value the wisdom found in a circle/community, where everyone is a participant and leadership is shared. This is not to discount the brilliant scholar whose forte is lecturing; there is a place for this in teaching. But a circle locates authority in more than one lone voice, and it results in more diverse pedagogical styles. In the changing landscape of Protestant America, as churches shrink in size and many find themselves unable to pay for a full-time pastor, laypeople will likely have to take on some of the jobs traditionally done by an ordained person. Many voices will break open the Word, not just one.

Changes in My Understanding of Ministry. My understanding of ministry has changed substantially since seminary. I see all work toward social justice as ministry now. A chronic illness has led me to consider many kinds of healing as ministry. Several of my colleagues have thriving writing ministries.

Speaking of writers, theological education would be greatly enriched by embracing the arts as a doorway to the sacred. My own church has a small art gallery, a theater, and a literary witness committee that has brought dozens of poets to our community. The response has been tremendous: 1,600 people came to hear Mary Oliver; 800, to hear Gary Snyder. The arts ought to have a larger place in theological education.

Teaching. One of the most delightful surprises of my career was finding, and teaching in, an interdisciplinary graduate program at Hamline University in Saint Paul, Minnesota. Classes attract students from the ages of twenty-five to eighty, and they are team taught—so a physicist will teach with an art historian, or an ethicist with a theologian. Some of the courses I have taught include Prophets and Mystics (with a Judaica scholar), Poetry and the Sacred, Pilgrimage Stories, Spiritual Memoir, The Soul in the Workplace (with a public administrator), Religion and Hope, and Vocation and Money. An area of great interest in my teaching has been the subject of hope, which includes my long bout with a chronic illness.[12]

Teaching Spiritual Practice. In both university teaching and spiritual direction, the core of my work is helping busy people tend their prayer lives and

---

12. Julie E. Neraas, *Apprenticed to Hope: A Sourcebook for Difficult Times,* Living Well (Minneapolis: Augsburg, 2009).

find the sacred in the everyday. Its focus is the deep taproot at the core of all religions that anchors us in our source. If someone had given me the term *spiritual director* (from the Irish practice of having an *anam cara*, "soul friend") in seminary, it would have saved me considerable anguish. This is the kind of work I wanted to do, but I did not have the words for it, nor did the inner life have much of a place in our classes. In those days few of us knew about centering prayer or mindfulness practices. They are such helpful tools for people in anxiety and stress. Many ministers have spoken to me about their sense of inadequacy around spiritual practices.

A 1994 survey of its graduates from across the decades found that only 15 percent of responders remembered their PTS years as spiritual in nature. This was a shocking discovery to the PTS Alumni/ae Advisory Board, of which I was a part at the time.

People are so open these days about their hunger for spiritual experience and practices that anchor them. If they can't find what they desire in their own religious tradition, they will look in other places, sometimes sailing past Christianity altogether. It is good that spiritual direction has become an area of study at the seminary.

Religious Diversity, Religious Pluralism. Because religion is hugely important to a majority of earth's people, because it lies at the nadir of many of our conflicts, and because America has become the most religiously diverse country in the world, seminaries must further their students' knowledge and understanding of traditions beyond their own. We simply cannot afford ignorance about these core teachings. As Prof. Diana Eck of Harvard's Pluralism Project says, religious diversity is a given; pluralism, a schooled understanding of religions, must be earned.

As a professor teaching religion to undergraduates, I have come to see how important religious literacy is, and I celebrate having access to the world's wisdom traditions as never before.

The BIG STORY of Which We Are a Part. The greatest influence on my faith in the last two decades has come from the spellbinding discoveries about our universe. Thanks to the Hubble telescope, we now know that we are a tiny speck in a vast sea of planets, suns, and stars, billions of them. Our universe is three hundred billion light years across. This is dizzying, mindboggling, and profoundly humbling. It took somewhere in the neighborhood of fourteen billion years for human beings to arrive. Cosmologists Brian Swimme and Thomas Berry suggest that our species' ability to reflect means that we are the universe conscious of itself. What a responsibility! This is not just an interesting sidebar for people intrigued by science; it is a profound new consciousness of our place and purpose as human beings. If religious traditions are great, encompassing stories about the nature of reality, the universe story is the ultimate frame within which all these other stories play out. We must initiate our young into this story. It ought to be reflected in worship services and theological education.

Furthermore, human beings have become equal to one of the powers of the universe (gravity, for example). We are imperiling our planet at an astonishing rate. The earth's well-being must be a global priority. We must all be about the work of restoring the balance that a healthy earth requires if we are to have a future on our planet, faith communities included.

I am profoundly grateful for my theological education. It was a privilege to study at PTS. Yet if we are to keep pace with Spirit, who is always ahead of us, some of the seminary's practices must evolve and change. I am heartened by its desire to listen to its women graduates in particular for what some of those changes might be.

6

Church and Seminary Administration

**DANCING LIGHTS
BREAKING INTO THE
DARKNESS: CALLED TO BE
EXECUTIVE PRESBYTER**

Ruth Faith Santana-Grace

There is no denying that the dark nights of the human pilgrimage in this life are real. Those nights are formed by the brokenness of the world around us, along with the brokenness within us. They are formed by cycles of nature and circumstances beyond our control. All who walk this earth will experience the shroud of these dark moments—moments that can entomb our spirits and thus our lives.

My thirty-seven years prior to attending Princeton Seminary stand within and in contrast to this backdrop. The darkness of the night held the pain of abuse—hidden in the betrayal of "religious" individuals; the pain of self-denial—shaped by racism and cultural stereotypes; the pain of loss—as I held my dead daughter's newborn body; the pain of failure—accepting the reality of a youthful divorce. These moments sculptured an incomplete caricature of who I was or could be. However, because of a light breaking into the darkness, they would not become my story.

Over time I recognized a light moving in and around my life, defying the darkness. It was, and is, a light reflective of the aurora borealis, or the northern lights—a light that dances and cannot be contained. It comes in colors we're incapable of naming. It's a light that even whispers rhythmically in the darkness. It is this light—the light of God's unrelenting love—that has given me the hope of the resurrection through this, my earthly pilgrimage. The words in John 1:5 are pivotal to my spiritual understanding—"The light shines in the darkness, and the darkness did not overcome it."

The journey to Princeton Seminary reflects this reality. I was born into a Hispanic Presbyterian home, and the churches of "La Encrucijada" in Manhattan and "San Lucas" in Queens, New York, provided a foundation for my journey. Bound by rhythms of family, tradition, music, faith, and a parental determination for our education, I was shaped by resurrection possibilities. Our parents wanted more for us—and as I would learn, my parents even wanted more for themselves. At the age of forty, my dad, Felix, with an eighth-grade education, announced that he was moving us to Bangor, Maine, to study to become a Presbyterian pastor. Not to be outdone, my mom, Carmen, with a fifth-grade education, secretly got her high school equivalency. This moment, questionable at the time, loudly affirmed that the God of creation never stops believing in our possibilities. This was my first conscious acknowledgment of that dancing "Holy Spirit" light compelling us to resist human limitations imposed by the darkness. I would struggle to catch glimpses of these lights along my journey, as they would often be dim. Ultimately, they would not be contained.

My compromised spirit would enter young adulthood with the scars of uncertainty about my worth. It was a season of agnosticism and wilderness wandering—in a desperate effort to reconcile the darkness with the reality of dancing lights breaking their way into my soul. But this dancing light came from outside any formal community of faith, becoming one of the most foundational and transformational events in my life. An unlikely New York City congressional campaign would serve as the embodiment of resurrection possibilities. With the introduction of the Olivero family into my life, I was introduced to Latinos doing amazing things. I learned of my heritage in new ways. With their encouragement and network, I claimed my faith in the public sphere. I was introduced to education and opportunities. More important, I was introduced to me. The sounds of the northern lights sang into my heart with colors, giving me courage to defy stereotypes imposed by the culture.

With a new sense of self, I embarked upon Washington, DC, where I found a spiritual home in the welcoming of a "liberal" Presbyterian church and their pastor and wife—Sid and Shirley Skirvin. Their embracing witness spiritually grounded me while working with mayors and national leaders, and completing my Masters in Public Administration. They kept me grounded as I dated the man I would marry in 1987—Edward, an Irish American (then

Roman Catholic, with a doctorate from the Pontifical Seminary in Rome). He lived in Italy with his young son David. DC was surreal—meetings in the White House, spending time with national leaders. I found myself believing that I was indeed gifted to do something in this world. The colors of the aurora borealis broke through my soul with hues and shades more nuanced and complex.

It was my husband Edward's uncompromising spirit that would continue to challenge the insecurity within. His voice was the loudest in not allowing my spirit to be compromised by whatever darkness threatened—from the outside or from within. It was ultimately his courage that led us to pursue seminary education. We were active in the American churches in Rome and Florence, Italy. I even preached my first sermon at St. Paul's, within the walls in Rome. Looking back—the signs of my own personal call were there, but I was unable to recognize it. But after five years in Italy (Edward's twenty-four years), we found ourselves in Princeton, New Jersey, with new and unexpected challenges, shrouded in the darkness of institutional and cultural bias. I struggled to discern where God would call this NYC Latina with the hyphenated last name. Who would define or limit me? I wondered how an institution teaching resurrection hope could prompt a dark season of internal struggle. But like Jacob wrestling with God in the night, I could not let go of what I did not yet understand.

This darkness was different, however—during this struggle, I experienced glimmers of light faithfully breaking through. They were the lights embodied by Geddes Hanson—connecting theology to praxis; Daniel Migliore—providing words to what I intuitively believed; Choon-Leong Seow—whose mind and spirit were contagious; Dennis Olson—modeling covenant life throughout his teaching and our 1999 trip to Israel. They were the lights of Jane Dempsey Douglass—who, in addition to teaching me the relevance of history, taught me how to stand with grace and poise. And there was Tom Gillespie, providing insight into the power of relationships across theological divides, a moment defined by his refusal to uninvite Dr. Peter Gomes as commencement speaker because of an outcry of a small segment of students. My ultimate mentor at Princeton was music. My weekly discipline with the Seminary Singers and the Gospel Choir helped exorcise the paralyzing power of the darkness. It renewed my spirit—in ways little else could. The sounds of music, along with the corporate teachings and witness of these amazingly complex individuals, allowed the colors of the lights to break forth brightly. In spite of myself, the light insisted on dancing.

Nothing, however, would add more colors and movement to those lights than the birth of our son Dakota at Princeton. His reception into our seminary community was profound. His life would add dimensions, colors, sounds, music, and challenges—even to this day. His passion and compassion continue to grow our spirits. There is no denying that my experience at Princeton laid a transformative foundation to the theology of my leadership and praxis. Because of it—in all its complexity—I would bear a light of hope into a new season of service.

That season would begin at the First Presbyterian Church of Bethlehem, Pennsylvania, where I served as pastor for adult discipleship from 1993 to 2005. Through this three-thousand-member (98 percent Caucasian) "evangelical" community, I learned that poverty comes in forms other than economics. They helped to grow our then-little boy. They grieved with us when my dad died. Because of them, I am theologically bilingual. Their witness added bold colors to the lights compelling me forward.

Notwithstanding their blessing in our lives, serving as a cultural bridge would again cause wrestling with self-worth, as I allowed the darkness to claim a small part of my spirit. It was the darkness of discouragement—causing me to wonder about the limited opportunities within church structures. So when the invitation to go to San Gabriel Presbytery came, it was like a whirlwind. Would I enjoy this ministry? Could we move our seventh-grader from the only community he knew? Could we really move to southern California? With the encouragement of Edward, Dakota, my mom, and my sister Diana—I entered mid-council ministry with forty-four congregations, half of them worshiping in languages other than English. I would humbly enter the rich sounds of Thai, Mandarin, Cantonese, Arabic, Korean, Indonesian, Spanish, Tagalog, and more. I developed deep friendships in California and learned about my spiritual gifts in ways that would forever defy the temptation to see myself as "less than" because of cultural bias. The dancing lights of God vividly compelled me forward in creative and confident ways.

That confidence is claimed today as the first woman (and first person of color) installed as executive presbyter of the Presbytery of Philadelphia, with 130 communities of faith. Eighteen months into this ministry, I am aware that the darkness continues to threaten my soul and, frankly, the souls of the world. But now I am equally aware that the lights breaking through that darkness are far brighter. At times, because of the abundant blessings, I can even momentarily forget that the darkness exists. I am aware that I live in constant contradiction to the stereotypes of that darkness—serving on the board of the Presbyterian Foundation, serving as vice chair of the board of our seminary. I recently preached at Harvard, where our son is a senior—the significance of that symbol is not lost on me. These places are foreign to my "natural" frame of reference, and they can easily allow the darkness to second-guess my place in them.

The reality of the darkness makes the need for light more urgent—dancing lights in the form of mentors and leaders. That is part of our call. I am aware there have not been many women by whom I've been mentored. Notwithstanding this sad truth, Princeton has and continues to provide amazing guides, companions, and friends—male and female—who inspire me, providing a fascinating network of gifts along the way.

Because of the value of this network, today I intentionally encourage young women seeking to be in ministry. The seminary can be a catalyst in forming and encouraging networks of women in ministry—across race and theologies. It can teach the stories of women in the church from a place of significance. It can identify and celebrate women who can be presidents and vice presidents of our institutions. For me as a Latina, that need is even more urgent as we seek to find our voice in the church of Jesus Christ.

And as for that church—I believe that the church is reforming to find relevance for this time and place. This is both exciting and threatening. After more than twenty years in "formal" ministry, through a time when cultural fragmentation and polarization has been the norm, my understanding of our call has become simple. We are to proclaim God's grace through Jesus by "bearing and being" the Word in the world through the multicolored lights of our witness—defying the darkness that threatens God's creation. This witness of justice, mercy, compassion, joy, and worship happens both within and outside the walls of the church. We are to join in the dance of the aurora borealis reflective of God's redemptive work in Christ—shining light in the midst of the darkness.

There is no denying that the dark nights of the human pilgrimage are real. But light—the light that broke into the world in the form of Jesus, and that continues to dance with the colors and sounds and movements of the northern lights—that is our hope. It is the hope of who I continue to become.

SEMINARY PRESIDENT: ONE STEP AT A TIME

Carol E. Lytch

In one of the early scenes in the movie *Wild*, a young hiker (played by Reese Witherspoon) prepares to walk the thousand-mile Pacific Crest Trail. She's in a hotel room packing the gear she purchased for the hike. She stuffs the items one by one into her backpack, fills the internal pouch with drinking water, and tries to hoist the backpack on to her shoulders. The weight and size of the backpack are so great she can't even lift it. She lies on the floor and gets under it so her back and legs can help her lift it. She tries several times and can't stand. Finally she loads it on her back, and she gets her legs in standing position. But then she topples backward from the weight. It's a funny scene, but it also unnerved me because it reminded me of being a seminary president.

I have often thought of the role of president of a seminary as carrying a backpack around all the time. You bear a weight of responsibility that you feel constantly: there is the mission of your school; there is the legacy of your predecessors; there are alumni/ae and trustees who care deeply about the school; there are churches that care; there are faculty and staff who have devoted their lives to the school; there are employees who depend on you for their jobs and livelihood; there are students counting on graduating. You cannot be flippant about it. I remember even before I started, the executive assistant to the president handed me my name tag with the title "President." I made some lighthearted comment like, "Wow, I guess I'm really the president." And she was angry with me. I did not even know this woman, and she scolded me, saying, "We need a president here, and if you aren't the one, let us know." I was pretty shocked. But I learned not to joke about it.

Starting in 2009 when the economy tanked and seminaries' endowments shrank, the calling to be a seminary president often meant leading in the midst of crisis. Enrollments that had been steadily trending upward started to decrease by 1–2 percent each year, with enrollments at the mainline Protestant seminaries decreasing more steeply. The traditional donors who give the bulk of gifts to the annual fund were fewer as their generation ended. Denominations and charitable foundations were not offering the support they used to give. Thus the three revenue streams of a seminary—endowment income, net tuition revenue, and annual gifts and grants—were declining. Even before 2009, sociologists were documenting the decline in trends in church memberships and attendance, especially in mainline Protestant denominations; thus it became harder to make the case for the education of clergy in a less-churched society.

Dan Aleshire, executive director of the Association of Theological Schools, who was my boss in 2011 at the time I considered the call to become a president, was blunt about the challenge that faced anyone who considered a presidency of a seminary. He said, "It will be like walking in a fog. You won't be able to see what is in front of you. You will take one step at a time. And you have to keep walking slowly."

I knew something about fog. My husband and I were walking the Camino de Santiago de Compostela, a 500-mile pilgrimage across northern Spain, over a ten-year period. On the first day of the Camino, which we started a few summers earlier, I carried a heavy backpack over the Pyrenees Mountains, and at the top of the mountains we encountered heavy fog. We could not see ahead of us. We could hear the clanging of cowbells in the pastures alongside of us, but we could not see the cows. We could only look down at our feet and see the gravel path and sometimes the figure of someone walking just ahead of us. I liked the fog. It was mystical. It was like walking in the clouds, reminding me of the clouds that surround God's heavenly throne. For me, being a seminary president is an intensely spiritual journey. I have never depended so radically on God's daily provision of resources.

Looking back, I see a thread in the many experiences that shaped me spiritually and in other ways to accept this calling. I could start with my baptism and confirmation, but the distinctive calling to church leadership came when I was sixteen and was ordained as a Presbyterian elder. I was the first "youth elder" in my home church in Metuchen, New Jersey. This was not common in the early 1970s. I was a discontented teen in my church. I returned home from a nondenominational evangelical camp each summer unsatisfied with my home church that was, in my opinion, not as outwardly expressive of faith and high-level commitment to God. I attended prayer meetings and Bible studies elsewhere, even as I remained active in my local church.

Ordination as a youth elder in my junior year of high school started something new. It opened me to a lifelong exploration of the nature of the church, especially as it is an organization, the embodied community of faith that requires committee meetings, budgets, stewardship campaigns, and buildings. The church is a physical body and a social organization. A love of the church as an organization started to grow and mature into my current passion for vital congregations. Nothing makes my heart sing more than being present in a congregation that worships with joy and authenticity, engages in significant mission, demonstrates strong bonds of fellowship, rears children and youth in the faith, and exhibits radical hospitality. In these times when American society is so individualistic, the church is not. It is congregational; it is what individuals do in concert with each other to join in God's mission.

I went to seminary right out of college because, ironically, I did not want to be a minister. In my senior year of college, one of my professors nominated me for a fellowship funded by the Rockefellers designed to incentivize persons who did not want to be ministers but would attend seminary if given an opportunity. I loved studying the Bible, so seminary interested me. At that time in my life I was conservative theologically and influenced by complementarian views of gender. I did not know if women should be ministers. In 1977, I had only seen a few women ministers preach in the chapel at my women's college. I was more inclined to go into the overseas mission field, and I was appointed to a position in Korea by the Presbyterian Church. My parents did not want me to go off and become a missionary, so they encouraged the seminary alternative while also expressing doubt that I would be able to do anything significant as a woman with a seminary degree.

When I entered Princeton Seminary, I told the chair of the presbytery's committee that shepherded candidates toward ordination that I was not sure I was called. I did not sign up to enter the candidacy process. Within a couple of months, I phoned him back and said I was ready. In my field education setting, church members were telling me I had a calling. At the same time, in seminary I was able to wrestle with scriptural understandings of gender and ministry, and was satisfied that women could be ministers. At that time (1977–1980), approximately 25 percent of the students at Princeton were women. There were only a few female professors as well.

I had a very negative experience in my first semester at Princeton when a professor asked me out on a date, and I declined. In class he compared women who could preach to dogs who could stand on two legs. But that episode was counterbalanced by many more positive experiences with the faculty. The women professors were powerful role models. Many of the male professors strongly affirmed women; I later learned to call them "allies." John Mulder, in his Piety, Power, and Politics course, exposed me to the stories of early women in church leadership in the American context. It was an awakening for me, and I felt empowered.

I sensed that I was marked for pastoral ministry when Princeton Seminary awarded me the prize in pastoral ministry at graduation for a year's study and travel abroad. At that time, in 1980–1981, I became a role model to the very few women who were studying at the University of Edinburgh for ordination in the Church of Scotland. I was the first woman to serve the historic St. Cuthbert Church as "attached" clergy since its founding in the 12th century.

Upon return to the United States, my husband and I together became trailblazers for clergy couples. We were probably, in 1982, the first couple in the United Presbyterian Church to serve in two equal, full-time positions in a single congregation as copastors. The graciousness and flexibility of the First Presbyterian Church of Cranbury, New Jersey, made this possible as we had one child and then a second. Figuring out policies related to maternity and paternity leave and adjusting terms of call to accommodate family life were essential. Eventually I began a PhD, partly because I thought that the life of an academic had more flexibility for family life than the pastorate. I also wanted to study what made congregations vital. The church growth movement at the time consisted of techniques, with no theological or theoretical grounding. Once again I turned to my Princeton professors who named the field that I was interested in: congregational studies.

I pursued the PhD and completed the arduous terminal academic degree (without dying) because I thought that my calling was to teach. But it turned out not to be the case. Looking back, I believe that God was channeling me into administrative leadership in theological education. I first worked for Lilly Endowment, coordinating grants to seminaries, and then served as assistant executive director of the Association of Theological Schools (ATS), the agency that accredits seminaries. One tumultuous month in the spring of 2006, I was offered an endowed faculty chair at one seminary, was rejected for a teaching position at Princeton, and was offered the position at ATS. I discerned that God was calling me not to teaching but to administrative leadership in theological institutions. And oddly, it is because I love congregations that I eventually became the head of a different organization, that is, a seminary.

My work at Lilly Endowment and ATS prepared me to be a seminary president. In those organizations, I became knowledgeable about almost all the Catholic and Protestant seminaries in the United States and Canada. I learned about seminaries from the inside through being involved with their accreditation. I planned leadership training for presidents, and I worked with ATS's programs to advance the leadership of women in theological education. I got to know presidents personally. I met women presidents who were stellar in their roles and also very human and approachable. I remember one particular lunch conversation with Laura Mendenhall, who at the time was concluding her seven-year presidency at Columbia Theological Seminary. She told me that I could do the work of a president, and that gave me courage. I was getting invitations from presidential search committees, having been nominated by other presidents, both female and male, people whom I considered my mentors. The right invitation was extended to me to become president of Lancaster Theological Seminary, and I believe that God called me to this role.

In the four years since I became a seminary president in 2011, an increasing number of women are being called to presidential leadership in both liberal and conservative seminaries. Women are succeeding other women as presidents. The president and dean, the two top administrative positions, are sometimes held by a team of women. I believe that the changing perception of women's roles in society is impacting the church and seminary. The leadership training of women through ATS and the advocacy for women's leadership in different denominations are bearing fruit. What sustains me in this role now is the collegiality of other presidents, administrators, faculty, and church leaders. I keep in touch with Princeton Seminary friends who are also colleagues, both male and female. I meet for a weekend twice a year with four other senior women in theological education to reflect together and support one another in this calling.

This past summer my husband and I continued our backpacking pilgrimage across northern Spain, and it led us back into the mountains and up into the clouds. I was thrilled to experience again the physical sensation of what I live day to day as a president: God's daily provision and guidance when the way ahead is not clear. That is God's calling to me—to trust and hope in God as I lead a venerable institution that educates and nurtures leaders for God's ministry.

BEING A BISHOP, LIKE THE PUKEKO BIRD

Helen-Ann M. Hartley

Throughout my spiritual journey, I have been influenced by Luke's post-resurrection narrative of the disciples on the road to Emmaus (Luke 24). Caught up in their grief and unable to imagine a world outside their immediate experience, they share together thoughts about the events that have shattered their existence. The risen Jesus comes alongside them (rather like that annoying person who starts to invade a private conversation), and as the story unfolds, they are reminded not just who they are but *whose* they are. In being reminded of the "big picture" and in the breaking of bread, suddenly they see the stranger for who he is: Jesus Christ—and nothing again is the same. They don't just jog back to Jerusalem; they run as fast as they can! Jesus is there with them, on their journey, and most particularly at the times they felt most alone.

I have been a bishop for sixteen months, and the past year or so (2014) has woven a tapestry of intensity and exhilaration, creating a kaleidoscope of opportunity, bringing fresh insight. Bishops participate in the richness of the apostolic succession whilst working within the specifics of the context into which they are called. In any description of my ministry, I try to use the word "opportunity" rather than "challenge," not to downplay the reality of the latter but rather to acknowledge the positivity of the former. My pastoral staff, which was carved for me, has etched in it four "footprints" of the pukeko bird, which never steps backward but is always very intentionally forward-moving, with hugely exaggerated steps (just to make the point). This is how the episcopate (and indeed all leadership in ministry) works: forward moving through new surroundings, into new things and in new ways. Forward doesn't just mean one direction, however. It is possible that a path will be taken several times and in different directions, but its forwardness comes from an ability to think afresh about situations as they arise. This is the task of leadership that a bishop is called to fulfill. A former colleague of mine reminded me when I became bishop that "episcopal" is an anagram of a certain fizzy drink! So what, I wonder, gives my episcopacy its "lift" and "buoyancy"? This inevitably suggests a deeper sense of energy and being rather than the "doing" of the diary. Defining what a bishop "does" is less obvious than what a bishop "is," perhaps?

Being called into a role that you don't ever expect perhaps marks my reflection on my journey to this point. It is true to say that the journeys we take are full of unexpected twists and turns, much like the Emmaus road. My upbringing in a Christian home was very broad and ecumenical, a blend of Presbyterianism, Anglicanism, and Roman Catholicism. I was born "a daughter of the Manse" in the Scottish borders. However, a move "south of the border" to the northeast of England changed the emergent shape of my accent and set a path of formation that in my childhood and teenage years was key to who I am now. I attended an Anglican primary school, followed by a Roman Catholic secondary school (where the hymn line "Faith of our *Fathers*, living still, in spite of dungeon, fire, and sword" remains a memory), most of the while remaining in my Presbyterian denominational identity. My mother's illness, which forced her into hospital for what seemed an eternity to me as a child, planted the seed of denominational change for us as a family. Her frequent receiving of Holy Communion whilst in hospital caused her to attend our local Anglican church when she recovered. In time, as a whole family we started attending the Anglican parish church of St. Chad in Sunderland ourselves, and the rest, as they say, is history. I vividly recall attending my first service: the Bishop of Durham was visiting, and I wondered why on earth he was wearing so much "stuff." Of course, little did I know then that decades later I too would acquire the symbols of episcopal office, the mitre, pastoral staff, pectoral cross, and ring that so profoundly represent the bishop's ministry of teaching, shepherding, and guarding the unity of the whole church. Yet I look back on that now with a profound sense of that part of the Emmaus road being filled with discovery and surprise.

Formation in an Anglican context (while consciously celebrating my Presbyterian heritage through attending to the importance of the ministry of the Word) remained for me as a teenager and young adult within a "male" world. Women were not permitted to be ordained as a priest in the Church of England until the early 1990s while I was a theology undergraduate student at the University of St Andrew's in Scotland. I remember when the vote took place and the dozens of women who rejoiced at being the first to be an ordained priest. At the same time, thousands of miles away, in the Anglican Province of New Zealand (as it was then), the first woman became a diocesan bishop, Penny Jamieson. But I had no knowledge of that, nor of course any idea that I too would become a bishop in that context.

The opportunity to spend a year at Princeton Theological Seminary came at a time when I had a growing sense of my own vocation into ministry but while I lacked the clarity that often accompanies vocation. My year at

Princeton Theological Seminary was a year of immense challenge for me, both personally and spiritually, and indeed academically. Two things stand out. First, classes with Beverly Roberts Gaventa. I never was much of a fan of the apostle Paul, but Beverly changed my mind about that with an almost Damascene effect. Her scholarship and insight were key to unlocking a deep sense I had of vocational pull toward ministry. Paul became my champion, not my opponent. Second, AKMA (A. K. M. Adam). I think that most students at PTS in the mid-1990s probably have an AKMA story. I struggled with his classes and felt an almost constant sense of inability to understand the complexities of postmodern criticism. It was only later that the lightbulb moment came and I realized then, as I do now, what a tremendously inspiring man he was then—and is now. These two professors became key to my journey, in ways they never knew then, though may of course now in reading this.

Eventually, a doctorate followed at the University of Oxford, after a year as a pastoral intern at Westminster Presbyterian Church in Wilmington, Delaware, where its then senior pastor, Jon Walton, influenced my love of preaching. Next I spent a year immersed in the world of Jewish Studies at the Oxford Centre for Hebrew and Jewish Studies. My doctoral studies focused on Paul's use of the imagery of manual labor in his letters, and in my laboring with Paul, I finally found clarity to pursue my vocation formally within the Anglican church. I was ordained as a deacon in Christ Church Cathedral, Oxford, in 2005, and was priested a year later. From that time onward, my vocation became intimately woven with my love of teaching and communication. From groups of schoolchildren in primary school assemblies to lecture halls full of people in training for ordination, the opportunity to help others grow and deepen in their faith through theological education has been a passion of mine. In that sense, the opportunities that I have had in theological education could and should be open to everyone. However, my experience of such education in different parts of the world has shown me that many are denied this, and particularly and worryingly, quite often it is women who are prevented from accessing this right. It is appropriate here that I acknowledge the widely respected Anglican theologian Jenny Te-Paa Daniel, who brought me to Aotearoa, New Zealand, while on sabbatical at the College of St. John the Evangelist in Auckland and then as a colleague faculty member of that institution. Jenny is an inspiring leader whose many contributions, not least to my own journey, must be given full and due credit.

I arrived with my husband to Aotearoa in early 2012. I did not expect, a year and a half later, to be elected bishop of Waikato, New Zealand. The Diocese of Waikato and Taranaki (which covers 30,000 square kilometers in the north island) is unique in the Anglican Communion in having two coequal bishops who together must work in leading mission and ministry. I rejoice in this collaborative partnership and note its remarkable alignment with the Emmaus road story. Leadership that is collaborative and life-giving is important, and together we share in one another's joys and burdens, leading the whole people of God in living out God's mission.

Another biblical passage that has been important to my journey is the encounter between Jesus and the Samaritan woman at the well in John 4. Much has been written about this encounter and its unusual and risky narrative: why was Jesus with this woman alone in the middle of the day, for example? But in just one verse we learn something vital about Jesus' identity: the "Who do you say that I am?" question. An answer comes in verse 26, where Jesus says to the woman, "I am he, the one who is speaking to you"; in other words, "I am the one *in conversation* with you." If we want to engage in the question of who Jesus is, and if we want to engage with what might happen as a result of that discovery, then as a whole church (regardless of denomination), we are going to have to start thinking carefully about the language we use and the ways in which conversations are enabled. As we seek to follow the path of Jesus, making Jesus known in ways that speak into and out of our contexts, we need to attend to the depth and intimacy of knowledge together. In that sense, any call to share practical resources must always walk together with the call to share knowledge. That is where the unexpectedness of discipleship lies. It is essentially uncharted territory. Therein lies an immense and exciting opportunity that we are only just beginning to realize.

In her contribution to the St. Paul's Institute Symposium at St. Paul's Cathedral in London, in July 2014, the chaplain to the speaker at the British Parliament, the Reverend Rose Hudson-Wilkin, said, "The real crisis that we face is not so much one of a lack of equality in leadership. . . . I believe it is a failure to respect the other's humanity, a failure to respect women as human beings."[1] In that sense, "Who do you say I am?" is a question of profound importance that each member of the body of Christ ought to ask and face as a matter of great urgency. Theological education has the capacity and imagination to provide this.

My story cannot be completed without reference to five very important people whose lives are intricately woven with my own and who are role models to me: my parents, Jim and Pat; one of my aunts (Pam); my husband, Myles; and my episcopal colleague in ministry, Archbishop Philip Richardson. I include them all for very different reasons, but most of all for their unwavering commitment to help me grow, in fact to not stop growing, constantly

---

1. Rose Hudson-Wilkin, "Women in Leadership: What Needs to Change?" (lecture, St. Paul's Institute, London, July 16, 2014). Retrieved from http://www .stpaulsinstitute.org.uk/Reports.

expanding my horizons way beyond any self-imposed boundary I may have created. Ministry is always about holding on and letting go, like the disciples of the Emmaus road who were forced to hold on tightly to the wondrous, grand narrative of God's dealings in the world, while at the same time forced to let go of their inability to trust in God, who made all things new in Jesus Christ by the power of the Holy Spirit.

7

Creative Expression

BORN FROM GRIEF: A WRITING VOCATION

Amy Julia Becker

God's call upon my life, now that I am a thirty-eight-year-old mother of three, is the same call I heard as a teenager at a Young Life camp many summers ago. When I was fifteen years old, I had a decision to make about whether to return to boarding school, a place where my childhood faith had withered, or to stay at home for the remaining years of high school, where my faith had a far better chance of thriving. I heard a voice: "Go back to boarding school, and take me with you." It was my first experience of the personal call of God. Those words have shaped my life ever since.

It sounds a bit anthropocentric, I know, to say that I am the one taking God with me wherever I go. I cringe when I look back at my own bad theology. Of course God is already present wherever I go, and from a theological perspective what I'm doing is, by the guidance of the Spirit, participating in God's work. But I heard it as "Take me with you," and I'm grateful that God called me in language I could understand.

In boarding school and then in college, I ended up helping to start groups that introduced my peers to the idea that God loved them and loved them personally. In both cases, those peers were smart, educated, and successful—highly motivated, overachieving, headed toward med school and law school and corporate America. But they felt uncertain, shy, vulnerable when it came to anything spiritual. Still, the message of God's ever-present, loving reality intrigued and attracted many of them. They showed up for Bible studies. They wondered out loud about evil in the world. They wondered whether God really cared. Some of them even came to a lasting faith.

These fledgling groups grew and continued after I graduated, and I went on to work for a parachurch youth ministry, FOCUS (the Fellowship of Christians in Universities and Schools), for the next five years. The work was similar to those groups in college—teaching, speaking, leading Bible studies on the campuses of independent schools, seeking to introduce students to Jesus. I've always wanted to welcome people outside the church into the circle of believers. I've always wanted my peers to know that faith and achievement, faith and the intellect, are compatible with one another.

Eventually I decided to apply to seminary while my husband applied to teach in a boarding school. I thought that I wanted to become a school chaplain, to transition into a more formal version of the work I had been doing all those years. I didn't want to be ordained. I knew we might start a family, and I wasn't sure how all the pieces of our lives would fit together. But I figured that I would always be talking with people about the Bible and theology, whether in a formal or informal role, so seminary seemed a logical next step.

It was around that time—the summer of 2003—that I backed my way into my vocation as a writer, and I almost backed myself out the door of Princeton Seminary. My husband and I were moving to Lawrenceville, New Jersey, in August of that year—he to begin teaching at the Lawrenceville School; I to begin a Master of Divinity at PTS. In between the decision to head to New Jersey and the start of the school year came his mother's diagnosis of primary liver cancer. His mother lived alone in New Orleans, and she needed help. We moved down for the summer, and when the cancer returned in August, I decided to defer my enrollment at seminary.

Peter's mother died on September 11, 2003, far earlier than anyone had expected. I had the unusual privilege of spending most of the final week of her life with her. I held her hand and sang hymns and made decisions about when to call her sons and tell them it was time to come home.

I suppose that I could have rushed headlong into the first semester of school. Classes started a few days after she died. Instead, I waited. I helped arrange the funeral. I returned to New Orleans to sort through the items in her house. I unpacked the boxes in our new house in New Jersey. And I grieved.

In the midst of the packing and unpacking and grieving, I decided to type up the journal entries I had written during my mother-in-law's illness. I wanted a record of the hope and beauty and goodness that had pierced the darkness of the reality of death and dying throughout those months. As I started to type, the characters in my journals started to talk. I filled in memories that I hadn't originally written down. I wondered if I could write the experience as a memoir, not just a series of journal entries to be passed along to our children someday.

By the time I began my MDiv in January of 2004, instead of wanting to become a school chaplain, I wanted to write books. Moreover, I felt convinced that God was calling me to write books, to communicate something true and beautiful about the nature of reality—of our humanity and of God's love—through this story of a broken woman who found grace as she faced the end of her life. I wanted to write books that had Christian faith as their bedrock and yet would communicate that faith to an audience of people who resembled those friends of mine in college—educated achievers who didn't know what to make of spirituality, and especially of a theology of sin and grace.

Over the course of the next two years I continued my studies, but I used the summers and an independent study to work on the book. Every day, as I holed up in front of the computer to edit or to write, I wondered, *Shouldn't you be doing something more productive with your gifts? Isn't this just navel gazing, a way of hiding from real ministry?* But another voice countered, *Keep going. Trust me.*

And then, on December 30, 2005, our daughter Penny was born. Two hours later, the doctors told us they suspected that she had Down syndrome. Their suspicions proved correct—Penny was diagnosed through a blood test with trisomy 21. We didn't know then what her diagnosis would mean for our family, but we experienced familiar emotions. It was the feeling of grief, of dislocation, of losing someone—in this case, the child we thought we were having—forever.

I had completed two years of school at that point. I took one credit at a time for the next few years, still working on the memoir, but mostly spending time with Penny. I read a stack of practical and theological and personal books about Down syndrome and disability. We shuttled from one doctor or therapist to the next. By the time she was two, Penny had an occupational therapist, physical therapist, speech therapist, and special educator each come to the house once a week. They all gave us homework—exercises to do with her to help her develop her motor and cognitive skills. She needed tubes in her ears and glasses and a heart procedure.

But what happened with our grief after Penny's diagnosis wasn't the same as what happened after Peter's mom died. With his mom, the grief remained. We still get choked up on major occasions when we notice her absence. We still wish that she could hold her grandkids and spoil them. We still wish that we could call her and ask her what their dad was like as a child. But with Penny, the grief was transformed. Over time, we realized that we were mourning a hypothetical child, a child who had never existed, a child who did not need to be mourned. We realized that we had been given a child who deserved love, who offered great joy.

I journaled regularly about Penny. Once she was two years old, my grief had been replaced by gratitude, and I had hundreds of pages written down. The first book was more or less complete, and I was pregnant with our second baby. I started writing short opinion pieces, first for blogs, then for the *Philadelphia Inquirer*, later for other national news websites. Meanwhile, an agent approached me about writing a book about my experience as a mother of a child with Down syndrome. I decided to self-publish the memoir about my mother-in-law, take a leave of absence from seminary, and start writing this new book.

Penny is now almost ten years old. The book I wrote about her—*A Good and Perfect Gift*—languished as a manuscript rejected by forty-eight publishers while I went back to school and finished my degree. The day I completed my senior thesis, I received a contract for its publication by Bethany House. It eventually won a Christopher Award, and *Publisher's Weekly* named it one of the best religion books of 2011.[1]

It's hard to know how to make sense of God's providence, and yet I do look back and think that if I had gotten a contract for the book when I had wanted it, I never would have finished school. It felt like a sweet affirmation of my calling to minister through writing when that contract arrived, as if God wanted me to connect the dots of providential timing and see that none of it came by my own doing.

My husband and I still live on the campus of a boarding school, and I lead a Bible study for the students here. I preach on occasion in our church, and we lead an adult Bible study. I also volunteer as the director of Sunday school for the elementary aged kids. I'm writing another book now, and the ideas for three novels percolate in the back of my brain most of the time. I spend a lot of time with our three children—shuttling them to and from ballet and gymnastics and soccer, supervising playdates, reading out loud and singing and taking walks outside, making sure that we all participate in cleaning and cooking and other household chores.

It is quite possible that a decade from now, when our kids are all more self-sufficient and I have more relational energy to spare, I will pursue a call to a

---

1. Amy Julia Becker, *A Good and Perfect Gift: Faith, Expectations, and a Little Girl Named Penny* (Minneapolis: Bethany House, 2011).

local church or a course of study that could lead to teaching on a college level. I would like to find an institutional home for my ministry and my writing.

But still, as I look back on over twenty years of seeking to follow where God leads, what at times has appeared like a series of disjointed efforts instead begins to look like an intentional path. I have "taken God with me" into schools and friendships and online communities and family. I shouldn't be surprised to discover that God has been present—gracious, patient, loving—everywhere I go.

MUSIC AND WORSHIP: FROM INDONESIA TO THE GLOBAL CHURCH

Ester Pudjo Widiasih

Formation and Work. My interest in liturgical studies started with my fondness of singing in church choir, and some dancing and acting since I was in kindergarten. My parents were active church members and brought their three young daughters along with them to church worship and activities. My mother was a first-generation Christian. Her singing led her to be a self-taught choir conductor. My father, a third-generation Christian, was a dancer of Javanese classical dance. In the 1970s my father introduced Javanese dancing in a Javanese church in Jakarta. At that time, for many Christians, the local culture was still seen as an inappropriate means of telling the Gospels' stories. With my mother writing the scripts, my father choreographed Javanese ballets of biblical stories that were performed in our church. For my parents, being a Christian did not mean repudiating one's ethnic cultural identity. In spite of past missionary teaching, my parents proved that one can be both a Christian and a Javanese.

My parents' love for the church and the Javanese tradition, with its artistic expressions, influenced me tremendously. Not only did I decide to study theology and become ordained as a minister of Word and Sacrament, but I developed an interest in using creative artistic expressions for proclaiming the gospel, particularly in worship. I too believe that the church must embrace and express its faith in Jesus Christ, God's incarnation, through local cultures, where it belongs. For churches in Indonesia, especially those coming from the Dutch Reformed tradition, accepting and using one's own cultural tradition in worship have been challenging. In recent years, fortunately, there have been attempts to make Christianity more contextual by embracing local culture and identity. Along with this spirit, I believe that worship and other kinds of church ritual need to express the culture and social context of the people.

The Jakarta Theological Seminary (JTS) invited me to teach liturgy and music in the last year of my study at this oldest ecumenical seminary in Indonesia. This appointment created an opportunity to pursue graduate studies.

After my graduation, I did further study at the Asian Institute for Liturgy and Church Music in Manila, the Philippines; at Princeton Theological Seminary for a Master of Theology (ThM) degree with concentration in worship studies; and at the Theological School of Drew University, New Jersey, for a PhD degree in liturgical studies. These academic institutions equipped me to teach in seminary as well as to do my ministry in the church.

I taught classes on liturgical studies and church music at Jakarta Theological Seminary at the undergraduate and graduate levels. Besides teaching, I coordinated the liturgical life of the campus for daily and weekly worship and for special services. The chapel worship became an enhancement of, and a laboratory for, my liturgical classes. Led by students, staff members, and professors, the JTS has a Center for Liturgy that offers lectures, workshops, and training on worship and church music for church members and leaders in Indonesia. I was also responsible for organizing this center, planning its programs, giving lectures, and conducting workshops. The goal was to educate church members and leaders about contextual and creative worship.

After several years of teaching, I received an offer to work at the World Council of Churches as program executive for spiritual life. My main task includes planning, coordinating, and leading daily worship at the Ecumenical Center and the communal prayer of the WCC's meetings. My department is also responsible for collecting prayers, songs, Bible studies, and other worship materials in support of WCC's goal of realizing the unity of the church and WCC's programs on striving for justice and peace. Praying together is indeed an obvious action of fellowship in Christ. Christians from different confessional traditions and cultural and social backgrounds are united in worshiping God. A taste of the unity of the body of Christ is indeed manifested in worship.

Studying at Princeton Theological Seminary. I learned about Princeton Theological Seminary as I was looking for a theological school that had a concentration or department in liturgical/worship studies for a master's degree. PTS was appealing to me because the seminary has the same Reformed background as my church and JTS, but it also has students and professors from various confessional backgrounds. Another important factor in attending PTS was the scholarships for international students, for which I am very grateful. Another PTS program that was very beneficial for me was a chance to take classes at Westminster Choir College. I was preparing to teach subjects on liturgy and church music, and taking some classes on church music at Westminster Choir College helped with this preparation.

During my years at PTS, my classmates came from various confessional and ethnic backgrounds that made the discussions both inside and outside the classrooms interesting and enriching. The professors encouraged us to be open-minded to different theological views, but at the same time to value our own confessional traditions. We learned the teachings and practices of the church in the past as well as at present time. In a worship class taught by Rev. Dr. Leonora Tubbs Tisdale, for example, we learned about the history of worship as well as current issues in worship. We discussed the worship of the Presbyterian Church, but students were also encouraged to explore their own churches' worship traditions. This teaching approach pays attention to the balance between traditional and contextual, confessional and ecumenical. Professor Tisdale also inspired her students to perceive worship in more comprehensive and creative ways, involving our senses and various artistic dimensions as well as our cultural traditions. She reminded us that worship planners have to pay attention to the whole human self to make worship more meaningful and to engage congregants' participation. In other words, worship must not stress words and the cognitive dimension only—a practice that is so dear for the Reformed churches.

This class also emphasized that worship planners have to ensure that women's voices are heard and that they take part in the leadership. Liturgical elements such as prayers, songs, sermons, and so forth can be built upon theologies that are developed by women and based on women's daily experiences. Inclusivity in worship includes the assurance that congregants can participate fully and actively. Thus, efforts have to be made to assist worshipers with special needs that enable them to worship God with the community. The classes I took at PTS laid a strong foundation for how nowadays I plan, coordinate, and lead worship as well as for how I teach about worship and church music.

One of the unforgettable experiences at PTS was being selected to sing in the touring choir. The joy was not just about singing, an activity that I loved, but also about participating in different churches on Sundays. By attending those churches, I had the opportunity to meet people outside campus and to experience different styles of worship. Each church we attended had its own style of worship, which sometimes was determined by the cultural background of the majority of its members and not so much by its confessional tradition. This phenomenon made me realize the pluralistic nature of the United States and how influential a particular culture is in shaping church worship. I learned so much about American churches and the country's wider culture through my encounter with the worshipers in those various churches.

Looking to the Future for Women. I am blessed in having supportive parents who encouraged me to pursue the best education I could get and allowed me to follow my passions. I am aware that there are many women who are discouraged from pursuing higher education because of their gender. In Indonesia there are only a few women teaching in seminaries or theological schools, even though many churches have allowed women to be ordained and to work as pastors since the 1950s. There are even fewer women theologians and pastors who have doctoral degrees. The ordination of women is indeed an affirmation of women's leadership role in the church. However, in the midst of a strong patriarchal culture like in Indonesia, it is still rare to have women holding leadership positions in the church structure. I hope that in the future there will be more women having postgraduate degrees in theology and many more women becoming church leaders.

One important thing I learned from the classes I attended at Princeton Theological Seminary is the necessity for churches to listen to women's voices and to facilitate those voices to be widely heard and appreciated. In the worship class, for example, we learned not only about how to plan and organize worship, but also about how to make worship a space where women experience God's love and justice. It means that, in worship, stories of women are told, God's words are seen through women's eyes, women's presence and works are valued, and leadership roles are open to women. Worship thus becomes a place of acknowledging women as God's children who are equal to men, as well as a means of empowerment for all worshipers, women and men, to live out their baptismal faith: "There is no longer Jew or Greek, there is no longer slave or free, there is no longer male and female; for all of you are one in Christ Jesus" (Gal 3:28).

Looking to the future, I dream of a world without discrimination against women, where women are free and safe to be themselves and are given the same opportunity as men. I dream of churches acknowledging women's voices with full involvement and leadership. I believe that education is one of the key ways to make these dreams come true. Seminary education is influential in pastors' views. As a seedbed, seminary is a place to plant and grow the seeds of ministry. It is important, therefore, for seminary students, women and men, to learn about equal rights and justice for women and to empower women in daily life and ministry. Yet the lesson must not be taught only as an intellectual exercise, but also as a real experience for students, faculty, and staff members. It means that a seminary must become a community that affirms the equal rights of women and provides as many opportunities as possible for women to take part in leadership. Such a community must listen attentively to women's voices, ideas, and theologies; actively tell their stories in classes and other contexts; and encourage women to be themselves in their daily lives and in ministries.

KEY CHANGES: A MUSICIAN'S TRANSITIONS IN MINISTRY

Donna J. Garzinsky

"'Whom shall I send, and who will go for us?' . . . 'Here am I; send me!'" (Isa 6:8). This poignant text from Isaiah crystallized as I graduated from Westminster Choir College. Warren Martin, former Westminster Choir College professor, echoed this text in his "Anthem of Dedication" that all Westminster students learn and sing at commencement. It continues to be a powerful text for me.

But back to the beginning. I was baptized a Lutheran at my father's church and learned the faith and was confirmed in the Episcopal church, where my mother had been the organist for a number of years. One of the scriptural texts I took to heart from this time is Luke 10:27: "'You shall love the Lord your God with all your heart, and with all your soul, and with all your strength, and with all your mind; and your neighbor as yourself.'"

As a young child, I grew up hearing Mom practicing on the organ that Dad had built for her in their home's basement. Many of the pieces she played lodged deep in my memory, only to be rediscovered with delight over the course of time as I explored new sheet music and discovered an old friend.

My formal music studies began with piano lessons when I was seven or eight. In junior high school, I set my sights on becoming a doctor. While I loved being able to play many band instruments and had just switched to organ lessons, becoming a doctor would fulfill my desire to do something meaningful and to be of service. My dad and I had many conversations about how to achieve this goal. He must have sensed, though, that my soft heart and discomfort with traumatic wounds might cause problems. After a difficult discussion about how I would feel should I lose a patient in surgery, I began to rethink my goal. But if not medicine, then where was I headed? Suddenly my path seemed dim.

Sometime later, I began to study organ with William Payn, then director of music at the Presbyterian church in Morristown, New Jersey. The music he gave me to learn was challenging, but all of a sudden things started to click. I found that I could play the pedals and keep them coordinated with my hands. Now even Bach became exciting! The world of organ music opened up as I learned works by Vaughan Williams, Langlais, Franck, and Mulet. Dr. Payn invited me to sing with the high school choir and attend worship. This was a challenge, since I couldn't drive yet and Morristown was forty minutes away. With help from my brother, I was able to do both. What Dr. Payn did with music in worship was something new and very exciting. As my organ skills improved, he would occasionally allow me to play in worship— even more exciting! Then I heard the Widor "Toccata" one Christmas Eve and was so taken by it that, after finding my mom's copy of it, I learned most of it in one week. All of a sudden I knew what I wanted to do: become a church musician. I soon had my first church job: organist at a small Methodist church near home.

Difficult conversations with my parents ensued: Could I find a full-time church position? What if I couldn't find one? How would I support myself? The solution was to pursue a degree not just in church music but also in music education.

During my sophomore year in college, I became the music director at United Presbyterian Church in Plainfield, New Jersey, where I served nine years and introduced a variety of music ensembles. As a young college student, I was appreciative of how two members in particular, Helen Foerster and Jeanne Mayer, reached out to shepherd me into the fold. Helen was recovering from the death of her husband but still embodied community and love, and she helped to shape me. Jeanne was one of those church members who graciously did 80 percent of the work of the church. Her death from breast cancer affected me deeply and helped me to realize that I needed pastoral skills, even if I was not planning to be a pastor. Rev. Thomas E. S. (Ted) Miller was called to the church a few years after I arrived. Now retired, Ted was an excellent pastor, open to new ideas and new ways to engage and involve the congregation. He was passionate about mission and understood how growing congregations do active mission work. It was during our work together when I realized that despite having grown up in the church, I needed more education—more theological education. Ted encouraged me to explore my options.

New Brunswick Theological Seminary seemed like the best fit. It was within a reasonable commuting distance and offered a Masters of Theological Studies degree that could be pursued on a part-time basis—perfect for a working church musician. My Old Testament and New Testament professors engaged students with interesting insights into the history, themes, cultural context, and critical analysis of the Bible.

Partway into my studies, the seminary discontinued my degree program.

Princeton Theological Seminary offered a Masters of Art in Christian education degree and was willing to transfer many of my accumulated credits. Such a degree made sense to me because one aspect of music ministry is spiritual growth/faith formation.

I was excited to be at Princeton Seminary. My classes with professors such as Freda Gardner, Mark Taylor, Daniel L. Migliore, and Stanley Hauerwas all challenged me and—at the same time—confirmed that I was on the right path. The only downside was that as a part-time commuting student, I missed the wonderful fellowship, group study, and worship that seminary interns at my church had described and enjoyed.

In 1986, still a few credits short of my master's degree, I felt God calling me to something new. This was surprising, as I really felt that Plainfield was my spiritual home. How was I going to pull up roots? How could I finish my studies while starting a new position? Just after making the decision to go the Presbyterian church in Westfield, a deeply cherished relationship ended unexpectedly. Devastated, I wept and turned to God in prayers, reading psalms and hymns of comfort, and pouring my heart into composing. The will to move on gradually returned, and with it I discovered the wonderful work ahead of me in Westfield. With graduation behind me in 1987, I was able to immerse myself fully into the music ministry at this new church and to do volunteer work with its young adult and youth ministries. Working in such a vaunted church, I sometimes struggled to reconcile ministry there with what I had learned in seminary. After one seemingly successful handbell tour, I was stunned to learn that one ringer had not engaged spiritually. My primary goals in music ministry have been first, to encourage everyone to sing to God with enthusiasm (with God's spirit); second, to provide opportunities for all ages to develop and share their musical talents in choirs and ensembles or individually—all in service to God; and third, to support the musicians' spiritual growth and fellowship. This failure troubled me, and I have tried subsequently to be more intentional about engaging spiritually through prayer, poetry, devotionals, and sharing of joys and concerns.

God continued to work in mysterious ways in my life, bringing me together with someone who was patient and loved classical music, and coincidentally attended a Presbyterian church. In 1991 we married, I moved, and we hoped to start a family. Needing to reduce my hours and long commute from my new home, God opened a new door: First Memorial Presbyterian Church in Dover as its part-time director of music. It was a congregation with rich traditions, and I was soon learning new major organ pieces for Christmas and Easter and conducting annual performances of G. F. Handel's *Messiah*. My tenure at First Memorial Presbyterian Church came during a time of pastoral transition and, as it turned out, transition for me as well.

Faced with expensive infertility treatments, I searched out a variety of non-church jobs, hoping to find one that could use my skills and offer broad health insurance. The long road eventually led to work as a reading/language arts editor at Pearson Education. As my workload grew, something had to give, and so I said a sad goodbye to the good people at my church.

During the summer of 1998, I answered an ad for an organist at the Community Church of Mountain Lakes, a United Church of Christ church. The church had a well-developed, graded-level choir program and was looking for a good organist. I hesitated to apply, as I was unfamiliar with the denomination's worship and polity, but a door was opened, and I accepted the position. All pastors bring a unique focus and theology to their role. Rev. Dr. Larry Kalp's theology came at a good time for me—a theology of gratitude. Val Piederson, the director of music, shared her gifts of love of good music, high standards, and gentle spirit. I was privileged to work with her until she passed away from colon cancer in March 2003, a time when pastoral care was an important part of my work. Soon thereafter, Rev. Kalp retired and thus began a long pastoral transition. Toward the end of this time, I took on responsibility for oversight of the music program and directing the adult choir. The joy of working with these dedicated and talented people was rich with promise. And yet I began to feel the familiar nudge from God: it's time to do other work. Like all of the previous churches I had served, it was difficult to leave, and especially so after fourteen years.

The church I currently serve is one in which I never expected to be. It is an Evangelical Lutheran Church in America congregation, and I had applied for their interim position, anticipating that the church would want a Lutheran musician (which I was not) and would not consider changing the interim position to a permanent position. God had other plans. At the end of an intense first month as organist/handbell director, the interim music director, Ken Bryson, agreed to stay on for the entire first year, and so continued the whirlwind as I learned new liturgies, hymns, Lutheran theology, and many people. At the end of the year I struggled with what was to come next. Like me, my colleague Ken had experienced the same joy of directing wonderful singers and surely wanted to continue on. I, however, was supposed to take over. A transition period was created to allow us to find our way, asking God's guidance as we went. With prayer, open hearts, honest conversations, time, and grace, we arrived at a shared position giving each of us directing responsibilities. The position and congregation continues to evolve as we listen to God's Word and seek God's will for us in this time and place. I feel grateful to be serving among them.

Social media is big at St. John's, and yet I was reluctant to embrace it initially. I now tweet for the church and post YouTube worship videos. To stay up-to-date on a variety of topics and issues affecting worship and the church, I read widely. Certainly, the education I received at New Brunswick and Princeton Seminaries has been invaluable and has helped to open doors and inform my faith. While at Princeton, I had few women professors, and among them Freda Gardner stood out as an exemplary role model and teacher.

Most of the positions I've held have been part-time, even as they grew into full-time responsibilities. As my parents long ago suspected, it is difficult to support oneself with a part-time church-music position in this area, but I am grateful for all the opportunities I've had to serve God—*Soli Deo gloria*. As Psalm 92 begins, "It is good to give thanks to the LORD, to sing praises to your name, O Most High."

THE GRACE OF TALENT:
THE CALLING OF AN ARTIST

Heather Sturt Haaga

There is an art to art. There is a magic and a mystery to art that is hard to articulate. And the magic, the "God thing," is what permits the creation and the engagement. The process ranges from the small—children at vacation Bible school painting summer-themed pictures to share with their families—to the sublime—stained glass windows and majestic banners beckoning congregants to engage with God.

The act of creation is, to me, a true gift of grace. Unmerited favor. The ability to observe closely and to translate your sight with a pencil or a paintbrush onto a paper or canvas is the gift. Then, like all things, the gift requires nurturing and focus. Be it painting or piano, the gift of talent demands practice, repetition, and sometimes starting over. The gift requires one to look inward and recognize that the talent should be encouraged and used.

The art of art is about creation, clearly, but it is also about connection, the relationship between God and ourselves. His Creation inextricably connects all of us to Him and to one another. I think that this sense of connectedness, this need for connection, is a driver for artistic people—many times only on a subconscious level. The ultimate goal of the artist is to evoke a response, to make a connection with the viewer, to change a perception. When these things occur, you know that you have been successful, and, hopefully, used the gift God gave you to the best of your capability.

We have a handwritten note on our refrigerator that paraphrases the passage from Luke. It says, "Much is demanded of those to whom much has been given." Depending on where you are in life's arc, this can mean different things. But one constant for me has been to recognize that talent, unmerited favor, requires "doing."

I started drawing at an early age and won a contest at age six with a picture of Cinderella's coach. On the way through life I had high school art, a few Saturday morning art classes, and one disastrous college semester of studio art (read: drawing nudes). While I loved creating "crafty" things for our children, Sunday school, and AYSO soccer, I never thought to paint until I was forty-three. Our son, at that time twelve, said to me, "Mom, you are too old to start something new." Which, of course, had the expected effect of spurring me on. I've never looked back.

For the most part I am self-taught, though I worked in an atelier, of sorts, for several years surrounded by painters more experienced than myself who became helpful guides. In the beginning I painted in acrylics for the simple (and ridiculous) reason that the brushes were easier to clean. But acrylics have a downside. The paint dries very fast and is unforgiving. Oils, on the other hand, provide more depth and a deeper color. And at the end of the day, like all things that require a bit more effort, they are so worth using.

Many people ask me if painting is relaxing. It is not. Painting requires amazing concentration and focus. After completing a session, you can feel, physically, as if you've run a race. And sometimes, but not always, the magic, the "God thing," happens, and you look at your finished work and think, "Did I do that?" That is your glimpse of grace, unmerited favor.

There are two aspects of painting that are, in a way, ministerial. One is the connecting piece—the creation of an emotional or spiritual connection among the Creator, the artist, and the viewer. Painting allows—no, demands—a focus on creation, an intense scrutiny of a place or an object that, for the most part, does not occur in everyday life. You must concentrate on the lemon, the tree, and study every aspect carefully. This process underscores the complexity and providence of God's plan.

The connection is visual as well as creative. Because I primarily paint landscapes and still lifes, the paintings have a sense of place. All paintings receive a title as well as a short accompanying story—perhaps only a few sentences long—that explains or suggests the background of the piece. And then the viewers, because they are then connected, become a part of the painting. An example of this might be a painting titled *Normandy Vista*, whose story is as follows:

> So quiet now, so serene the fields where once smoke swirled and gunfire peppered the landscape. Where men dashed through the fields and hedgerows, hoping to come out alive on the other side. So quiet now. The fields are healed, but we will never forget.

The other ministerial aspect is the teaching piece. People always ask a painter questions: How do you draw it? How long does it take? Do you paint from life or imagination? The practice of creation causes people to engage, to ask questions, and, perhaps, to consider their own gifts of grace and how they might be fostered.

Often people say, "I can't draw a straight line." Which is funny but completely untrue. Yes, talent comes in varying amounts, and we all do not have the same capabilities. But there is something to be said for learning how to look more closely and observe life around you, being willing to take a chance and to maybe fail at first. Encouragement to try is sometimes the only catalyst necessary, and with that you are launched. If nothing else, when you attempt to paint, to play an instrument, to throw a pot, to write a story, you better understand the challenge, the commitment, and the sheer hard work creativity demands. You will never look at a painting in the same way again.

I am blessed, and I am grateful. It is a wonderful gift to be able to encourage others to try. It is a wonderful gift to be able to bring others pleasure through my work. My happiest moment is when that connection occurs and another person has a glimpse into a process that is grace driven.

CATHEDRAL ARTS: BRINGING HOPE TO DISADVANTAGED CHILDREN

Kimberly Hyatt

"What are creation's needs for full functioning?" asks Tillie Olsen in her book *Silences*.[2] To answer this question, near the top of my list are the arts, the Divine, and myself. Choosing the arts, which empower me to make sense of the world, as the focus for ministry transformed me from a silenced woman with music and the written word as trusted friends into an advocate for economically disadvantaged and culturally diverse children.

The 1987 statement "A Call to Church Involvement in the Renewal of Public Education" urged Presbyterians to support education and ensure the development of aesthetic appreciation and skills.[3] The statement spoke of children's needs in these areas as being "of life-giving or life-denying proportions." My role as pastor in leading the Cathedral Arts Project in Jacksonville, Florida, is my attempt to do just that, responding to the Holy Spirit, the Lord and Giver of Life.

Through the Cathedral Arts Project, we help some of our community's most vulnerable children uncover the treasure buried in their lives through unleashing their creative spirits. Among the myriad of intrinsic and instrumental benefits of arts education, children come to see their own creative potential as ones bearing the *imago Dei, the image of God*. Since all children bear this mark, they all deserve opportunities for arts learning. Without us ever talking about God, children find ways to transcend the limits of their circumstances by focusing on that which lies within and beyond. I know this because it is my story too, a story in which the arts were not only a faithful companion but also a life giver.

In the early 1970s, as a little girl in rural South Carolina, I would sit alone on my metal Sears swing set, bellowing out the bluegrass gospel songs we sang at the quaint Baptist church every Wednesday and Sunday night. The

2. Tillie Olsen, *Silences* (New York: Delacorte, 1979).
3. "A Call to Church Involvement in the Renewal of Public Education," adopted as a resolution by the 199th General Assembly of the Presbyterian Church (U.S.A.), 1987.

faster the song, the higher I could swing. Growing up on a little farm with no one around to play with, music was my steadfast ally in taking me from where I was to where I wanted to be.

I am from tobacco, corn, and soybeans. We didn't have much—but marigolds, roses, and azaleas beautifully framed our little house. Pecan trees and tobacco barns dotted the forty acres around me—land from which my grandmother cleared the pines on her own with a hand axe. I was a skinny girl with big ears, who spent summers working on the farm and served as church pianist while my Daddy led the singing. Life was simple, hard, and far from glamorous. I felt like a misfit. Something inside me longed for a better life that somehow involved carrying a briefcase, like the sophisticated people I saw on TV.

At twelve years old, I responded to an altar call one Sunday night to be saved. All the talk about hell didn't make any sense to me, but I thought I should hedge my bets and try to do the right thing. Once becoming an official Christian, I was convinced that I could never swing high enough to experience a single ounce of happiness the rest of my life.

An awkward entry into teenage life made for an especially poor relationship with God. Rural communities can sometimes be vulnerable places for young, developing girls living among farm hands. One of the men working on our farm made being on my own land an unsafe space. I felt confused and disconnected as his hands overpowered parts of my body. I pushed what happened to the back of my mind. I spent hours every day under the headphones. Once again, it was music that proved my salvation and transported me to a different place and time.

High school senior year came quickly. An African American student named Rupert and I were named most intellectual and had our picture taken together at Dr. Wilson's, the grandest home in our town. I was surprised that my parents did not seem proud. Eventually, I realized that it was because I was coupled as an equal with "a colored boy." I knew that it wasn't right. Just like every Saturday when my mother and I would take Cora to the grocery store. The African American woman was made to sit in the back seat of the car "where she belonged." She was called by her first name, unlike Mrs. Graham, a white woman we sometimes drove to church who was always given the front seat. We lived in contradictions, treating some people differently, tossing about the N-word, while saying that we followed Jesus, who loved all the children—red and yellow, black and white. I was perplexed and angered.

Feeling like a misfit in so many ways, one Sunday afternoon while my parents were in their room listening to a preacher yelling about God's love and going to hell on the radio, I imagined picking up a shotgun leaning in the coat closet, wrapping my lips around it and being done with it all—the contradictions, the dreams, the briefcase. Then Millie entered my thoughts. She was a girl I met the summer before during a program at Presbyterian College. She knew a different God. I put down the gun in my mind's eye, and I picked up a pen and wrote a long letter to Millie. She must have written back instantly. Her letter described how she and others in her church cared and would be praying for me. The good news of the gospel became incarnate in a letter from Millie, tucked in a light-blue envelope with a twenty-cent stamp. The propositions of Christianity still didn't register as truth for me, but I did love the music, and now I had the feeling that people, albeit people hours away, cared for me. It was enough.

I had not yet entertained going into the ministry. I knew that I wanted to go to Presbyterian College because Millie would be there. I ended up majoring in political science, and I graduated cognizant for the first time of my responsibility to help others—*dum vivimus servimus*, while we live we serve.

My first job was as a newspaper reporter in my hometown, where I covered a few Ku Klux Klan parades and a cross burning one night in a remote field. The contradictions of what Christians did in the name of Christ seared into my mind, this time with sounds, smells, and images. Shortly after, I made the impulsive decision to move to Washington, DC. I was hired as a secretary in the government relations division of a large association and quickly moved up the ranks. I loved being a lobbyist, and I loved DC. For the first time, I felt like I belonged. I never dreamed of having such an exciting job in a cosmopolitan city. Here I was—this poor farm girl mingling with heads of business and government. And I finally got to carry that briefcase!

In Washington, DC, I found a style of worship that felt right. For the first time, I encountered a woman as clergy and found refuge and inspiration from the arts—art museums, the ballet, and choral productions. The beauty of Scripture as poetry came into focus at a Good Friday concert at the Kennedy Center. Leaving the hall, I noticed the lights reflecting on the Potomac and let the words I just heard linger—the stars, Orion, and darkness becoming light. The arts were giving me life and a new way to glorify and enjoy God.

Having gone from considering suicide to being happier than I could have imagined, I now faced giving it all up to go to seminary. Just as Millie helped me discover a new way of experiencing the Divine, I wanted to do the same for others. I found a path of life and felt called to go and do likewise.

As soon as I visited Princeton Theological Seminary, I knew that it was the place for me. It was nothing like my childhood. I loved the beauty of the campus, the charm of the town, and, most of all, the attention to scholarship.

Seminary was full of challenges before I started. First, I was all but kicked out of a Bible study at my church for pointing out that two accounts of the same story could not both be true. And then the letter arrived confirming logistical details, including my student mailbox number: 666. It startled me, but I felt compelled to keep it. Walter, the mailroom coordinator, told me that I was the first student ever to keep that box.

I saw life's challenges through the lens of 666. I came down with strep throat during orientation and missed opportunities to form initial friendships that would be vital to feel included. There were record-breaking heat waves with no air conditioning; record-breaking blizzards came with no heat. During my first year, my father had a heart attack. During my senior year, he was diagnosed with cancer and died. Transitioning from the farm to DC had been so easy, but Princeton was another story. It made me wonder if my student mailbox number was God's way of telling me to stay in DC.

In many ways, I was my own worst enemy. I entered seminary with an enormous ego, a condescending attitude, and the very self-righteousness that had turned me off from Christianity as a child. I quickly found myself occupying a lonely space.

Initially very involved with a conservative group, I found that the positions they took during the ongoing debates about human sexuality and the "Re-Imagining" gathering (a conference incorporating feminist theology) did not ring true to me. I resigned from my leadership position there yet still rolled my eyes whenever feminist theology came up elsewhere. I had not even come out to myself as a lesbian. I never sought out a progressive group.

I was the conservative misfit living in Hodge Hall among liberals. I was sure that God had placed me there to save them; turns out, they were the ones leading me to wholeness. A woman down the hall turned me on to Tillich's trinity as creative power, saving love, and ecstatic transformation. I began to appreciate diversity of thought, ambiguity, and freedom of conscience. The radical openness of *ecclesia reformata, semper reformanda secundum verbum Dei* (the church reformed, always reforming according to the word of God) resonated. Classes in liberation theology and Niebuhr helped me see the inadequacies of an individualistic faith and gave context for the anger I had always felt over the dividing walls of hostility and perceived superiority between whites and African Americans. Ministry broadened to encompass compassion, justice, reconciliation, and social righteousness. I arrived at Princeton Theological Seminary very right of center. I graduated left of center. I began to find my voice.

Since I was a little girl, the arts have been a life-giving means of grace. Appropriating the arts as a vessel for ministry is my way of service. If it is true, as Howard Gardner posits, that there are multiple forms of intelligences, then we need the arts to have a fuller experience of life, of God, even.[4] I see many

---

4. Howard Gardner, *Frames of Mind: The Theory of Multiple Intelligences* (New York: Basic Books, 1983).

adults who struggle with the notion of God because they are constrained by the contradictions of propositional truths. I often wonder, why not consider the aesthetic dimension to apprehend Divine revelation? It is a sensibility that can set captives free.

The thousands of children we serve through the Cathedral Arts Project will be able to call on their aesthetic sense as they grow older and make their way along the path of life. We see time and time again how the arts are a catalyst for extraordinary change in the lives of children, especially those like me, who feel like misfits.

To me, religion is but another art form, and to some, the arts are religion. They accomplish the same purposes. By using whatever materials are at hand, both the artist and the religious person endeavor to find refuge, to make sense of what is and to bring forth that which is not yet.

8

Innovative Ministries

EMERGING CHURCH, EMERGING WRITER

Danielle Shroyer

I have been fascinated by God for as long as I can remember. I didn't have language for it at the time, but looking back, what I most enjoyed doing both out loud and in the solitude of my own head was theological inquiry. I liked asking questions, probing the stories, questioning assumptions. I felt defensive when others tried to make God too easy almost as much as I felt defensive when others tried to pass God off as too small. Even today, it's the "aliveness" of God that most captivates me. God's reality always slips just through our fingers and beyond our grasps, despite all the words and doctrines and traditions with which we try to hold God. As much as that frustrates me, it is also what I love about God the most.

It is also what has made my journey of ministry somewhat unorthodox and complicated. I've always been wary of totalizing, or even semidefinite, claims on God, which has given me hesitant and complicated relationships with institutions, denominations, and systematic theologians, just for starters. It isn't that I believe that we should shy away from saying something about God; I more find fault with how we hold our beliefs. One of my college professors said that we should hold theology like a porcupine. As far as I can tell, most everyone I know holds their theology with hands that must be bleeding.

I felt called into ministry the summer after my junior year of high school, which surprised me almost as much as it did everyone else. I was not the star girl of Sunday school or the leader of youth group. I was the girl who often came to church by herself and had a lot of questions and opinions. At least in west Texas, I would hardly pass for a bona fide church kid. In my religion classes at Baylor, many of my classmates would say that they were going into ministry as third-generation pastors or that they had been aware of their call their whole lives. I had no idea how that felt, any more than I had an idea of what ministry would look like for me. But I knew that I had always been desperately interested in God—not vaguely interested, not passively interested, *desperately* interested, like a detective in relentless pursuit of the clues that would solve the world's greatest mysteries. Whatever the calling, I hoped that it was at heart an invitation to grab my magnifying glass and start searching.

My first and best official clues came my freshman year of college, when I finagled my way into Hebrew class as my chosen language requirement. Those enigmatic boxy symbols held a poetic universe of meaning within them. I could hardly bear to set down my chestnut brown *Biblia Hebraica* to give attention to my other classes. Certainly, I thought, my calling was to the academy, where I would be encouraged to study with flourish. My other religion classes whetted my appetite for theological rigor as well, and I all but assumed that I was destined one day to don the robes of a tenured PhD professor.

And then I experienced something that would completely alter my trajectory. Because Baylor's version of sorority hazing was mandatory church attendance while pledging, I found myself in the pews of University Baptist Church of Waco on its first ever gathering. In addition to its location in an old house, I remember two other things: the pastor wore jeans and the benediction song was "Hold My Hand" by Hootie and the Blowfish. What I remember most, though—what I will remember forever—is how it dawned on me that church could be changed. Traditions, after all, are simply new ideas people felt inclined to keep around. What if I simply gave myself permission to come up with new traditions?

I finished my undergraduate studies with an eye toward seminary and hoped for a place with intellectual rigor, a stellar faculty, and a strong community. I willingly listened to the counsel of my professors when they steered me toward Princeton Seminary. When the dean of Princeton Theological

Seminary came to campus for a visit and mentioned all of these things plus flag football, I was officially sold. One of my professors felt so strongly about it that he flatly refused to send a letter of recommendation anywhere else. Princeton, he said, was a perfect fit.

And it was. I found at Princeton a community of thoughtful, bright, interesting people who differed in many respects but held in common a commitment to the good news. I found professors who pushed me, stretched me, and inspired me. I found the academic rigor I hoped for, and I graduated with a clear sense of the unfolding history of the church and the theological questions that continually begged for answers. And I played flag football every season.

What I did not find as easily was a group of people who shared my out-of-the-box ideas about church structure and practice. So when in my middler year of seminary I became part of the leadership team of a new church plant called Journey Church in Dallas, I felt that I had found a calling that could give me wings. I moved to Dallas that year to pursue a full-time internship so that my fiancé could accept an internship himself. Though I was placed in the chaplain's office at Southern Methodist University, a mutual friend connected me to the founding pastor of Journey, who asked me to join their team. At the time, Journey had only hosted a couple of Sunday gatherings, so over that year I was able to watch and be part of its founding. I had no idea that Journey would become one of the first independent emerging churches in the country, nor that I would later return to become its second pastor.

Through my friend Jason Mitchell at Journey, I was invited to join an exciting project that would again alter my trajectory. A small group of pastors were putting together a group of people who were interested in rethinking church, theology, worship, and mission. They called it the Terranova Theology Project. Jason mentioned that they were looking for some young (and preferably female) voices and asked if I was interested. I practically bombarded him with enthusiasm. A few days later, I received a phone call from Brian McLaren, a then-unknown pastor from Maryland. We had what I can only call an interview, and afterward I was invited to join the Terranova Theology Project. There I met a group of people who would become my close friends, mentors, and traveling partners.

That group became Emergent Village, an organization that described itself as a generative friendship among missional Christians. For me, *generative* is the operative word. Emergent generated questions, ideas, new thoughts, and new forms of old practices in ways that brought life to me, and I hope, through me. Early on, many of us were preoccupied with deconstructing questions, but we became far more interested in constructive reimagining, where we pondered what mattered most and how we could design communities of faith to engage and embrace it. I served in various capacities within Emergent Village over the next decade, including two years as cochair of the board.

One of my favorite contributions of Emergent Village was Theological Conversation, an annual conference that brought a renowned theologian together with a few hundred pastors and lay leaders. We hoped to spark fire in both directions so that theologians would be required to bring their work to a practical level and pastors would be required to bring their practical issues to a theological level. We hosted conversations with Walter Brueggemann, Jürgen Moltmann, Musa Dube, Miroslav Volf, Nancey Murphy, and John Caputo, among others.

I felt so alive and at home at the theological conversations, bringing thoughtful and deep engagement to the practical realities of daily faith life. I found my pastoral identity and voice in that space, and for the first time I could picture myself leading Sunday gatherings to explore a text or an idea in ways that would hopefully be of interest as well as consequence. Thankfully, my experience at Journey provided me with an example of a faith community that not only allowed but encouraged such a posture.

After my full-time internship, I returned to Princeton, with my new husband Dan in tow, to complete my MDiv program. The experiences from the previous year gave me fresh eyes with which to see my studies as well as an invigorated sense of call. Without even thinking consciously about it, my call moved from centrally academic to ministry focused. When conversations of ministry arose in the classroom, I'd find myself wondering, "Would this work at Journey? Why or why not?" For the first time, I was preparing myself for a ministry I could actually envision.

In May of 2002 I had in my arms a Master of Divinity degree and a five-month-old daughter. Over the next two years I served (thanks to a PTS woman alum) as an assistant chaplain at Meadow Lakes retirement community and on staff at a local church. I had just given birth to my son when I received a call from the pastor of Journey, letting me know that he was stepping down to pursue counseling full-time. Soon after, I received a call from the Pastor Search Posse, as they called themselves, inquiring whether I would like to apply for the position. Though at the time the idea of moving to Dallas and pastoring a church with two very young children seemed daunting if not impossible, over the next few months it was as if all of the pieces fell into place. I began my journey as pastor of Journey on my twenty-ninth birthday.

For the next eight years, the community grew, changed, and moved locations three times. Our rhythm of life was something like an accordion, stretching out in seasons and shrinking back together in the next. I learned to ride the waves of change that were our only constant: people with varying degrees of faith crisis, inconsistent attendance, up-and-down finances, and seemingly endless transience as people moved for job relocation or graduate school or internships. Through it all, though, together we held a strong center, and I watched my community grow and mature spiritually. As often happens with a young pastor, I found that I grew up and changed alongside my community members, stretching into new theological terrain and spiritual practices as well.

For over a year I lived in the tension of my deep love and loyalty to Journey and a sense that a new chapter was on the horizon. Because I loved Journey so much, I spent a good deal of time repressing this new call, unwilling to sever ties with the people and community I held so dear. In the summer of 2013, however, I realized I could not flee this new call any longer. I asked the elders to release me from being the pastor in charge and allow me to renegotiate my role in a way I wasn't even sure how to describe. The community was beyond gracious, and patient, and unbelievably supportive.

As I discerned my new sense of call, I began to pursue writing and speaking full-time. What I longed for most of all was to return to the wide-open space of inquiry, where I could ponder the biggest questions over a long period of time. In a season of spiritual ambivalence in America, there is much to ponder, and I wanted to think deeply about those matters and share them as they came to fruition. As for Journey, I now serve as theologian-in-residence, speaking on occasion and supporting the pastor in fostering the spiritual direction of the community.

Since I have stepped down from my role as pastor, a number of people have asked me if it feels strange to have left ministry. While it does feel strange to call myself a writer, it feels no more strange than when people first began calling me pastor, or, for that matter, when my children first began calling me mom. Whatever identities we carry, they take time before we wear them like second skin. But I don't feel that I have left ministry at all, only changed the form of ministry in which I serve. I view my ordination not as a calling to a particular position but a particular posture. I have been commissioned to be a certain kind of person in the world, one who seeks to abide by and in the life of Christ and who seeks to bear witness to that life in word and deed. More deeply, I'd say that I have been commissioned to be a watcher of the sacred, a keeper of the holy, a teller of the true. Rather than living into that calling through leading weekly discussions at Journey, I do so through my writing.

In the next century, I imagine that ministry will both widen and deepen in American society. Our understanding of ministry will need to widen to encompass the diverse ways the people of God are bearing faithful witness to the life of Christ in the world. And because the need for sacred connection will only grow, our understanding of ministry must deepen, so that we foster an ability to honor and connect with the holy in profound and meaningful ways.

What will remain constant, I believe, is the need for theological acumen, deep biblical literacy, and an understanding of church history. To do ministry in this new millennium, what we need most is thoughtful people capable of critical engagement while holding onto a theology of playful hope and multiconnectional imagination. Princeton may not have prepared me for the specifics of ministry at Journey, but it prepared me for something far better. It gave me a deep well of knowing from which I could draw what I needed and how to find what might be missing. Princeton shaped me as a person and rooted me in faith and tradition, so that I could innovate with integrity. I stand ever grateful for the professors who guided me and for the countless women trailblazers of faith who made my path possible.

"PASSIONATELY SEEKING": MINISTRY IN THE RICE FIELDS OF THE PHILIPPINES

Esther M. Berg

The path to adventures with God is not a grand one. It is the fact that God himself is our partner in the journey that makes it grand.

As long as I can remember, I have been a woman of faith, feeling a burning desire to serve God with my whole life. As a child, I looked forward to the nightly Bible stories my parents would read, especially the story of Queen Esther. I often wondered if God might use my life to live up to that great name. That passion to learn and be a part of God's story only grew when I got my first Bible and I could read it on my own. One day I attended Catholic catechism class with a friend and saw women serving God. I knew at that moment (in the simplicity of my eight-year-old mind) that I wanted to be a nun and bring that opportunity for women to my own church. I had decided that I would start my own order of Presbyterian nuns. The passion was there. I needed only to find a pathway.

I grew up with several female role models: intelligent crime fighters like Nancy Drew and Wonder Woman; dynamic sisterhoods, united for a common goal, like Charlie's Angels; and egalitarian teams of men and women working side by side, such as the X-Men and the Fantastic Four. Yes, my childhood was overflowing with female role models at every turn—everywhere, that is, but in the church. I saw plenty of amazing women working hard behind the scenes, but I didn't want to make the cookies for the youth group; I wanted to lead it. I didn't feel called to sit quietly and learn. I had burning questions and wanted to study.

During my junior high years, my Sunday school teacher was an open-minded man who encouraged my passion. When I would read ahead and bring a list of questions, he loved it and said I made him a better teacher. Rather than discouraging my hunger, he fed it, setting the stage for my youth pastor who would change the direction of my life. My youth pastor nurtured my faith and put me in leadership immediately; I got to teach, and even preach. He was the first person who told me that women could be pastors. When I was choosing my university and major, it was his voice encouraging me to follow my gifts and begin my journey to truly serve God to the fullest as a vocation and occupation.

During my college years, my grandmothers started speaking to me as a woman, passing on their wisdom and faith. I was amazed to see how ahead of their time these ladies were and was so grateful for their sharing.

I loved my grandmother Ruth's stories of being a pastor's wife during the Depression. During WWII she was left in the manse with her two small children and her mother, as her chaplain husband left for war. She took in another chaplain's wife who was also left behind, and she trained the young new pastor, who allowed them to stay in the manse in exchange for cooking and cleaning. All her sacrifices built her true leadership in the community of faith, holding the congregation together as a pastoral figure, even when there was no pastor.

My grandmother Winifred was active in everything from scouting to prayer group and golf. She was instrumental in the country club opening to women. She was constantly pushing barriers while maintaining her femininity, leading and serving in all areas of her church and her community. As she aged and became housebound, she remained active and was a leader of the prayer team at church until the day she died. In her eyes it was simple: "I can still use the phone, and I can pray." These women taught me to open my eyes to see God's opportunity even when our paths take unexpected turns and lead us through significant obstacles.

Seminary at Princeton was one of the best seasons of my life, although the path was not always what I expected. I guess, in part, that I'd hoped for the real-life version of my fictional childhood role models: a place where smart women were not afraid to speak out, where women weren't competitive with one another but rather banded together to create their own unique harmony; where egalitarian relationships flourished and dialogues opened hearts, minds, and doors. I briefly joined the women's center, where we shared our disappointments, challenges, and hopes. However, I quickly realized that the aim of the women's center was more focused on advocacy, and I wasn't interested in being politically correct. I wanted to be a rebel for God's transforming power. In the end, I found my greatest joy in the myriads of relationships with my fellow students and professors, also fellow sojourners. One of my favorite groups was the breakfast club, a mixed group of folks who would meet for breakfast. We were able to discuss our courses, beliefs, and questions while disagreeing with grace. That inspired a group of us to start a Friday night fellowship to continue to encourage each other in our journeys.

As I left seminary for my first professional pastorate, I was given a box of photos, letters, and a diary that belonged to my great-grandmother, Effie. She and her husband (Princeton grad, 1899) spent their marriage on the mission field as the first Presbyterian missionaries in Busan, Korea. Those items were an amazing treasure: symbols of calling and caution, the joy and the cost of service, the dance of laying down and taking up. I seriously considered entering the mission field at that point, but I was not yet ready to take the leap. I spent the next decade in pastoral ministry, each year growing in my desire for and support of mission. While I dearly loved each congregation I served, I could not shake the conviction that there was something more. Having grown up with the God who can do exceedingly and abundantly more than we could ask or imagine, I knew in my core that this "more" calling me was the springboard into mission.

On a spiritual retreat, my daughter and I felt that God was urging us to go "out" to Korea, the land where our ancestors had served only one hundred years before.

With only our confidence in God's leading, we held a garage sale, raised the cost of our tickets, and went. For ten days we visited with members of a Busan church. We toured, I preached, but mostly we prayed. Again and again we felt the confirmation of the Lord, culminating with an invitation from the church to both of us (Kate to teach at their school and me to be a pastor in the English service). Korea was the place where we would be trained and molded for long-term mission service.

We sold everything we had and returned to Korea, ready to learn and walk in the footsteps of my great-grandparents. It was humbling to receive the overwhelming gratitude and recognition of the Christians in Busan for the service of my ancestors.

However, life steeped in cultural differences was painful. We had to face ourselves and let go of the many aspects we had thought of as "faith" that were actually just cultural contexts. This was our first lesson in how easy it is to "go" without truly leaving. If we wanted to be missionaries, we had to let go of institutionalism and cultural biases, and submit our ways, thoughts, and emotions to God so that we could reach God's people in Asia through a context that they could understand.

The path of "letting go" of self and culture was even more liberating than being free of our possessions. We began to see a purer gospel, less hindered by the history and values of our own culture. Our understanding of Scripture blossomed in new ways with the simplicity of a faith truly lived.

In the midst of our training, our eyes were still looking toward the majority world where we could make a difference for those who truly were the "least of these." The Philippines came to the forefront during our time in Korea. Many Filipinos come to Korea to work in factories or in hotels, where their monthly salary often exceeds their annual income back home. Our Korean church had a Filipino fellowship and did mission each year in the Philippines. When a typhoon destroyed the hometown of one of our members, we traveled to the Philippines prepared to help rebuild and to encourage those who'd lost their homes and church. While in the Philippines, we saw churches on every corner, yet saw devastating poverty, abandoned children, and little help or compassion.

It was into this gap that we felt God calling. In our preparations, it was surprising to discover how unsupportive many mission organizations were. My own presbytery refused to even consider affirming my call because I'd have no "oversight," and most mission organizations were so firmly rooted in American culture that their requirements for income raised were well beyond what was actually needed to live among the poor.

Rather than give up, we felt that the path forward was to form our own mission organization. Having learned through our cross-cultural experiences that truth shines in simplicity, we began to search Scripture for clear statements of purpose. Two struck us immediately: Luke 4:18–19 and Matthew 10:7–8. Jesus was so clear about his mission: he came to bring good news to the poor, free the prisoner, give sight to the blind, free the oppressed, and he sent his disciples out to do the same, as freely as we ourselves received it. In our studies, a single Greek word began to appear again and again: *zéteo*, meaning "passionately seeking." The path became clear when we read it in Luke 19 as Jesus declared that the Son of Man came to *passionately seek* and save the lost. With our destination before us, we set out to passionately seek what God seeks. The first step was beginning to see the world as God sees it, loving what God loves and teaching others to do the same.

Personal faith and holiness without action in the world is emptiness— merely a clanging gong or cymbal. It goes against the most foundational commandment to love others. It is this crisis of being right without living rightly that is addressed in Isaiah 58, and the remedy is to "spend yourself." From these ideas Zeteo Missions was born. Our way to participate in Jesus' purpose: God's transforming reconciliation.

And so I find myself living in the middle of a rice field building an orphanage, growing crops, training others, being an ad hoc doctor for those who have no alternative, speaking God's love and freedom to a land enslaved in poverty, making disciples, and building community leaders. My passion has found its path, and I am home.

MINISTRY, MAYHEM, AND MAGIC: CALLED TO CONFLICT RESOLUTION AND CONCILIATION

Cynthia S. Mazur

After 9/11, a volunteer who was assisting near the search-and-rescue workers' command post in New York City called me, asking for help with a workplace problem. Her poor relationship with her boss was starting to undermine her health. She told me this story: she had called the international volunteer organization shortly after 9/11 to ask if she could help. As a remarkable demonstration of her determination to be of service, she specified that she wanted the worst job they had to offer, along with the least desirable hours. The organization asked her to be the pot scrubber on the graveyard shift. She readily accepted. She wanted to "help the helpers."

As the Alternative Dispute Resolution (ADR) director for the Federal Emergency Management Agency (FEMA), I help the helpers, the unsung heroes of disaster services. These people work behind the scenes, do their jobs with heart and devotion, work in unbelievably stressful conditions, and often withstand a certain amount of negative press. Most disaster employees would say that they do not need praise from the press or thanks from the public. I am employed to make sure that these employees have access to fair and honest processes that can help them with problem solving, conflict management, and dispute resolution in their jobs.

While I was working as a chaplain in the summer of 1978 at a psychiatric hospital, I knew that I had a calling. Residents would always return to questions of theodicy. "What does God have in mind for me?" "How can God create and sustain a broken human?" "Where can I find God in the midst of loss and confusion?" Many people wanted to better understand their place in relation to God. Those were the conversations I wanted to be having. I graduated from PTS in 1980 and was ordained at Christ Congregation in Princeton.

My PTS years were filled with friends and mentors. This year, 2015, started with my attendance at a same-sex wedding for two PTS graduates. Although the ceremony was small, all the people who were present, even the presiding minister, were PTS graduates. These are ties of more than thirty-five years.

Many PTS administrators and professors were exceptionally supportive: Dr. Doris Donnelly, Bill Brower, James Loder, and the registrar Judy Lang, who approved my request to graduate in two years as opposed to three. She stated that I was the first student to have such a request approved. My two clinical pastoral education (CPE) experiences were thoughtful glimpses of mental illness and prison life, respectively. Reverends Fred Arnold and Fred Bucher were legendary chaplains and instructors, each adding richness and depth to my understanding of the role of spirit in lives marked by disruption and dislocation. As I considered the future, I thought that I would like some-day to do international relief work for Church World Service.

I had been raised Roman Catholic. When I decided that I wanted to be ordained, I had to find a denomination that was fully supportive of women's ordination. The Congregationalist Church, which ordained Antoinette Brown Blackwell in 1853, was open, affirming, and inclusive. After much research and reflection, I selected the United Church of Christ as my denomination.

I wanted my first church to be multiracial. Eldridge Cleaver is quoted as saying that Sunday morning is the most segregated hour of the week. My first pastorate was located in New Town, on an Indian reservation, in North Dakota. Oddly enough, due to a mix-up by the federal government, the Fort Berthold Indian Reservation had been opened up to white settlers in the 1800s. The reservation was home to three affiliated tribes: the Mandan, Hidatsa, and Arikara, and to non-Indians. The land was beautiful, perched on the bluffs of the Missouri River. And Sakakawea (or Sacagawea) had jour-neyed through it with Lewis and Clark.

Although clergy were respected in my town, they were not seen as change agents. The key players in advancing greater rights on the reservation were the lawyers. Indeed, while I was there, the lawyers won a thirty-million-dollar settlement for the tribes from the federal government. The lawyers were the advocates, advancing fair treatment and better policies. They were having a direct impact on the community. To be a true champion, I decided, a law credential would be of immense value.

I entered law school and came to understand the dark illusion of using courts to obtain justice. It can happen, but, generally speaking, individual lawsuits exact a tremendous toll, and even people who win in court often do not feel satisfied. I became interested in the legal and spiritual tools available to the average person to avoid litigation. People can be transformed by the power of words to de-escalate and create mutual respect, and by the biblical call to make amends and be reconciled.

Upon graduation, I took a two-year job working on prisoner civil rights issues for the Fourth Circuit Court of Appeals in Richmond, Virginia, and then I took a job at a large law firm in DC. The latter job demanded crush-ing hours and paid handsomely, and I knew instantly that it wasn't for me. I started applying for teaching jobs at local universities. Georgetown Law School (GT) offered me an opportunity to teach and get my Master of Laws in prisoner civil rights issues, and within short order I accepted a job that would begin the following academic year.

One evening, after a long day at the firm, I came home and turned on the TV. I discovered that the United States had a domestic disaster relief agency. I watched the footage of the Loma Prieta earthquake, and the banner at the bottom of the screen referenced the Federal Emergency Management Agency (FEMA). I made up my mind that night. Once my GT job was drawing to a close, I sent my resume to FEMA, was interviewed, and was offered a job in their legal department. I had earned a scholarship to study international human rights in France for one month at the close of GT, and, when I returned, I started working at FEMA in 1991.

When I moved to DC from Richmond, I joined the First Congregational UCC in downtown DC and found it vibrant and full of opportunities for social action. As a church member, I was working on inner-city problems such as affordable housing, living wages, and access to services. I was part of a strong homeless advocacy group headed by the national icon Mitch Snyder. Marion Barry was larger than life. During this time I was also doing many weddings, funerals, and baptisms for the unchurched.

A member of my church, Ruth Shinn, sister to the theologian Roger Shinn, became my best friend, and she introduced me to two things that would become foundational. First, there would be a lifelong commitment without fail to tithe a set percentage of all income from all sources. Second, Ruth introduced me to her volunteer work at the court-annexed mediation program at the DC Superior Court. The court accepted me into their program, trained me as a mediator for family and child protection cases, and ultimately made me a mentor mediator for the next twenty-five years.

I was learning and developing the skills to help people avoid onerous, protracted, and painful litigation. The DC Bar selected me to be one of their arbitrators and to chair some of their panels, which were offered at no expense to members of the public who had complaints against their attorneys for malpractice and fee disputes. In 1999 the administrator of my agency asked me if I wanted to be the director of ADR for FEMA. Janet Reno was pushing all federal agencies to use alternative dispute resolution for both external and internal disputes. She had a vision, and she wanted the public and federal employees to be better served through negotiation, mediation, and a commitment to honest and forthright resolution when appropriate.

With regard to workplace disputes, people don't necessarily get the outcome they seek at the beginning. Nonetheless, almost always, with a transparent process based on fairness and good faith, the problem shifts in some constructive manner. ADR puts the focus and energy on what is important to the participants, their "interests," and on finding an open and honest means to meet the interests of both sides if possible. People are encouraged to resolve issues through direct communication, emotional intelligence, and personal responsibility. These conversations are not based on legal rights and entitlements. They are based on win/win principles of negotiation.

In 2003 I was asked to chair the Workplace Conflict Management section of the Interagency ADR Working Group (IADRWG). The IADRWG is a very active federal committee initiated by President Clinton and based on legislation authorized by the first President Bush. It works to promote alternative dispute resolution across the federal government. As chair of the workplace section, I help federal agencies develop robust ADR programs, and as a group we share the latest ADR developments and emerging trends in the workplace.

Over the years I have been called upon to mediate disputes for pastors, congregants, and divided churches. To deepen my understanding of conflict resolution and conciliation, I decided to pursue a PhD at the School for Conflict Analysis and Resolution (SCAR) at George Mason University. SCAR has its roots in the civil rights, social justice, and peace movements, and it is a conflict resolution practice center, developing conflict intervention as a scholarly, academic field.

I was interested in the role of religion and religious leaders in peacemaking and resolving international, violent conflict. During my studies I visited the Initiatives of Change School in Caux, Switzerland (formally Moral Re-Armament). The group had been founded in 1938 by a U.S. Lutheran minister, Frank Buchman, to promote reconciliation between the French and German people. It continues to pursue reconciliation around the world to this day.

For my dissertation I planned a series of interfaith dialogues between two Protestant churches in the DC metro area, one very conservative and one very liberal. I spent more than two years with many false starts before I fully grasped the depth of fear that religious groups have of each other. I shifted my agenda and wrote my dissertation on communication, crisis management, emergency management, and conflict resolution in the midst of Hurricane Katrina.

Whether at the metalevel of a national disaster or in the microcosm of the workplace, the mission is to reestablish hope, meaning, and connection in peoples' lives. With mercy and empathy, people create order out of chaos; they often can find significance in the midst of mayhem. FEMA's mantra is "Safer, stronger, smarter." These conversations search out growth and the lessons learned.

With every crisis, people create a new normal that can be full of potential and possibilities. As people problem-solve, I see them commit to integrity and their highest values. People may need a bridge, or a guide, or a peacemaker, as they find the magic to regenerate their lives. Transformation will almost certainly involve grieving, forgiveness, and compassion. I often see people at their worst and at their best. Most people will deepen their inner resources of gratitude, resilience, and honor.

My life has been a process of enlarging my maps and expanding the definition of my ministry. I have reframed my call to ministry as helping people be their highest and best as they serve others. My ministry is everywhere and every day for the overworked, underappreciated employee. These people do not have glamorous jobs and are not paid particularly well. Yet they serve with great dedication and devotion to help people in need.

I work with the modern-day tools of words, good process, courage, commitment, and intention in order that people can heal, take responsibility, and create powerful workplaces. I answered the 9/11 call from the pot scrubber and worked with her and her boss over a period of a few weeks. When we finished, the volunteer thanked me and told me that I had made huge difference in her health, commitment, and workplace satisfaction. My ministry is a privilege beyond words.

NURSING AS MINISTRY
TO THE WHOLE PERSON

Catherine Rutledge-Gorman

A life based on faith promises moments of grace coupled with times of uncertainty. My life's journey thus far is a good example of those components. I am a part of a loving, supportive, and intellectually challenging community, and I am called to a career where my work helps transform people's lives. I am blessed in many ways. As a nurse educator, I teach nursing students to become compassionate caregivers in a modern, stressful, complex health care system. Thirty years ago I would never have predicted this outcome. Here is what led me to this point.

Being raised in the Presbyterian Church, and the daughter of a pastor, I grew up in a community of faith where love reigned and challenges were addressed with faith as well as logic. I still name countless church members as mentors and surrogate parents and grandparents. They supported and guided me during those impressionable growing years. So when I felt the call to ministry, I knew that I brought a wealth of experience and "good instincts," as one head of staff remarked, about how people from various backgrounds and theological leanings can come together to be the church, sharing the good news of the gospel.

I applied to PTS because my dad graduated in the class of 1955, and he always said that it was the best. I relished the opportunity to study in a place of such historical significance and stellar reputation—plus exploring the east coast was a bonus. Forays into NYC and Philadelphia with fellow seminarians were unforgettable times. I have many fond memories, including, ironically, an amusing Communion service on a Sunday evening. A dozen weary seminary students, returned from a long day of church work, stood around the Communion table. The worship leader struggled to "break the bread" because the "body of Christ" was too big for her petite hands and the tenacious braids of the challah loaf would not unravel. While she wrestled with the bread, my tired, overactive imagination filled in images of Jesus calling to Peter to get a bread knife from the kitchen in the upper room. Finally, after wrangling with the bread for what seemed like several minutes of tense silence, she secured half of the loaf on the Communion table with her left hand while pulling the other half up in the air with her right. Her expression during the struggle revealed no humor, and the incident serves as a reminder to be strong, steadfast leaders who are also willing to appreciate the humor that helps us breathe a little deeper and enjoy life a little more.

Women in ministry have always needed to prove themselves worthy. While completing a clinical pastoral education (CPE) program, I was called to the room of a patient who had requested a priest. Unable to find a priest, the chaplain sent me—a young, female, Protestant, first-year seminary student—into the patient's room. Recognizing the incongruence of the situation, I boldly walked in and said, "I understand that you asked for a priest," and with my hands in the air, continued, "but you've got me." Fortunately the patient laughed, and I felt God's presence minister to us both that evening.

Scriptural text and themes still have relevance in my life, and I miss the daily, varied, worshipful services at Miller Chapel during my seminary days. I remember one of my own favorite sermons, titled "It's Not Our Party" (Luke 15:11–32). I focused on the older son who dutifully stayed with his father, not the returning, younger, prodigal son. Preaching to a predominantly white, middle-class congregation, I emphasized that for most of us, we are more like the older brother who dutifully worked hard and followed cultural norms. Such actions can lead to a sense of entitlement that gets in the way of seeing God's grace in our midst. We, like the older brother in the parable, begrudgingly complain that we deserve a party for all our hard work and dedication. Yet such a sentiment ignores the roots of our good fortune, as a privileged class and race full of opportunities that fit into conventional expectations. It is my hope that when we appreciate our good fortune, we better understand how God uses different paths to reveal God's grace.

Women pastors were not radically new when I started in the late 1980s, but that does not mean that they were overly common. As the first woman to be ordained in my home church, I fully recognized the influence of several role models in my ordination journey. My early role model, besides my father, a pastor for forty-plus years, was a woman pastor in my home presbytery. She kindly agreed to meet me when I began to consider a call to ministry. My questions for her were more practical than theological. I remember inquiring, if I became a pastor, would I ever date again? She kindly did not laugh at my myopic query, and her thoughtful, supportive answers helped me clear the way to embrace my calling and forge ahead.

Once at PTS, it was my great privilege to take several classes with Dr. Freda Gardner. I learned much from her, including stories about the early women associated with PTS. I remember a funny story she told about the first faculty dinner she attended at the president's home. An awkward moment arose when, as the first female faculty member, she was not invited to smoke cigars along with the rest of her all male colleagues. The president's wife graciously invited Dr. Gardner to accompany the faculty wives' gathering instead. Dr. Gardner's gracious yet often prophetic voice served as a role model for the inevitable awkward moments awaiting women in ministry.

I fully enjoyed my three years at PTS. Upon reflection, I offer the following suggestions to improve the experience for women in ministry today. I remember a time, after graduation, when I was offered a significantly lower salary than the man I was replacing. I successfully negotiated an equitable package, yet I know several colleagues who did not. A class that teaches such human resource skills would be helpful to incorporate into the PTS curriculum.

Ministry is challenging, and any efforts to support a healthy work-life balance would benefit both pastor and church. Emphasizing practical approaches such as expense accounts for gym memberships and regular intervals for rest and relaxation would help in equipping women for ministry.

I graduated from PTS in 1989 and served as a pastor for ten-plus years in various churches. My experiences were some of the most inspiring and fulfilling of my life coupled with some of the most gut-wrenching and disappointing. Baptizing children, preaching the good news, welcoming new members, conducting weddings and memorial services, and visiting the hospitalized and homebound parishioners rank as highlights. It is a humble privilege to be with people at some of the most significant times of their lives. I cherish those experiences as insights into what God's creation can be. Life is a fragile gift, and when we acknowledge that gift with humility, grace, and thanks, we better understand God's love for us all.

Unfortunately, I also worked in two separate churches shattered by the unprofessional conduct of the head of staff. It is impossible to quantify the damage such actions inflict. Although my years as a pastor included a lot of tension between more conservative and liberal members, often grappling with issues such as ordination of openly gay and lesbian members, ultimately the widespread damage of working with several unprofessional pastors led me to question my place in organized church leadership. I remember a little girl asking me if her baptism was still "valid" when she learned that the head of staff had resigned. Of course I assured her that it was, but my heart ached for her anyway. My spiritual journey at this point was filled with disappointment and exhaustion.

After much angst and soul searching, I decided to become a stay-at-home mom while my two boys were young. Once they started school, I felt the need to use my gifts and energy to a broader extent. Nursing school seemed like a good combination between my scientific background (having majored in chemistry in college) and my interpersonal skills developed in ministry. Becoming a nurse was the right role for me to continue serving others at significant times of their lives.

Presently, I have minimal contact with the organized PC(USA) church. I still have a number of family and friends from my time as a pastor, and they all understand my reasons for leaving and recognize my new career as a continuation of my ministry. I am blessed to have such supportive people in my life.

Regardless of my reasons for leaving the ministry, I believe that I am a better nurse because I was a pastor first. There are numerous transferable skills between pastoral ministry and nursing. For example:

- I listen to what people say and also what they leave unspoken. Frequently, the absence of words helps to explain the main concern of a patient or parishioner.
- I care for the whole person, not just a diagnosis.
- I understand the importance of family-centered care. If a wife suffers a stroke, her care inevitably includes her spouse. Physical and spiritual needs must be addressed to ensure the best quality of life possible.
- I know how to welcome people into new environments and finds ways to get them involved. Whether first-time visitors to a church or first-year nursing students in the school, people tend to learn and grow when they feel a part of something greater than themselves, especially when it adds to the greater good.
- I excel at working with teams, exploring options and building consensus.
- I know how to teach in effective and meaningful ways so that people can use that knowledge to improve their lives.

I've often said that nursing is like ministry, except that the terminology is slightly different.

My pastoral experiences serve as a foundation on which I build my nursing career. I am grateful for the journey I traveled; I believe that God's call for me still exists; and I am thankful to serve.

SACRED CONNECTIONS
THROUGH WORLD RELIGIONS

Elizabeth Barry Haynes

Recently I attended an interfaith service in my hometown of St. Augustine, Florida. It was an event connected with St. Augustine's 450th birthday as the oldest European settlement in America. Native Americans, Buddhists, Hindus, a Roman Catholic priest, several Protestant ministers, a rabbi, and the imam from the local mosque offered readings, blessings, prayers, and music.

The theme was compassion and understanding in a town that had often in its long history seen its inhabitants engage in deadly clashes between religions and cultures—beginning in 1565 with the massacre of French Huguenot soldiers by founder Pedro Menéndez de Avilés of Spain. Many in St. Augustine today have tried to learn from the past by being more tolerant of each other's diverse beliefs. Even so, there was a confrontation in 2015 by a few fundamentalist Christians shouting hostile words in front of the local mosque.

As an instructor of world religions at Flagler College in St. Augustine, I also try to encourage students to practice compassion and understanding as they study what various peoples believe within the context of a particular time and culture. My premise is that spirituality is part of their humanity and that a look at other peoples' beliefs may give them a fresh perspective on their own.

I have been teaching at Flagler for ten years, which I much enjoy—not only because there is always something new to learn but also because it's great to encourage students to engage the theology, history, traditions, and art of each religion we study.

When I enrolled in a course on world religions at Princeton Theological Seminary (PTS), I had no idea that I would be teaching it myself one day. However, even though I only teach part-time, I feel a strong sense of call to teach this subject. I myself have learned much about various faiths and cultures through both my work and my travels. For example, I tell my students of hearing the call to prayer at a mosque overlooking Cairo while the sun set behind the pyramids in the distance, and meeting with a Russian Orthodox priest in a remote part of the Caucasus Mountains in Russia. I share with them the time my family and I hiked to a cliff in Wyoming to view sacred Native American paintings on the cliff walls. In Alaska, a Tlingit guide explained potlatches and totems. In Jerusalem, I prayed at the Western Wall.

Over the years, my students have experienced yoga and tai chi, blessings from a Hindu swami, and a Chinese scholar's explanation of neo-Confucianism in China. Until recently we also had the rare opportunity to meet with one of the rabbis in town who had been a Holocaust survivor. As we sat with him in the synagogue, he told his harrowing tale of survival and faith after losing most of his family.

I also draw upon my experiences as an international business lawyer. Before I attended PTS, I had practiced law for many years. Both as an in-house corporate lawyer and as a member of a large international firm, I met clients from many parts of the world. I learned something about Buddhism and Shintoism to better understand the culture and beliefs of our Asian clients. One of my firm's lawyers was a Sikh—a religion I knew nothing about. He was very helpful in giving me some insight to his faith—knowledge that I was able to pass on to my students many years later.

My experiences at PTS have also enriched my teaching. I was blessed with being part of a wonderful study group of friends from diverse backgrounds. In addition to working together as a study group, we would also go on retreats at a great old inn up in the Delaware Water Gap. As we visited there and in one another's churches, I learned about some Hispanic and African American traditions to which I had not previously had much exposure. Likewise, PTS provided many opportunities in chapel and other programs to experience worship from the perspective of many cultures.

Another significant experience at PTS was my job connected with the fiftieth anniversary of the discovery of the Dead Sea Scrolls. Scholars from Jewish, Muslim, and Christian traditions gathered at PTS in 1997 for a symposium. My job included helping participants with any personal assistance required. While doing this, I got to meet the names behind the footnotes from my studies. I also witnessed colleagues of different faiths working together in pursuit of their shared interest in the Dead Sea Scrolls.

I recall the time when scholars, engineers from Rochester Institute of Technology (RIT), corporate sponsors, a film crew, and members of the PTS community all gathered in Speer Library. The engineers had developed technology that could safely reveal words on scrolls that had previously been unreadable. A small fragment of scroll from Cave 1 had been brought to the library by an Orthodox priest from a monastery in Lodi, New Jersey.

As everyone stood in hushed silence, Professor James Charlesworth of PTS and the RIT engineers set up the equipment and placed the scroll where it could be viewed. As he read out the words and translated them, I was amazed to think that I was hearing words being read aloud for the first time in nearly two thousand years—words possibly last heard at a worship service in Qumran. Even the corporate sponsors and the jaded film crew stood in silence that long ago afternoon as we all took in the importance of what we had heard.

I still pass that story on to my students, and you can hear a pin drop when I tell it. That is one of my goals in teaching world religions—to make students aware of connections to the sacred in the midst of ordinary life. That is because I encounter so many students who label themselves "nonreligious."

Out of each class, there may be half or more who have been raised without religious affiliation. For them, any religion is suspect—full of fanatics and hypocrites—and the idea of God is often regarded as old-fashioned, a mere superstition from an earlier age. They are taking the course to fulfill a requirement, but their spiritual curiosity is lacking. They arrive in my class presuming that religion is irrelevant and generally unnecessary.

I also have the other kind of students—the ones whose own faith is so narrowly defined that they are a little suspicious and afraid of other faiths and beliefs. That is why I require all my students to do two "event reports" during the semester, in which they must attend a worship event (a service, wedding, funeral, or ceremony) and write about the nature of the event, the participation of the worshipers, and their own reaction or reflections.

These reports have intrigued me. Some students express surprise at the nature of a worship service—it was not what they expected. Some students are blunt in their dislike of the event. Others are so interested or moved that they actually think that they might go again. As a teacher I must remain neutral in my evaluation of these reports, but as a pastor I take delight when I read that a student has been opened up to new spiritual possibilities previously unknown or ignored.

I have also been fascinated by what students notice when they choose a church service as one of their "events." So many folks in a congregation feel that the pastor is key to attracting new members. Perhaps. But my students have rarely mentioned the pastor or other worship leaders in the ten years I have been reading these reports. What students comment on the most is the nature of worshipers. Do they look interested in the service? Are they friendly? Do they sing and read liturgy and prayers with faith and passion, or do they look bored? I have truly been surprised at how much more impact the worshipers have on the visitor than the worship leaders. I am not sure that people attending worship realize how influential they are on visitors or how closely they are being observed by the strangers in the room.

I have devoted most of this article to what I am most passionate about at this time in my life. I see my calling at Flagler College to include opening up students to the nature of faith and to what people regard as sacred or divine.

At the very least, I hope to expand spiritual awareness in students living outside the walls of belief.

Frankly, my other ministry experiences since graduating from PTS in 1997 (MDiv) and 1998 (ThM) have not been what I expected they would be. I was ordained and served as a solo pastor of a small church in Jacksonville, Florida, for three years. I was told that half the membership left without ever meeting me just because they did not want a woman pastor. The remaining congregation and I worked hard to build up membership, but there was little money. The roof leaked, the HVAC died, the plumbing was cantankerous, and there were bullet holes in the windows.

Our many community-oriented events—such as basketball camp, vacation Bible school, neighborhood play days, and free weekly bread lines—were all well attended. However, our congregation was predominantly elderly and white in a neighborhood that was neither, and we were Presbyterian in a neighborhood that was inclined toward nondenominational churches. Although we added a few members, eventually the congregation became unable to support a full-time pastor.

It was after my pastoral ministry ended that I began teaching at Flagler College—teaching courses in world religions, business law, and a course I designed called Team Building in Business, in which I worked with students all semester while they learned to function together as a team in order to complete goals on a service project.

Students chose their own projects, including collecting rugs for refugees in the Sudan, raising money to build a halfway house in Moldova, and collecting food and clothing for the local homeless shelter. Other teams worked with unwed mothers, created an art program for deaf children, or cleaned up the beaches. I was very impressed with the giving spirit of students in that course and the enthusiasm they had for helping those in need.

In addition to teaching, I have served as a guest pastor in many churches, a parish associate, a tutor to boys from a group foster home, and the coordinator and an instructor for the presbytery's Commissioned Lay Pastor program. All of these activities provided me with great insight into ministry both inside and outside the walls of the church.

Unfortunately, although these activities were considered a "validated ministry" by my presbytery, they did not pay the bills. However, I was able to continue juggling these various jobs for a while because I was also assisting my mother, who had developed some health and eye issues. By serving as a part-time caregiver for both her and our large old family home, I was able to keep up these various ministries and still stay afloat financially.

This all changed in 2012 when, around the same time, my mother died and I myself became quite ill. My illness has lasted for over three years—sometimes bringing me close to death, and certainly causing me terrible chronic pain. I have had to cut out most activities and reduce my teaching schedule to just one course—World Religion—the teaching of which has kept me going even during the worst of my illness.

I have had to learn during this time to trust God more than ever, since I have been faced with huge medical bills without insurance and without enough strength to work. Last year and the year before, I spent most of my life savings on medical supplies and hospitals, but I was still sick and getting worse. I read through Job and Lamentations repeatedly, hoping to understand God's plan in the midst of my pain and discomfort.

Finally, my prayers were answered when my niece, sister, and physical therapist combined forces to locate a wonderful medical team who knew how to heal me. The treatments have been excruciating, but I was willing to endure them because it eventually worked after many months and many prayers.

During the long, lonely, and painful journey of my illness, I was once more made aware of how much the church means to me when circle friends brought meals and drove me to the doctor and when the congregation regularly prayed for me and provided financial support. It felt strange and very humbling after all the years of helping others to be on the receiving end of church assistance, but I welcomed the help with profound gratitude.

I must also say that even though my illness has been both frightening and miserable, it has provided me with fresh insight into God's graciousness and steadfast love. Every time I found myself in serious trouble, God always managed to send me what I needed most to keep going.

Even though I am still in the healing stages, I hope that I soon have an opportunity for an expanded role in ministry in addition to my teaching. After such an overwhelming experience, I have fresh insights to share about what it means to be connected to God—trusting in that sacred link to sustain me in all things and at all times. That is what I count on, and that sacred connection is what I hope to continue to pass on to others.

PART III

Explorations in Ministry
and Theological Education

INTRODUCTION

This final section of the book builds on the previous material on women pioneers and trailblazers and women's own stories of ministry to consider what their experience has taught us about ministry and seminary education. It consists of two chapters.

Chapter 9 explores the nature of ministry and God's call to all people informed by women's perspectives. It provides a broader understanding of ministry, moving beyond the more traditional focus on only clergy. The second half of the chapter narrows the lens from this broader understanding of ministry to focus on clergywomen, not because they are more important but because they can become change agents for the recognition of all women's ministry. Clergywomen's experiences and status are considered within the wider context of the place of women both personally and professionally in our society.

Chapter 10 concludes the book with an overview of theological education, examining its various components and then sharing a new vision for whole-person theological education that is rooted in the Judeo-Christian understanding of the whole person. This vision includes the following parts: growing in the intellectual life; pursuing physical, emotional, and mental health; deepening the spiritual life; and cultivating the moral life in community.

9

Ministry Redefined

*Biblical and Theological Perspectives
and Women's Experience
in the American Cultural Context*

The history and stories of Princeton Seminary women and insights from research on alumnae have helped to broaden our understanding of Christian ministry by providing a context for these closing chapters on ministry and theological education. They have expanded the scope of what constitutes ministry as serving God and others in diverse ways and places. As noted, even in the early years of PTS's history in the nineteenth century, women practiced ministries of hospitality, teaching, and encouragement to the students as they blazed their own trails in ways open to them or even created new ways to minister. The contemporary trailblazers did not let the church's "No" to their leadership become the last word. Instead, they raised their voices in a resounding "Yes" to serving the church not only locally as the first woman pastor in a church but also internationally in Christian world organizations, churches, and agencies. Our contributors' stories display their great diversity of ministries across the globe. When God called, they answered.

The first section of this chapter will examine an expanded understanding of ministry and God's call in light of the Bible and Christian tradition. This leads to our broadened definition of Christian ministry as the work of all baptized Christians who understand themselves to be called to serve God and others. An exploration of the concepts of call, vocation, job, work, and profession helps to place the ministry of ordained clergy in the context of the ministry of all baptized Christians.

The second section presents a snapshot of the status of U.S. women, providing a baseline for comparison with the particular situation of clergywomen.

189

Material from a survey of PTS women[1] illustrates the issues and concerns. The social realities faced by women generally and by women clergy in particular highlight challenges that continue to face women as they seek to follow God's call to ministry in traditionally male-dominated settings.

GENERAL PERSPECTIVES ON THE NATURE OF MINISTRY

Many have believed that ministry refers to the particular pastoral functions of the clergy, that is, performing the sacraments, preaching, teaching, evangelizing, and pastoral care.[2] Yet the word "ministry," *diakonia* ("service"), in Romans 12 links ministry, service, and gifts. Does this broad definition of ministry make all acts of love and service ministry? In one sense it does. A distinction may be helpful between ministries as doing versus "minister," the person. There is a danger of a professionalization of ministry, in which only the ordained are viewed as doing ministry. This distinction becomes especially important for those who decide to leave their first career to go to seminary to become "ministers," as they may already be doing ministry. Likewise, those who leave a clergy role to enter another field of work may still be doing ministry; not only clergy but also laity do ministry.

Thus, we may think of *Ministry* (with an uppercase *M*) as referring to what clergy do, where call, vocation, profession, and ministry become one and the same, while *ministry* (with a lowercase *m*) is defined as loving and serving God and others in the name of Christ. Hence, all Christians may practice ministry as part of their lives, whether in the context of their employment, volunteer work, or retirement or whether they are unemployed, well, or extremely ill. In other words, doing ministry is not tied to social standing, job, health status, gender, or mental or physical challenges. There is no hierarchy suggested by these distinctions but simply a clarification of the difference between the ministries of the laity and of ordained clergy. (We recognize that in some traditions there are also ordained elders and deacons, but here we are referring to ordained clergy.)

---

1. See the introduction to the book for details about this survey. Hereafter, references to the survey will be referenced as "the Survey."

2. The gift of healing in the early church was also believed to be important. See Abigail R. Evans, *The Healing Church: Practical Programs for Health Ministries* (Cleveland: United Church Press, 1999), 6. "In early Christianity, according to Hippolytus, proof of the ability to do miraculous healing was necessary for being a bishop so was considered an important gift as well."

Call to Ministry

Given this perspective on the nature of ministry, the question becomes "Do we need a call from God to validate that what we do is ministry?" Regarding this question, there are several important points to be made. All Christians are called by God; that is, there is a general Christian call to obedience. We also have a specific call to use our God-given gifts; our gifts are to be used most specifically to build up the body of Christ for the good of the church and community, the service to others that is our ministry.

All Christians Are Called by God

The concept of call raises a series of questions: Who calls us? What are we called to do? What is the nature and context of our call? In the New Testament, *call* (*klēsis*) refers to the general call of all Christians. The understanding of the church is likewise based on the New Testament Greek, *eklēsia*, as God's called-out people. In fact, *klēsis* is the term for the governing body of the Old Dutch Reformed Church and the Reformed Church of America, which still use the term "classis."

The universality of God's call is the basis for all the stories of God's interaction with humankind, what theologians refer to as *Heilsgeschichte* (God's holy history). "The command of God is the call to wake up, to recognize ourselves and to take ourselves seriously in the totality of what we can actually do."[3] In Karl Barth's view, we choose what God has chosen for us, and God's call to obedience is our calling and vocation.[4] Thus, the following definition of call is offered: All Christians are called by God to obedience; responding to this call becomes the catalyst to lead a life in Christ. This is God's general call. (We are not suggesting that God calls only Christians, as God loves the whole world, but this chapter is about the Christian life.)

Our response to God's call is first a spiritual response: "'Find a place in your heart,' implores Theophan the Recluse, 'and speak there with the Lord. It is the Lord's reception room.'"[5] This is an attitude of readiness—the classical virtue of *alertia*, attentiveness—of being centered, being open. Hence, our response to God's call is dependent on our discernment—to discern is to distinguish, determine, and sort out. Discerning God's will in our lives, however, often feels like seeing through a glass darkly (1 Cor 13:12).

---

3. Karl Barth, *Church Dogmatics*, ed. G. W. Bromiley and T. F. Torrance (New York: T. & T. Clark, 1961), III/4:626.
4. Ibid., III/4:597.
5. Suzanne G. Farnham et al., *Listening Hearts: Discerning Call in Community* (Harrisburg, PA: Morehouse, 1991), 1.

The Biblical Tradition and Women's Experience of Call

When we consider the lives of the faithful in Scripture, we see, on the one hand, the universality of God's call and, on the other hand, its great variety and particularity. God does not use one method of call or call people to one type of service, so in both method and kind there is great diversity. Likewise, God calls all kinds of people into service to fulfill specific tasks. Acceptance of the call is showing obedience to God.

Within the biblical tradition there are a few dramatic stories of God's call to particular service; those of five men are perhaps the most well-known: Abraham (Gen 12), Moses (Exod 3), the prophets Isaiah (chap. 6) and Jeremiah (chap. 1), and the apostle Paul (Acts 9). All of these narratives involve God's voice, and some are reinforced by fire, light, or a vision. Some recount initial resistance by the one called; others portray immediate obedience. The tasks are varied; no task is easy; and God's supportive, ongoing presence is a constant, even when it sometimes seems far off in the midst of difficult circumstances. These same features appear in various configurations not only in lesser-known biblical stories but also in God's call to myriad forms of service throughout history.

The biblical tradition further offers significant examples of God's followers moving into new work or new directions in response to God's ongoing call. A call to a particular form of ministry is not necessarily a lifelong call to that form. Paul, for example, more than once realized that he needed to redirect his ministry to unexpected venues, even within the broad framework of his missionary calling. The book of Acts famously records the change of his missionary itinerary in response to a vision calling him to Macedonia (Acts 16:6–10). Moses' life offered an even more dramatic change of focus: his call to confront Pharaoh and his call to deal with the apostasy of the golden calf were two very different kinds of ministry. Ruth's loyalty to Naomi called forth very different decisions and actions over the course of time.

Yet the call of God in biblical understanding is not restricted to those individuals whose call experiences are narrated in detail, nor is God's call limited to those whose names are given to us in the biblical text. All of God's people are called to be faithful in their daily lives, whether their service involves high-profile leadership or the supposedly ordinary tasks of life in family and community. Biblical stories of God's people are sometimes about their faithful actions and sometimes about their failures to live up to their callings; both kinds of stories help us to reflect on our own lives and ministries. The examples that follow here are offered not as "proof" that women are called by God (for surely God does call all)[6] but rather as an explicit reminder that beginning with the people of Israel and the earliest church, God had indeed called women as well as men to all kinds of heralded and unheralded service.[7]

The Bible includes just a few examples of women whose call experience is described in a detailed narrative; these women are most typically called to bear an important male child. The story of the annunciation to Mary, mother of Jesus, is the most striking example (Luke 1:26–38). Sarah, mother of Isaac, may be placed in this group, although her call is less direct, as she initially overhears a man (really an angel of God) speaking to her husband, Abraham, about the child she is to bear as heir of the promise (Gen 18:9–15). There is also the unnamed wife of Manoah; an angel appears to her to announce that she will bear a son (Samson; Judg 13:2–24). In honoring God's call in such stories, we must keep in mind both the very different cultural context of the ancient biblical world and God's continuing call in every generation to the vocation of parenting. Alongside such stories we may place the very different story of the women who went to Jesus' tomb and were commissioned explicitly to bear witness to his resurrection (Matt 28:1–7). In these narratives we observe a wide range of human responses, including disbelief, puzzlement, fear, acceptance, and joy. Such varied and evolving responses offer comfort and courage to the faithful of every generation as they experience God's call on their lives.

Among biblical women in sustained public leadership we may think of Miriam (musician), Deborah (judge), Huldah (prophet), Phoebe (deacon), and Priscilla (missionary and church leader).[8] Certainly these women should be understood as called by God, although we do not have a recorded call story for any of them. Some biblical women may be portrayed as receiving their call indirectly. Queen Esther, for example, is told by her cousin Mordecai that she might be in her position "for just such a time as this," even though there is no explicit mention of God (Esth 4:14).

"Ordinary" women also have a variety of roles in the ongoing life of God's people. They serve God and others (i.e., they "minister") even though we

6. The authors of this book stand in a long tradition of affirming that God may call women to any position of religious leadership, ordained or not; that viewpoint has been well argued elsewhere both biblically and theologically, and the reasoning will not be rehearsed here. This section focuses rather on the many varieties of call and service, whether to "lay" or "ordained" ministries.

7. For a full cataloging of biblical women, see Carol Meyers, ed., *Women in Scripture: A Dictionary of Named and Unnamed Women in the Hebrew Bible, the Apocryphal/Deuterocanonical Books, and the New Testament* (Boston: Houghton Mifflin, 2000).

8. See Exod 15:20–21; Judg 4:4–5; 2 Kgs 22:14–20; Rom 16:1–2; Acts 18.

cannot recover any call narrative and they are not in public leadership. The midwives Shiphrah and Puah, for instance, disobey the Pharaoh's orders to kill Hebrew boy babies (Exod 1). The daughters of Zelophehad challenge Moses' legal ruling about land possession; the result is a divine pronouncement supporting their proposed change in inheritance rights (Num 27). Here ordinary women speak out to make a difference for others in the future. Ruth's faithfulness to Naomi is presented by the narrator as an embodiment of divine faithfulness. The unnamed woman who poured costly ointment on Jesus' head is remembered in perpetuity as bearing witness to his divine significance (Matt 26). Mary the mother of John Mark hosted Christians in her home in a time of fear and persecution (Acts 12).

Even this very limited selection of biblical examples helps us to recognize not only the glorious differences among us as human beings and the great variety of tasks that God has for different individuals in God's work of justice and mercy but also something about God, God's very nature. The fact that God uses so many ways to get our attention, to speak to us, says something about who God is—not a static monolith but a dynamic spirit, who blows where She will. As we experience the biblical witness, and as we listen to, respond to, and support and love one another, we learn that the one, constant, unchanging God who calls us comes to us in wondrously complex and varied ways. God may speak directly to us in a momentary experience or sudden awareness; God may speak through other individuals; and God may speak through the cosmos—the grand design that leads us to see a design in our life, interwoven with the larger tapestry of life.

The variety of ways of experiencing God's call was evident in the responses to the PTS Survey. While 77 percent of the women stated that they received their call in the church or another ministry setting, others reported dramatic experiences of receiving their call. For example, one respondent shared a "call dream" that she had at age fourteen while living in the Netherlands. "The dream involved my preaching in Spanish in the Southwest of the United States in an adobe-styled church. I did not speak Spanish at the time of my call dream, and I had never been to the U.S., nor had any intention of coming here. Now I am in the States ministering with a Spanish-speaking congregation. God moves in mysterious ways."

Amazingly, God's call is often born out of the times of our greatest despair, weakness, and failure—when we feel the emptiness of our lives and when all else fails; it is then that we are open to hear God's words in a powerful and confirming way. And yet sometimes God's workings seem abstruse or difficult. One PTS seminarian wrote in a paper on call and spiritual journey, "I am not sure I belong in seminary; maybe I overheard my neighbor's call." Or, like many of our biblical forebears, we may hear God's call clearly but not want to respond. God's call, as Elizabeth O'Connor writes, "asks that we set out from a place that is familiar and relatively secure for a destination that can only be dimly perceived, and that we cannot be at all certain of reaching, so many are the obstacles that will loom along the way."[9] Hearing it and responding are two very different actions.

Many PTS women recount their struggles over how to respond to God's call, and they take circuitous paths before being confirmed that the ministry they are doing is precisely what God wants them to do. Yet alongside stories of resistance and struggle, they also give testimony to just how wonderful and surprising God's call can be and how it changes over time.[10] Indeed, 83 percent of the Survey respondents noted the changing nature of their call. Here are some examples of what they said:

- Because I've had the wonder of being present in life-changing moments—deaths, births, rebirths, reconciliation, speechless tragedy, and bold mission—I have come to realize that I get to be with people at the most significant times of their lives.
- As I've matured, my call has become more meaningful, more precious, more substantive, and more joyful.
- [My call was] always opening the heart and mind. . . . A privilege, a joy, a sacrifice, a hope, an offering.

Hearing one's call is akin to discovering oneself—thus our spiritual journey, our self-discovery, our call to the Christian life, and our vocation all become intertwined.

Specific Call to Our Vocation

So there is a general and universal call to all Christians, but also a call to a specific ministry. In today's society not many people talk about their call or vocation; instead, they talk about their career, profession, job, or work. *Call, vocation, profession, career, job*—these terms may be used interchangeably, but they are very different concepts. A career deals more with questions of upward mobility and job-related income. A profession is a career/occupation within certain disciplines that requires formal qualifications, education, and mastery of skills, for example, as a doctor, lawyer, or clergyperson. So for clergy, Ministry is their profession. Vocation, etymologically coming from *vocare*, "to call," is here defined as using our gifts, talents, and aptitudes in obedience to God. Perhaps it is clearer to state that, for Christians, our vocation is our

---

9. Elizabeth O'Connor, *Cry Pain, Cry Hope: Thresholds to Purpose* (Waco, TX: Word, 1987), 82.

10. The authors' PTS Survey.

ministry. For Barth, vocation corresponds to divine calling, but it is also what constitutes who we are as individuals.[11] Barth uses *vocation* in two senses: the technical sense of job and the sense of obedience to God's call—so here even the unemployed have a vocation. As our life unfolds, it will bring to light whether what we are doing is God's call. Our vocation is not simply a result of our own intuition but needs the confirmation of others (though this can be slow in coming).

Vocation is the "place of the special responsibility of each in relation to the divine calling, the place of his freedom in limitation."[12] There is both a discontinuity and continuity, because God's call is continually unfolding and our response should be one of obedience. This is our indispensable orientation toward obedience.[13] And the form of one's calling will manifest itself as one is obedient. However, we are more than our vocation in Barth's technical sense. Vocation is our specific sphere of operation, but "the important thing is not the sphere of operation which a man has. It is what the man is within it, and not within it alone, but within the total limitation of his temporal existence."[14] Barth discusses at length each person's calling.[15] Here his focus is on obedience, not on remaining in our station in life. Barth argues that the general calling to be a Christian means that "every man has his special historical situation."[16]

One way of looking at this is that vocation is a sense of the "divine ought" in a particular situation—a response of obedience to God's call. Obedience means that we should not rely on the past as an interpretation of the future, for the past can be untrustworthy. Rather, we should attend to the questions, claims, promises, and demands of the moment, the command of God controlled by the hidden decree of God, whether or not we discern the command correctly. All stations in life are equally good. The historical situation of all persons is to be understood as the place of their readiness for their call and not as their determination. Our occupation may be that of a lawyer, physician, government bureaucrat, homemaker, carpenter, or businessperson; through any occupation we may manifest our vocation as we serve the needs of others in the name of Christ.

11. Barth, *Church Dogmatics*, III/4:599.
12. Ibid., III/4:607. Generic masculine human language is retained in direct quotations.
13. Ibid., III/4:597.
14. Ibid., III/4:632.
15. Ibid., III/4:600–607.
16. Ibid., III/4:618.

Gifts for Our Vocation

Vocation is also tied to our gifts. The concept of *charisms* (gifts) gives witness to concrete incarnation and the possible forms that vocation can assume. Vocation and aptitude are linked; our gifts are given by God's grace, though we have a responsibility to use and develop them. Many people called to a particular vocation feel that they do not possess the proper gifts. For example, Moses says to God, "'O my Lord, I have never been eloquent, neither in the past nor even now that you have spoken to your servant; but I am slow of speech and slow of tongue'" (Exod 4:10). Throughout history, others have been called to tasks for which they thought themselves ill equipped and have discovered new gifts and abilities emerging in the crucible of need.

What am I called to do? How am I called to embody Christ in my life? As reflected in the chapters on pioneers, trailblazers, and first-person stories, the vocations of these women arose from gifts of hospitality, administration, teaching, and preaching. As Howard Thurman points out, there must be a relationship between the ways we journey to our goal, under the aegis of our commitment to it, and the goal itself.[17]

The Unfolding Nature of One's Call

God's call is not static, although it is consistent as to its source. As our life unfolds, God opens up new paths and opportunities. In other words, we are not assigned to one occupation or position for life. Rather, ours is a dynamic God who has wonders in store for us of which we are unaware. This same sentiment is echoed in the Survey:

- I understand it [my calling] to have been my principal calling to the church. Even though my life included getting married in between working at a college and then military chaplain and mom, I never doubted in the in-between times the call had changed. I see what I do as directly related to the gospel. I married a Princeton Seminary alum and even his service to the church expanded and led the family from Maryland to Texas; I knew there was a time and a place for my ordination, and when I matched up with CPE in a hospital, I knew this was it! I laughed because most of my life was chaplaincy ministry. I never connected the dots God provided until now, this position as a hospital chaplain.
- My understanding of my call to ministry has morphed and changed over time, influenced by the variety of ministry settings I have worked or volunteered in. In addition to work with prisoners, the homeless, and the

17. Howard Thurman, *Disciplines of the Spirit* (New York: Harper & Row, 1963), 35.

addicted, I served as a parish associate . . . where I developed my worship leadership skills, finding my voice. After some difficult and painful experiences there when the pastor left, I needed some time away from church leadership. After moving . . . I wasn't able to consider looking for a church position for some time. Then when I was asked to provide pulpit supply in a small, rural congregation, God opened my heart to parish ministry again. I was called there as a designated pastor to help the congregation discern God's plan for their future. Ultimately, we discerned that God was calling the church's ministry to completion. . . . My first call ended when the church closed. Some of my experiences in the church as well as during CPE helped me discern a new direction in my call—to hospice chaplaincy.

• Initially, I served as a military chaplain with the desire to create a new role model for women. Two years into it, I changed from that to simply surviving the Navy experience. Following those three years, I have been engaged in co-pastoral parish work with my husband and all of that has actually been creating new role models. At last, after twenty-five years of ordination, I was installed as the solo pastor of a congregation, something I wished I had done earlier, but it was a great experience. Now, I/we have a daughter who is a parish pastor who is continuing to create new ways of doing ministry—deeply rooted in the great tradition of the church and yet bringing exceedingly creative models to the practice of ministry. She is, by the way, the offspring of four generations of professional church leaders (pastors, missionaries) on both sides of her family. My call has greater roots and fruits than I ever imagined!

• [My call first came] through an in-depth Bible study that made me hunger for more, so I went to seminary. Then by excitement in studying the Old Testament. Next by encouragement from faculty. At the end of my senior year, at the PTS Maundy Thursday service I felt an intense questioning within and wandered the streets until I felt a very strong answer of "yes." Finally, at my last review at my home presbytery, a Navy chaplain connected me with new possibility for ministry—the new openings for women in military chaplaincy. Up to that point I had not found an opening in the church that called me or interested me. This new option for ordination was the final and strong call, not only for ordination, but the strength of my sense of call that held me throughout a very difficult three years.

• We all have a calling, and I think my call now is about fulfilling the vows I made when I became ordained instead of working towards a future goal of "someday." I am living into that ministry with the work I do every day.

• My call has aged like a good wine over time. I realized I needed in some crazy way to be maybe one of the longest timed candidates for ministry, close to twenty-five years before I was ready. And now that I am serving and ordained in my ministry, it makes for such a wonderful perspective in acute-care, public-hospital people ministry. I love it.

• I tended to over-function and felt constantly the need to prove my worthiness for this work. I was apologetic and angry, all at the same time. But over a couple of decades I have found peace in doing my work alongside people who appreciate my gifts and respect my calling, and I have found freedom from the haters by just letting them go. I don't need to persuade them; that's not my ministry. I know what I know.

• The program I created and direct provides group and individual therapy and education for at-risk children and adolescents who have experienced sexual and physical abuse, domestic violence, substance abuse, and traumatic loss, in the context of a faith-based after-school center. The work comes directly from God's call on my life through Isaiah 61: "The Spirit of the Sovereign Lord is upon me. . . . "

The truth of the matter, however, is that sometimes we prefer to resist or not respond to God's call; it can be very difficult to bring change into our lives. The seeker needs certain attitudes or habits to be able to hear God when God talks: trust, listening without preconceptions, prayer, knowledge of Scripture, humility, discipline, perseverance, perspective, awareness of possible obstacles, and a sense of patience held in tension with an awareness of urgency. Another alumna picks up the theme: "In my early thirties, I started recognizing a nearly lifelong sense of restlessness as God's calling me to something 'else.' It was a slow process of trying to stay open to whatever the possibilities might be. The Almighty is patient, insistent . . . and has a definite sense of humor!"[18]

The call of each person means that "[w]e must know the truth, and we must love the truth we know, and we must act according to the measure of our love."[19] Leonardo Boff, a Brazilian liberation theologian, suggests that part of our call is to set our sights on an eschatological hope. This includes not just thinking in terms of the primacy of agape, but the love of the "least of these," following Christ's life of service and sacrifice.[20]

God's Call Is Rooted in Community

Our call is not simply individual but is rooted in Christian community. This is the basis of ordination in the Presbyterian Church, in that individuals who feel called to ordained ministry spend years under the guidance of the presbytery in what is traditionally called "the trials of ordination" as the presbytery validates a person's call. The call of clergy is thus confirmed in community.

18. The Survey.
19. Thomas Merton, *The Ascent to Truth* (New York: Harcourt, Brace, 1951), 8.
20. Leonardo Boff and Clodovis Boff, *Introducing Liberation Theology* (Maryknoll, NY: Orbis, 1987), 44–46.

There is an interconnection between our calling and the calling of others. The gifts of ministry listed in Ephesians 4, 1 Corinthians 12, and Romans 12 are depicted in relation to one another as well as representing how we belong to the body of Christ. Barth emphasizes the interconnection between our calling and the callings of others. "This sphere will more or less touch and intersect the spheres of operation of others."[21] Each member is important, but the sum exceeds the parts. Community arises from a common call, diverse gifts, and our mutual brokenness. We are bound together by our need of forgiveness by God's grace. For Dietrich Bonhoeffer, the key to spirituality rests with the community but is not exclusive to it. Bonhoeffer's beatitude expresses this perspective: "Blessed is he who is alone in the strength of the fellowship and blessed is he who keeps the fellowship in the strength of aloneness." Writing on community, he states, "The church is Christ existing as community."[22]

Call and ministry are intricately connected. Our call, born out of our community prayers, is to serve others, especially confronting social injustices together. Bonhoeffer certainly wrestled with social injustice, and it led him to martyrdom.[23] As we reflect on call and community, we note how they are connected to the church. But this does not mean that they only can be expressed in the church. It is certainly ministry when Christians serve God and others in a variety of settings outside the church.

A Broader View of Ministry

The exploration of the nature of ministry is an important one that the stories of Princeton Seminary women have helped to expand. The Survey respondents demonstrated a certain congruency of their perspectives on the nature

21. Barth, *Church Dogmatics*, III/4:630.
22. Dietrich Bonhoeffer, *Life Together: A Discussion of Christian Fellowship*, trans. John W. Doberstein (New York: Harper & Row, 1954), 89.
23. Abigail Evans, personal conversation with Eberhard Bethge, 1973. Bonhoeffer came from a prestigious family. He was a scholar, an athlete, a pacifist, and a Lutheran Christian. When in the 1930s he came to Union Theological Seminary in New York City, he worshiped at Broadway Presbyterian Church and Abyssinian Baptist Church. Bonhoeffer's perspectives do much to help shape our understanding of what life together should be in the church. Bonhoeffer was born into privilege and was headed for a brilliant career as a theologian—he came to see his calling as dedicated to rescuing those who suffered under Nazi rule, and it cost him his life. Bonhoeffer aimed for healthy, sober, and everyday life. He deplored wishful dreaming and idealized community. As an example, one of his seminary students, Eberhard Bethge, arrived at Finkenwalde looking for the famous scholar, Bonhoeffer, expecting to find him buried in a book. He could not find him and started watching a pickup soccer game. He noticed a particularly aggressive and energetic player, whom he later learned was Bonhoeffer.

of ministry—though many were based on their own particular ministries.[24] In other words, one's context affects one's understanding of ministry. Furthermore, women's experiences of call are intricately bound to their conception of ministry. Call leads to ministry, and the process of doing a certain type of ministry may lead to a calling to a new form of ministry.

Ministry of the Laity

Since God calls all people, we have a broad definition of ministry that includes more than clergy. In the Protestant tradition, when we refer to the ministry of the laity, this concept has unfortunately often been understood as the lawyer who teaches Sunday school or the bricklayer who is a church officer rather than as their lawyering and bricklaying providing occasions for ministry. Our work or profession itself may provide opportunities for ministry if we do it in service to God and others.

This is well illustrated by Maxine, whose description of her work as a supermarket cashier, which carries moments of ministry, appears in the book *Of Human Hands* under the title "Compassion Is the Most Vital Tool of My Trade":

> Cashiering in a supermarket may not seem like a very rewarding position to most, but to me it is. You see, I feel that my job consists of a lot more than ringing up orders, taking people's money, and bagging their groceries. The most important part of my job is not the obvious. Rather, it's the manner in which I present myself to others that will determine whether my customers will leave the store feeling better or worse because of their brief encounter with me. For by doing my job well I know I have a chance to do God's work too. . . . Observation and perception are the two tools I use most often to do God's work while doing mine. . . . Compassion, however, is the most vital tool of my trade. There are many sad stories to be heard while ringing up grocery orders. . . . During such times I try my utmost to listen with my heart, not just my ears. Often a single word of understanding or a mere look of genuine concern is just the right dose of medicine to help heal a bruised heart. When I succeed in easing some of the pain of another human being, it is then that I realize just how important my job as a simple cashier is.[25]

As we broaden the definition of ministry, the question arises, "What is

---

24. Survey Question 27: "How do you understand your current paid or volunteer position as ministry?" Question 28: "How did you first experience your call to ministry?"

25. Gregory F. Augustine Pierce, ed., *Of Human Hands: A Reader in the Spirituality of Work* (Minneapolis: Augsburg Fortress, 1991), 49–51.

special about 'ordained' ministers?" On the one hand, Boff refers to the special responsibility of the "religious" in the Roman Catholic sense of the word. He believes that for them there is a congruency between life and work. On the other hand, Barth represents the viewpoint that there is no special aspect to being an ordained minister, for the obedience of all Christians to God's call is the same. There are not first-class Christians—for example, the religious who have a vocation as contrasted to others who do not have one.[26] God's call cuts across all vocations. Within the one call and ministry, however, there are the differentiations of many gifts, as noted in Romans 12, 1 Corinthians 12, and Ephesians 4. Therefore, this broader definition of ministry in no way should undermine the important work of clergy who have been called to the particular ministry of Word and Sacrament: teaching, preaching, and pastoral care. In the Reformed tradition, one of the most important roles of the ordained minister is to equip the people to do ministry, that is, mutuality in ministry. For example, when Evans was associate pastor and Roger Hull senior pastor in the 1970s at Broadway Presbyterian Church in New York City, the sign on the front of the church building facing Broadway read, "Teaching elders: Hull and Evans; Ministers: all members."

Diversity of Clergy Ministries

One of the main themes running through this book is the diversity of ministry among women as well as among clergy as a whole. Some of this diversity is tied to the changing nature of the church and society, which necessitates changes in theological education (see chap. 10). Here, however, we will reflect how, especially for women, new avenues of ministry mean new opportunities, while other doors still remain closed. Women's creativity has enriched our understanding of ministry, and definitions of what constitutes ministry have also expanded. Even within the local church, pastors are exploring new ways to conceive of ministry. Here are some of the ways the Survey respondents defined *ministry*:

- Equipping the Saints for the work of ministry.
- To name the gifts of those around me and to cultivate those gifts for the various ministries to which we each are called.
- Vocation is not limited to a professional calling, as we are all called as members of the royal priesthood.

Serving God and others is also a recurring theme in the respondents' definitions of *ministry*:

---

26. Barth, *Church Dogmatics*, III/4:601, 603.

- As an Army chaplain, I am representing God to other military personnel, and I pray that I am an effective servant of God and to others.

- I live out my call to ministry as the full-time, solo pastor of a wonderful congregation. My role is to walk with people as they live out their faith in their daily lives. I support, challenge, encourage, love, and learn from them.

- My understanding of ministry is that our purpose is to serve after the manner of Christ, with authenticity and humility.

- Pretty much everything I do is in the service of God and of the church of Jesus Christ.

Many responses reflect diverse views of the respondents' ministry with congregations:

- I am the pastor of a very small church (25 in worship) that is doing very big things. In addition to the usual preaching, teaching, visitation, etc., I am the secretary and building manager, which take most of my time. We converted 20 unused classrooms to artist studios and now have 15 resident artists who are able to launch careers because of the type of space we provide. We have had newly released prisoners working with some of these artists, which gives them a second chance in life. We host a Presbyterian Church of America (PCA) congregation that worships in our building, and we do some ministry together. In short, most of our ministry is focused on those who are not members of the congregation.

- I am a minister of Word and Sacrament; I am a paid minister to a particular congregation and the community around it. That is easiest for me to see, understand, and believe. It is far more difficult to see my service to my family and our home as ministry. However, this might be the most important ministry I am doing—modeling close up and personally for our children and our family what it means to be a disciple of Jesus Christ, and how what I do for them is service based on my Christian faith.

- I have served my current congregation for more than 8 years. I am planning a sabbatical for next January–March, as I have become more of a manager than a spiritual director! I have just started spiritual direction as a preparation for this time! I am in the midst, therefore, of making changes to the way I operate and understand my ministry so that I can be more spirit focused and centered. My understanding of ministry is that our purpose is to serve after the manner of Christ, with authenticity and humility.

There are also respondents who have a more "outside the box" view of their ministry:

- At the YMCA I seek to serve others in the humble task of cleaning exercise equipment, washing the towels, etc. I see this as ministry as I seek to treat others as I would like to be treated. I believe that every person deserves to be treated with dignity in life and in the process of dying. Being with the dying and their loved ones as the end nears is holy work, a time when many experience the presence of God. As a hospice chaplain (which I start in April), I will seek to be a calming presence by allowing the light of Christ to shine through me (at least this is my prayer!).

• I am, for the first time in two decades of "professional" ministry, an evangelist. My church planting work is dedicated to scooping up spiritual refugees, especially young adults, especially LGBTQ folks and the people who love them. I'm swimming against the tide of "bad religion" to bring the good news of God's inclusive love to those who have found traditional churches to be boring, irrelevant, exclusive, and even painful. I have let go of so many assumptions about what "good church" looks like and am living in to Jesus' challenge to love my neighbor outside of my demographic comfort zone.

• Though my primary responsibility is teaching mathematics, I see . . . loving students and giving them hope and encouragement [as my ministry].

• My ministry . . . is to be the spiritual leader of the [senior living] community, providing pastoral care, worship services, memorial services, Bible studies, and other spiritual formation and direction to residents who are between the ages of 63–106 and staff members. I am called to provide opportunities for the residents to be engaged in active ministry to those they are able to reach. For example, I have started a Stephen Ministry, training and equipping and commissioning and activating residents. So far, the oldest resident who was trained was age 93 and is still active at 95. There have been many other resident involvements in ministry at the homes as well as in the churches.

• I work with college faculty and students to support and develop their sense of vocation to do justice work. I recruit, train, and support other volunteers for this work. God calls us all to work for justice, so nurturing others' call to work for justice is surely ministry.

• Presently, I work for a nonprofit youth advocacy agency whose purpose is to advocate for the best interests of the child currently in foster care. I recruit, train, teach, and supervise those volunteers who are the hands-on advocates. We do not provide any direct service; instead, we are a presence in the child/ youth's life, advocating to secure their right to a permanent home, education, personal safety, physical and mental health for the most vulnerable of children—those in foster care.

• I think that the modality of my ministry has changed, but my understanding has remained pretty much the same. I am called to be present—in the moment with the one to whom I am sent and/or who is sent/put in my path. That in the moment, the Holy can use me to empower, enliven, encourage to see, taste, know the One who is ever present ready to heal, embolden, renew. Now, this moment can occur in the teaching and/or preaching of the Word, in the midst of Bible study, on the playground, in the line waiting for a free bag of groceries, and sometimes while people are waiting to sample the latest "taste of crack" the "candy man" is dispensing.[27]

27. The Survey.

CLERGYWOMEN IN THE CONTEXT OF SOCIETAL REALITIES FOR AMERICAN WOMEN

Moving from a general analysis of ministry, call, and vocation, we will now focus on women in ordained ministry. This discussion is set within the context of the status of women in society working in other previously male-dominated fields. Some of these fields, however, seem to be moving more quickly than the pastorate toward equality between men and women. The relevant question is whether the church is in the vanguard or is lagging behind society regarding parity for women clergy. Is the church prophetic, on the cutting edge, or is it resisting change and new possibilities for women? How do these perspectives affect women who define themselves as ordained clergy? We know that some women leave professional church work for other fields because of the prejudice and exclusion that they experience there. Such prejudices cause some women who attend theological seminaries to end up in ministry outside of church structures. Should seminaries attend to these challenges?

Women's Status in Society Today

The feminist movement, in its phase from the 1960s forward, has been characterized as the most successful social movement of the twentieth century. Some believe that women's liberation meant being freed from housework while receiving higher earnings in the workplace. There is little doubt, however, that the most important gain of the women's movement was the expansion of choices for women—choices that were not available to their mothers and grandmothers. The reality is that many women now seem to believe that because new options are available, they need to do it all. In other words, the feminist movement opened new doors but did not necessarily equip women to choose which doors to enter.

By examining a number of statistics regarding education, employment, earnings, women's role in the family, and motherhood, a clearer picture emerges of how opportunities and daily life have changed and developed for women generally since the 1960s and specifically for clergywomen.

Education

Women today are more highly educated than ever before. In the fall of 2012, women made up 56 percent of the student body in colleges and universities.[28]

---

28. "Undergraduate Enrollment," National Center for Education Statistics, last modified May 2015, https://nces.ed.gov/programs/coe/indicator_cha.asp.

In 1970, that figure was 42 percent.[29] In 2014, 34.2 percent of U.S. women at age twenty-nine had obtained at least a bachelor's degree, compared to 25.9 percent of men.[30] In 2015, women made up 33.4 percent of the total enrollment of 71,182 in all degree programs in all Association of Theological Schools (ATS) member schools. Within this total enrollment, only 28.8 percent of the 29,512 MDiv students were women, but 45.8 percent of the 21,725 non-MDiv master's degree students were women.[31] In 2012 women received 52.2 percent of doctoral degrees, in all fields, awarded by graduate schools in the United States.[32] This is a general figure to compare with the 28.8 percent (of 462 total) ThD/PhD degrees awarded to women in 2015 at all ATS member schools.[33] What are the reasons for this significantly lower percentage of women earning doctorates in theological schools compared to the general figure for doctorates in all fields? Possible reasons include fewer positions, less interest in teaching than in the pastorate or other faith-related work, fewer role models, or cost of degree versus future salary.

Employment

For most women today, having a paid job is an expected part of life. Overall, women constitute 47 percent of the total U.S. labor force—a big change from past decades.[34] In the United States today, traditionally female professions still employ the largest percentage of working women. In traditional female occupations, such as elementary and middle school teachers, secretaries, and nurses, 75 percent or more of all workers in 2014 were women.[35] Although

29. "Trends in Educational Equity of Girls and Women," National Center for Education Statistics, http://nces.ed.gov/pubs2000/2000030.pdf.

30. "America's Young Adults at 29: Labor Market Activity, Education and Partner Status: Results from a Longitudinal Survey," U.S. Bureau of Labor Statistics, last modified April 8, 2016, table 1, http://www.bls.gov/news.release/nlsyth.nr0.htm.

31. "2015–2016 Annual Data Tables," Association of Theological Schools, table 2.12-A, http://www.ats.edu/uploads/resources/institutional-data/annual-data-tables/2015-2016-annual-data-tables.pdf.

32. "Women Earned Majority of Doctoral Degrees in 2012 for 4th Straight Year, and Outnumber Men in Grad School 141 to 100," American Enterprise Institute, September 30, 2013, http://www.aei.org/publication/women-earned-majority-of-doctoral-degrees-in-2012-for-4th-straight-year-and-outnumber-men-in-grad-school-141-to-100/.

33. "2015–2016 Annual Data Tables," Association of Theological Schools, table 2.18-A, http://www.ats.edu/uploads/resources/institutional-data/annual-data-tables/2015-2016-annual-data-tables.pdf.

34. "Women in Leadership," The Pew Research Center, January 14, 2015, http://www.pewsocialtrends.org/2015/01/14/chapter-1-women-in-leadership/#fn-20118-10/.

35. "Most Common Occupations for Women," U.S. Bureau of Labor Statistics, 2014 Survey, https://www.dol.gov/wb/stats/most_common_occupations_for_women.htm.

the percentage of women in some traditionally male-dominant professions has progressed significantly (law, medicine, business),[36] the percentage of women in other such professions remains very low (firefighters, police officers, military).[37] Some might argue that the situation in the latter group of professions is tied to the physical strength and stamina needed for them, even though women can certainly be superior athletes, police captains, and the like. The physical-strength argument cannot explain the differences in science, however. In science, technology, engineering, or math-related (STEM) professions, it is a mixed picture, with the lowest percentage of women in math and engineering.[38] Some have suggested that women do not have a natural aptitude in science, and the American Association of University Women (AAUW) is mounting a huge campaign to challenge these perspectives.

Earnings

Although women are obtaining higher levels of education and many more women are working and running businesses, the facts on earnings do not reflect a comparable degree of change. While there is no doubt that women have come a long way from the discrimination and struggles they faced in the previous century, the reality is that women still face inequality in the workplace. In the United States in 2014, women made 78 cents for every dollar that men earned. "Across all industries, women make about 22% less than all men."[39] Many economists attribute this disparity to the choices women make concerning personal fulfillment, child rearing, and hours at work. However, a more staggering statistic points to a more disturbing truth: women earn less than men in 99 percent of all occupations.[40]

Some of the wage disparities for women are due to the kinds of jobs many women fill in the workplace. Lower-paid service and administrative professions are still dominated by women. Women make up two-thirds of U.S. workers

36. Fifty percent of those working in law, 48 percent of those working in medicine, and 55 percent of those working in business are women. "Women in the Labor Force: A Databook," U.S. Bureau of Labor Statistics, December 2014, http://www.bls.gov /opub/reports/cps/women-in-the-labor-force-a-databook-2014.pdf. For law, this percentage includes female judges, lawyers, paralegals, and other judicial assistants.

37. Ibid.; 3.5 percent of firefighters, 13 percent of police officers, and 13 percent of military personnel are women.

38. Ibid., table 11. In 2013 women held 46 percent of the jobs in life, physical, and social science occupations (including 39 percent in the chemistry and material sciences category); 26.1 percent in computer and mathematical occupations; 14.1 percent in architecture and engineering occupations.

39. "The Gender Pay Gap Explained," Center for American Progress, April 14, 2015, https://www.americanprogress.org/issues/women/news/2015/04/14/111058/the-gender -pay-gap-explained/.

40. Ibid.

earning $10.10 hourly or less.[41] By today's standards, this is not a living wage. Today, unmarried mothers maintain about 25 percent of U.S. households;[42] certainly many women and their families are struggling.

Socioeconomic factors, class, and race contribute significantly to the uneven earning of men and women. Minority women's incomes fare the worst. In comparison to white men, African American women earn 64 cents per dollar, and Hispanic or Latina women earn just 54 cents per dollar.[43] Many college-educated women are able to work full-time because their housekeepers' and child-care workers' wages are so low, and of course many of these domestics are minority women. Over the past two decades, on average, about 55 percent of women with a college degree or more who took parental leave were paid during that leave. By contrast, only 35 percent of women with a high school degree and just 25 percent of women with less than a high school degree were paid during their parental leaves.[44] Is progress being made if some women's successes are made on the backs of other women? Whichever of these factors are in effect, it is clear that the male-female playing field is not level. What role might clergywomen take to help eliminate these disparities?

In terms of women clergy, it is more difficult to compare their earnings with those of their male colleagues because women generally serve smaller, poorer churches. Jackson W. Carroll reports,

> In our *Pulpit & Pew* sample, the majority of men and women solo and senior pastors had comparable salaries. For mainline [Protestant] pastors earning less than $60,000—who comprise 85 percent of all mainline senior or solo pastors—there was little or no difference in average salaries for men and women with the same education, years of ministry experience, size of congregation, and average income level of laity. . . . It is important to balance these indisputably positive gains with the problems that remain. First, women make up a disproportionately large[r] percentage of associate pastors [and pastors of smaller churches]. . . . Second, while women may receive equal pay for equal work, they may still face unequal access to higher-paying positions.[45]

41. Ibid.

42. "Working Mothers in the U.S.," U.S. Department of Labor, 2015, http://www.dol.gov/wb/Infographic_on_working_mothers.pdf.

43. "Gender Pay Gap," Center for American Progress.

44. "Job Protection Isn't Enough: Why America Needs Paid Parental Leave," Center for American Progress, December 2013, https://www.americanprogress.org/wp-content/uploads/2013/12/ParentalLeave-report-3.pdf.

45. Jackson W. Carroll, *God's Potters: Pastoral Leadership and the Shaping of Congregations* (Grand Rapids: Eerdmans, 2006), 70–71.

In the Episcopal Church as recently as 2006, not only was there a disproportionate number of women assistant and associate pastors, but clergywomen's median salary was $10,000 less than clergymen in parish ministry, and even those who became senior rectors made $13,000 less per year than their male counterparts.[46] With regard to the PC(USA), the denomination's board of pensions found in 2008 that "women have a lower average effective salary [total compensation, including cash salary, housing, and benefits] as compared to men as both pastors and associate pastors in nearly all congregational size categories."[47] A 2014 PC(USA) study concluded that "widespread anecdotal evidence seems to confirm that the conclusions of that [2008] report remain valid."[48] One of the challenges that numerous PTS alumnae identified in a variety of pastoral positions was inadequate pay.

Women's Role in the Family

In the decades prior to the feminist movement, women were expected to marry and become housekeepers and child rearers. Today, the picture for married women has shifted, with more dual-income couples, more stay-at-home fathers, and a more equal distribution of housework. Have these shifts in work changed the facts about housework? In general, it seems that men are doing more housework than they did in the 1970s, but women still bear the brunt of those responsibilities. According to a 2013 study conducted by the U.S. Bureau of Labor, on an average day, 19 percent of men did housework, such as cleaning or doing laundry, compared with 49 percent of women. Forty-two percent of men did food preparation or cleanup, compared with 68 percent of women.[49]

Motherhood

The realities of motherhood have also changed for U.S. women in recent decades. The number of women having children at all has significantly decreased; "nearly one-in-five American women ends her childbearing years without

46. Adair T. Lummis, "Forever Pruning? The Path to Ordained Women's Full Participation in the Episcopal Church of the USA," in *Women and Ordination in the Christian Churches: International Perspectives*, ed. Ian Jones, Janet Wootton, and Kirsty Thorpe (London: T. & T. Clark, 2008), 157–76, here 170. Statistics from 2006.

47. "God's Work in Women's Hands: Pay Equity and Just Compensation," PC(USA) Advisory Committee on Social Witness Policy, 25, http://oga.pcusa.org /site_media/media/uploads/oga/pdf/mid_council_ministries/acswppayequity.pdf.

48. "Fairness in Ministerial Compensation: Incentives and Solidarity," 2014, PC(USA) Advisory Committee on Social Witness Policy, 7, http://www.pcusa.org /site_media/media/uploads/acswp/pdf/fairness_in_ministerial_compensation.pdf.

49. "American Time Use Survey Summary," U.S. Bureau of Labor Statistics, last modified June 24, 2015, http://www.bls.gov/news.release/atus.nr0.htm.

having borne a child, compared with one-in-ten in the 1970s."[50] Additionally, many more unmarried women have children; 40.6 percent of all births in the United States are to unmarried women.[51] Among participants in the Survey, 67 percent have at least one child, and 68 percent of those who work in congregational ministries have at least one child. For women ministers, the responsibilities of motherhood may lead some to seek more flexible vocations through specialized forms of ministry. According to the PTS active alumni/ae database as of March 2016, 22 percent of active alumnae (women) are serving in specialized ministry and 21 percent in other types of service, for a total of 43 percent of women serving in nonparish settings. For comparison, 14 percent of the alumni (men) are serving in specialized ministry and 15 percent in other types of service, for a total of 29 percent of men serving in nonparish settings. This preference among women for specialized ministry is reflected in the study conducted by Barbara Finlay.[52] In a survey of seminarians and their goals, Finlay found that women were more likely than men to prefer to work in various chaplaincies, in retirement homes, and in urban ministries. It is not easy to know if this is by virtue of what might be available or if it is indicative of actual preference.

In summary, realities for women have changed dramatically since the feminist movement began. Women enjoy higher education in staggering numbers, outnumbering men in colleges and universities. Most women work outside the home, either by choice or by necessity, and many own and run successful businesses. Less changed is the reality that minorities are especially likely to suffer poor wages. Family life has adjusted less dramatically; men do more housework than previously, but women still do the majority of it. Getting married, having children, and then staying home to raise them is no longer the model for many women. The modern American family now includes single mothers, stay-at-home fathers, dual-income households, fewer children, two working partners with no children, same-sex couples, women who earn more than their husbands, and unmarried couples raising children.

---

50. "Childlessness Up among All Women; Down among Women with Advanced Degrees," Pew Research Center, June 25, 2010, http://www.pewsocialtrends.org /2010/06/25/childlessness-up-among-all-women-down-among-women-with-advanced -degrees/.

51. "Unmarried Childbearing," Centers for Disease Control and Prevention, last updated September 30, 2015, http://www.cdc.gov/nchs/fastats/unmarried-childbearing .htm.

52. Barbara Finlay, *Facing the Stained Glass Ceiling: Gender in a Protestant Seminary* (Lanham, MD: University Press of America, 2003), 49.

Current Status and Experiences of Clergywomen

Having noted that clergywomen are behind their counterparts in other professions, how would we describe their current position? First, our understanding of ordained ministry has changed drastically in the last decades. In the United States up to the late 1960s, ordained ministry was conducted overwhelmingly by male clergy—only about 2 percent of clergy were women. With the emergence of the trifold liberation movements of blacks, women, and gays, who were united in their feelings of marginalization and were antiestablishment, the church (as other social institutions) was affected. No longer did a certain role or position guarantee power or automatic followers. The seeds of change in the role of clergy were planted then, and they came to fruition in the late 1990s and have continued progressively into the present time. The question is, how much did the entrance of women into the ranks of ordained clergy in mainline Protestant denominations influence this move away from a hierarchical model, and to what extent are these changes a reflection of general cultural change? In 2010 the percentage of women clergy ranged from 8 percent (in evangelical denominations) to 25 percent (in old-line Protestant denominations), with an average of 12 percent across the board.[53] In 2014 in the PC(USA) 37 percent of active ordained clergy and 28 percent of all ordained clergy were women.[54] When compared to the previously referenced statistics about employment from the U.S. Bureau of Labor Statistics report, it seems that women clergy have made relatively small gains in comparison to women in the fields of law, medicine, and business. At the same time, women clergy have made relatively large gains in comparison to the professions of firefighting, police work, and some STEM fields.

The picture for women clergy in comparison to other professions is instructive. Having highlighted some of the gains experienced by women in society as a whole, we examine further the question of whether women clergy fare better or worse than women in other previously male-dominated professions. Generally speaking, it appears that women fare better in professions that entail more personal interaction with people, with a high value given to the caring dimension of the profession; for example, the statistics seem to show that female physicians are better accepted than female firefighters and police officers. From this perspective, one might expect women to make huge

53. "2010 National Survey of Congregations," Faith Communities Today, http://faithcommunitiestoday.org/sites/faithcommunitiestoday.org/files/2010FrequenciesV1.pdf.
54. "2014 Comparative Statistics of the Presbyterian Church (U.S.A.)," Presbyterian Church (U.S.A.), 10, http://www.pcusa.org/site_media/media/uploads/research/pdfs/comparative_statistics_2014.pdf.

gains in the ranks of the clergy, since physical strength is not the issue. But their situation is also affected by the fact that some Christians have theological objections to ordaining women, so that no matter how capable, they are not accepted in clergy roles. Percentages of women clergy also lag behind other professions because so many female seminary graduates are older and pursuing a second career and thus have more difficulty in receiving an ordainable position.

Studies from 2001 show that "when we look at the perception of the match [between a pastor and his/her congregation] in relation to the gender of the pastor, the results show that laity are significantly more likely to believe that there is a good match when the pastor is a male rather than a female—a relationship that holds regardless of denominational tradition."[55] Given the ongoing struggles of women clergy, it appears that the church is falling behind other professions in terms of embracing women in leadership roles.

We note that most of the discussion in this book focuses on female clergy in the United States; we recognize that there may be vast differences for those in other countries. In addition, women of color in the United States may have markedly different experiences than their Anglo counterparts, both historically and today.

Here we include two examples of such differences. First, in the black church there is a rich history of the "mothers of the church" who are strong and revered leaders, though they may not specifically enter the ranks of the ordained. Also, the "church nurse" was an important part of the ministry of the black church for those who were literally overcome by the Spirit and required special ministrations.[56] In the 1800s there were wonderful African American women preachers, such as Jarena Lee, Julia A. J. Foote, Zilpha Elaw, and others.[57] Yet, as numerous African American writers have shown, many segments of the black church continue to insist on a subordinate role for women, even as they use Galatians 3:28 to challenge societal racism.[58] Some insist that racism is more important to eliminate than sexism, while others believe that both are of equal import. Vashti McKenzie notes that African

55. Carroll, *God's Potters*, 87. See "U.S. Congregational Life Survey," Association of Religion Data Archives, data from fall 2008 and spring 2009, http://thearda.com /Archive/Files/Descriptions/CLS08ATT.asp; also http://www.uscongregations.org/. More recent studies were not available.

56. See Evans, *The Healing Church*, 153–75.

57. Sue E. Houchins, *Spiritual Narratives* (Schomburg Library of Nineteenth-Century Black Women Writers; New York: Oxford University Press, 1988); Vashti M. McKenzie, *Not Without a Struggle: Leadership Development for African American Women in Ministry* (Cleveland: Pilgrim Press, 2011).

58. See Demetrius K. Williams, *An End to This Strife: The Politics of Gender in the African-American Churches* (Minneapolis: Fortress Press, 2004), 188–89.

American clergywomen remain under "pressure to prove their competence" in a racist and sexist environment; such pressure can lead them to put on a brave public face while experiencing personal isolation in the face of instances of painful humiliation.[59] McKenzie's survey found that womanist clergy leadership included Eurocentric models but also incorporated distinctively African American attitudes and strategies, such as focusing on liberation or African roots.[60]

As a second example, we note that other women of color also face many more challenges than their white counterparts. The book *Here I Am: Faith Stories of Korean American Clergywomen* chronicles the stories of brave Korean American Presbyterian clergy who have shown courage and resilience in the face of prejudice and discrimination by both the church and society.[61] For example, some of these women are asked, "Do you speak English?" even if they have lived in the United States most of their lives. The church asks others, "Why do you want to be a pastor? Perhaps you can work with the women and children." One woman, who was already serving in a church while going through the ordination trials, was told that she could not have a public ordination but only a quiet one with three or four people, for fear that this Korean American Presbyterian congregation would not approve of her being an ordained minister. Despite such challenges, these Korean American Presbyterian women have persevered, and as of April 2013, there were ninety ordained clergywomen, sixteen inquirers, and eighteen candidates who were pursuing ordination in the Presbyterian Church. Yet there is only one working as head of staff.[62] For them, the church can be a place of solace and identity, but it can also pose difficulties for finding their place. The idea of an *Ajumma* theology (a Korean term for a woman who demonstrates self-assertion and power) is emerging as a way of speaking truth to power.[63]

Styles of Female Clergy Leadership

There is some ambivalence on the part of women clergy themselves and others about whether there is a distinctive style of leadership for clergywomen. In both the secular world and in the church, different perspectives are articulated about this ambivalence. It is interesting that in the early 1970s and

59. McKenzie, *Not Without a Struggle*, 92–99.
60. Ibid., 104–9.
61. Grace Ji-Sun Kim, ed., *Here I Am: Faith Stories of Korean American Clergywomen* (Valley Forge, PA: Judson Press, 2015).
62. Ibid., 25.
63. Ibid., 19.

1980s, conversations by writers such as Elizabeth Nickles, who defined alpha and beta styles of leadership, rarely entered the mainstream of conversations about women in ministry. Nickles and others distinguished the male alpha style, which is more authoritarian and hierarchal, from the female beta style, which is more consultative and inclusive, claiming that the beta style would dominate in the future because it is more effective.[64]

Women's leadership in the church, especially in the ordained ministry, seems to have followed Rosemary Radford Ruether's three stages of liberation: emulating the dominant culture, being over and against the mainstream, and in the last stage finding their own voice and way, although of course these stages are not hermetically sealed, and individual women may go back and forth between them.[65] We may now be entering a fourth stage where transformation of church and society is in the forefront as women's attention moves beyond being heard to becoming a leaven for the inclusion of all God's people around the table.[66] One modest idea for this transformation in the parish setting might be to prepare the homily out of the community reflection on the text, as has been practiced in many of the base communities in Latin America and in some U.S. congregations. Eunjoo Mary Kim has suggested a variety of strategies for more interactive preaching.[67]

Ruether points out that in the early stage women were so consumed with getting ordained that they were not questioning the nature of women or of ordained ministry. "Women in ministry, like all women trying to function in public roles under male rules, find themselves in a double bind. They are allowed success only by being better than men at the games of masculinity, while at the same time they are rebuked for having lost their femininity."[68] The aim for women was usually to be better than men in what they do rather than to be different. The second stage of over and against was reflected, for example, in the struggles for inclusive language for human beings and God and in the interpretation of key biblical passages concerning women. Today, many women clergy believe that they have found a different voice, à la Carol

---

64. Elizabeth Nickles and Laura Ashcraft, *The Coming Matriarchy: How Women Will Gain the Balance of Power* (New York: Seaview Press, 1981).

65. Rosemary Radford Ruether, *Sexism and God-Talk: Toward a Feminist Theology* (Boston: Beacon Press, 1983).

66. See, for example, Letty M. Russell, *Church in the Round: Feminist Interpretation of the Church* (Louisville, KY: Westminster/John Knox Press, 1993).

67. Eunjoo Mary Kim, "Preaching as an Art of Shared Leadership," in *Women, Church, and Leadership: New Paradigms; Essays in Honor of Jean Miller Schmidt*, ed. Eunjoo Mary Kim and Deborah Beth Creamer (Eugene, OR: Pickwick, 2012), 69–88, esp. 85–86.

68. Ruether, *Sexism and God-Talk*, 168.

Gilligan.[69] Thus, women may bring different perspectives, styles, or "women's ways of knowing."

When women in small numbers enter male-defined roles, they face many challenges. In focusing only on acceptance, usually defined in male categories, they may miss the opportunity to change the character of ministry as well as the mission of the church. There have been significant changes since women have entered the clergy, but the picture is uneven and much remains to be done. Women often suffer from a perfectionism complex, workaholism and its companion stress, and a tendency toward multitasking, at least partly in response to their struggle for acceptance. All of these things can take their toll. Here is what some of the Survey respondents had to say on these subjects:

- Male clergy in ministerium are not sure how to work with me. Lots of teaching to do with them. Already set the bar high on what I expect of them and how we can work collaboratively.

- Having been in my position with the same church for 15+ years, I'm not aware of my gender enhancing or inhibiting my ministry. People know who I am and where I stand on issues. They know my strengths and my weaknesses and this makes [it] much easier to handle. Being a woman, or at least being myself, I have a hard time saying "no" to any request for help, but as I age I am learning what my physical and emotional limits are. I really don't like to do a half-hearted job or to become stressed with too much work. Balance is the key.

- My current position allows a high degree of flexibility and grace. For this, I am extremely grateful when snow days, snow delays, colds, cheerleading tryouts, groceries, etc.—whatever family need beckons—I am overall able to respond. I am 100 percent the biggest inhibition in my life [because of] my inability to exercise. My body needs this. Even more so, my soul and mind and spirit need this. This feels like the one tipping point that I have difficulty integrating into my daily disciplines.

- Other than feeling the need to be available to my congregation 24/7, I don't feel that my gender enhances or inhibits my ministry among my congregants. In my community, it is a factor, however. During my last new members class, for instance, I was told by a couple joining the church that they were chastised by a neighbor for joining my congregation because "It's not a true church, you know; they have a woman pastor." I am currently serving a mid-size church in the Midwest and patriarchy runs deep!

Women clergy show especially strong advocacy for social justice issues. The second wave of feminism, launched by Betty Friedan's *The Feminine Mystique* in 1963, reached mainline Protestant churches by the 1970s, when opportunities for women in church leadership, including ordination, were

69. Carol Gilligan, *In a Different Voice: Psychological Theory and Women's Development* (Cambridge, MA: Harvard University Press, 1982).

expanding. During this time, many feminist scholars published critiques in hopes of changing the male-dominated theological language generally used in worship.[70] Various organizations—such as the Commission on Women in Ministry (COWIM), which was a division of the National Council of Churches of Christ (NCCC)—took the lead in efforts to end discrimination against women leaders. In light of this history, clergywomen have been perceived, and rightfully so, as more liberal than their male counterparts on many issues (abortion, homosexuality, etc.) according to various studies.[71]

Of course, the underlying question remains whether there is in fact an inherent difference in male and female styles of leadership. Are there traits that can be present in both sexes (e.g., a nurturing approach, or relational rather than hierarchal approaches to decision making), or are there inherent differences in the sexes? It is interesting to note that 78 percent of the Survey respondents answered yes to the question "Is there anything about your ministry or leadership style that you think is unique to your being a woman?" In written responses to this question, the three words they most commonly used to describe their unique gifts were "collaboration," "relationship," and "nurture." That said, 22 percent of respondents expressed some ambivalence in their answer to this question, indicating they were not sure if gender makes a difference.

These differing responses reflect the complexity of discerning whether or how much gender makes a difference in gifts for ministry. Rosie Ward points out that biblical leadership, patterned after the leadership of Christ, gives no warrant for separate gifts based on gender.[72] Yet she concedes that anthropological research identifies distinctions between leadership styles.[73] Clergywomen may seem more naturally suited to the relational, nurturing side of ministry, but prejudice against them is still often based on their gender rather than their suitability for parish ministry. Other gifts they appear to bring include capacities for vision casting, problem solving, facilitation, delegation, and collaboration.[74] In response to these apparent distinctions, Ward highlights that the Trinitarian model emphasizes collaboration in the use of these distinct gifts. It is not about who is more "purposeful or relational"; it is about these two attributes working in tandem. She writes, "The gender wars began in the garden but should end at the cross." As a result, Ward suggests

70. Lummis, "Forever Pruning?" 159.
71. Ibid., 164–65.
72. Rosie Ward, "Doing Leadership Differently? Women and Senior Leadership in the Church of England," in Jones et al., *Women and Ordination in the Christian Churches*, 76–86, here 78.
73. Ibid., 80.
74. Ibid., 83.

that the unique gift that women may be able to bring to clergy for the good of the church is a willingness to collaborate: the idea that "we can do things better together."[75]

In a study of male and female clergy, Edward C. Lehman Jr. set out to test cultural (maximalist) feminist assumptions about how gender affects ministry. Do different approaches to ministry actually cohere as identifiably male or female, and do male and female clergy actually differ in the extent to which each type is empirically associated with them?[76] The study determined that while there are masculine and feminine approaches to ministry, these do not correspond with the sex of the minister.[77] That is, a male clergy does not predict a masculine approach to ministry, and a female clergy does not predict a feminine approach to ministry.[78]

Ambivalence around gender-specific styles of clergy leadership is seen also in studies of congregants. For example, when church members were interviewed several decades ago about whether they wanted a woman minister and whether she would bring different gifts, they offered a variety of explanations. Primarily, all respondents expressed distaste for using sex as a factor in choosing a minister, either negatively or positively. Rather, they preferred to consider professional qualifications regardless of sex. "Women are people. Let them not be given positions because they are women!"[79] A number of the lay leaders further commented that having a woman minister has changed opinions in their congregations as to whether a woman can be as qualified as a man for pastoral leadership. But as illustrated in the following quote, most lay leaders still did not approve of seeking a woman specifically: "We are so pleased with our woman minister, and the growth her efforts have brought our church, that this position in the future would be open equally to male and female candidates—choice based solely on competency."[80] Nonetheless, a number of lay leaders, though believing that sex should not be a criterion in selecting a minister, still wanted a man, especially as senior pastor. The following remarks indicate degrees of awareness or discomfort that lay leaders experienced with their own ambivalence on this issue:

75. Ibid., 84.

76. Edward C. Lehman Jr., *Gender and Work: The Case of the Clergy* (SUNY Series in Religion, Culture, and Society; Albany: State University of New York Press, 1993). The authors found this to be true in their PTS courses in the 1980s, 1990s, and 2000s on women in pastoral ministry.

77. Ibid., 50.

78. Ibid., 79–80.

79. Jackson W. Carroll, Barbara Hargrove, and Adair T. Lummis, *Women of the Cloth: A New Opportunity for the Churches* (New York: Harper & Row, 1983), 147.

80. Ibid., 148.

- Our married co-pastors are doing an excellent job in shepherding our congregation, with their youthful exuberance and Christian devotion. They share equally in the work and are accepted equally. Still, personally, I would prefer a man if there was to be only one pastor, even though I know a woman would be as able.

- While I have no strong feelings personally and my Pastor is one of the few successful female ministers . . . experience leads me to admit men are superior local pastors.

- I believe sex or race should not be a factor in seeking a new minister; however, all other qualifications being equal, and having experienced both men and women's effectiveness as pastor, I would prefer the men.

- Even though I am a modern, moderately liberal, extremely active grandmother, who feels women are capable of doing anything in the church as well as men, I prefer a male senior minister. I do not even know why![81]

A reality in the last ten years or so is that multiple staff churches often desire at least one woman for the counseling ministry in case someone of the same gender as the counselee is desired.

> When we look at the perception of match [between a pastor and his/her congregation] in relation to gender of the pastor, the results show that laity are significantly more likely to believe that there is a good match when the pastor is male rather than female—a relationship that holds regardless of denominational tradition.[82]

Although it might be considered an overgeneralization, on the whole the first wave of ordained women in the "mainline denominations" seem to have focused on traditional patterns of leadership with expectations of 24/7 availability, while the second wave looked for redefining the pastorate more as a contract with parameters. This often led to their seeking positions in specialized ministry, which afforded more flexibility. Are we now entering a third phase, in which women have an opportunity to broaden our understanding of ministry and bring more balance to the call to ministry? It is instructive to hear what women clergy themselves have to say.[83]

- I was a frightened conservative when I went to seminary, unsure about being a female in ministry. I am considerably socially, politically, and theologically liberal now, and understand my call as a call to all different kinds of people just as I understand God's house to be a house of prayer for all people. I have also become less concerned about going off and creating a perfect product to bring back to God's people and am more concerned with how we all work together to do something that delights God.

81. Ibid.
82. Carroll, *God's Potters*, 87. See also "U.S. Congregational Life Survey."
83. The Survey.

- Since my ministry is to empower the ministry of others, I know that women and girls who get to see me do what I'm called to do are also inspired to figure out what they're called to do and do it too.

- My current position is enhanced in the areas of outreach and welcome, since I am highly involved in the traditional female roles in our community as a mother of a young child. In other words, I am at the school events, sporting events, and social events for small children in a prominent role as mom and clergy. I have been inhibited in my role as clergy when it comes to civil events due to my gender.

Challenges for Clergy in Ministry

Based on the discussion in this chapter, it is clear that there are many challenges for clergy in ministry. There are two aspects of these challenges to be considered. First, what special challenges do clergywomen face? Second, what general challenges do all clergy face in a changing world where the organized church may be considered less relevant and the fastest growing religious group is the "nones" (i.e., those having no religious affiliation)?

First, regarding challenges to women ministers, here we focus especially on ordained clergywomen serving local congregations. (It should be noted that a fairly large number of women may leave the pastorate seeking specialized ministries both inside and outside the church, although fewer specialized positions are now available.) There is a mixed picture of how women have fared. Books such as *A Church of Her Own: What Happens When a Woman Takes the Pulpit* give a rather discouraging picture of women's experiences.[84] Sarah Sentilles notes that many women are silenced, humiliated, and abused in the ordination process in Protestant denominations; many of those she interviewed experienced deep misogyny. She writes, "We Protestants like to pretend sexism does not exist in our churches, and yet ordained ministry continues to be one of the most male-dominated of all professions."[85] Sentilles notes studies in recent decades that track the trends of women leaving ministry.[86] It is not illegal for churches to refuse to ordain certain people based on sex, sexual preference, and, of course, theology.

84. Sarah Sentilles, *A Church of Her Own: What Happens When a Woman Takes the Pulpit* (New York: Houghton Mifflin Harcourt, 2008).
85. Ibid., 4.
86. Ibid., 16–17. In 2010–2012, the United Methodist Church conducted a follow-up study on the 1993 study that Sentilles cites. This more recent study found that although the percentage of women clergy who are serving in local congregations has increased significantly over the past two decades, the number of women who left local congregational work and who cited "lack of support from the hierarchical system" as their reason for leaving actually increased as well. See http://www.umc.org /news-and-media/women-pastors-growing-in-numbers.

Some Survey respondents reflected discouragement over the challenges of ministry, even moving away from the term "ministry":

- I don't really think in the terms of ministry anymore. Frankly, it's been very healthy for me to get away from Christian terminology. Ministry is loaded with a sense of obligation, sometimes even pride and the need to be needed. Now I do what I do because I find it personally meaningful. The landscape of social service is vast and overwhelming. I would love to make systemic change, but I don't see myself giving my God-given gifts to the world anymore. I see myself learning and growing by encountering the other and having fun doing it. I am shifting my focus to thinking about how I can spend my time in a way that makes me happy and puts food on the table. That happens to involve being a part of trying to end poverty in my community.
- Oy. I am so burnt out. I find that the church I am currently serving blocks ministry in all kinds of ways. Most of my ministry right now is trying to put a spiritual base for decision-making, but my arm is tired. So, I understand my vocation currently as a guide of sorts, I suppose. "Not that way, over here." I wonder if I am being faithful to God, and hope he doesn't strike me dead with a bolt of lightning for having such a sucky attitude about these stiff-necked people.

What all future pastors face is the challenge of how the church can be involved in the concerns of the world, moved by compassion to respond to the needs of others, while at the same time cultivating the inner spiritual life and our walk with God. The classic analysis by H. Richard Niebuhr in *Christ and Culture* still holds true.[87] The church is at the crossroads in a society that is less and less interested in organized religion.[88] The new byword is "spirituality without religion."[89] So the church is poised to determine if its relationship to culture is one of opposition, identity, transcendence, tension, or conversion. The classic struggle between identity and conversion still continues today. As the church relates to the culture and we expand our

87. H. Richard Niebuhr, *Christ and Culture* (New York: Harper, 1951).

88. Surveys conducted by the Pew Research Center show that the percentage of the U.S. population that is religiously unaffiliated (i.e., describing themselves as atheist, agnostic, or "nothing in particular") has risen from 16.1 percent in 2007 to 22.8 percent in 2014. "America's Changing Religious Landscape: Christians Decline Sharply as Share of Population; Unaffiliated and Other Faiths Continue to Grow," Pew Research Center, May 12, 2015, http://www.pewforum.org/2015/05/12/americas-changing-religious-landscape/.

89. Eighteen percent of the U.S. general public identifies as "spiritual only [i.e., not religious]," compared to the 65 percent who identify as "religious" and 15 percent who identify as neither. "'Nones' on the Rise: Religion and the Unaffiliated," Pew Research Center, October 9, 2012, http://www.pewforum.org/2012/10/09/nones-on-the-rise-religion/.

understanding of ministry, its leaders need to find ways to balance the pastoral and the prophetic.

The challenge of relating church to culture is not, of course, gender specific. But women may be faster to buck the mold and to balance the tension between conformity and resistance, the status quo versus change. The stories in previous chapters in this book reflect the creative ways that women are changing the church—breaking in and breaking out. They are seeking new ways for the church to be relevant to the world. We need to find new paths to open the doors of the church to all people and expand our understanding of the nature of ministry. Women are especially equipped for this job, as in their ministries so many have confronted prejudice, criticism, and resistance. For women (and men) to be prepared to be change agents, to be ready to serve wherever there are needs, especially in the church, theological education is a key step in such preparation. Seminaries have an important role in helping to prepare women and men for their future challenges and opportunities in ministry. It is to this topic that we turn our attention in the final chapter.

10

New Horizons
in Theological Education

This book concludes with reflections on theological education, since how we educate future pastors and specialized ministers will affect the face of the church and the ways in which clergy can be agents of change in society and the world. Our research on women's experiences in ministry lends impetus to the need for changes in theological education. Our thesis is that theological education needs to focus on the whole person. This approach sets forth a model in which the needs of body, mind, and spirit are attended to, if not in equal proportion to academic needs at least operating from a wholistic approach to education. (This wholistic view is reflected in some of the standards of the Association of Theological Schools [ATS].)

Such an approach can be challenging even for residential seminaries. It can be expensive, requiring a large faculty and staff, and the educational aim of a seminary might seem to be subsumed under too broad an umbrella. This chapter does not attempt to answer all the challenges of this model, but rather it will set forth a vision that can be adjusted to the realities of different contexts and institutions. This may seem to be an ambitious model at a time when seminaries appear to be in crisis. But at such a time, new paradigms have a chance to be heard—a new word spoken. In our research it has become clear that once in ministry, women realize that they needed not just academics in seminary but also attention to the whole person, as reflected in the stories in the previous chapters. As one of our Survey respondents emphasized, "Character, faith, maturity, integrity, wisdom, resilience . . . all these are essential for ministry." Or, as one of the Korean American Presbyterian clergy said, "I wish that theological education should be more toward holistic approach—holistic salvation and holistic mission." The voices of women cry for a more wholistic approach to learning and perhaps even a transformation of the seminary experience.

Given the dramatic increase in the number of female seminarians, it is important that theological education take into account women's experiences in ministry. In 1972 women constituted 10.2 percent of all enrollment in ATS-accredited schools; in 1980, this percentage had reached 21.8 percent.[1] As of 2015, the percentage of women had increased to 33.4 percent.[2] Very few studies of theological education have seriously addressed this dramatic change; they rather have focused on analyzing the crisis facing seminaries today.[3] There is no doubt, with shrinking church memberships and dwindling seminary enrollments, that there is a crisis. We should not focus simply on damage control, however, but also on seeking creative ways to equip women and men for ministry in the name of Christ. Systemic change is taking place rapidly in theological seminaries, and we hope to contribute to this conversation.

It is clear that we are in a changing world and church, with the increase of "nones" (or, to use the term coined by Rami Shapiro, the "spiritually independent"),[4] the shrinking of mainline churches, and the preference of spirituality over religion as an identifier.[5] Interestingly, Samuel G. Freedman noted in 2015 that there has been a "boomlet of students who are secular or unaffiliated with any religious denomination . . . attending divinity school."[6] We will focus principally on the MDiv degree in freestanding, mainline Protestant seminaries, not graduate schools of religion or divinity schools embedded in universities. Although we focus mainly on women and their

1. "Fact Book on Theological Education 1980–81," Association of Theological Schools, 9, http://www.ats.edu/uploads/resources/institutional-data/fact-books/1980-1981-fact-book.pdf.

2. "2015–2016 Annual Data Tables," Association of Theological Schools, table 2.12-A. http://www.ats.edu/uploads/resources/institutional-data/annual-data-tables/2015-2016-annual-data-tables.pdf.

3. Barbara Finlay, *Facing the Stained Glass Ceiling: Gender in a Protestant Seminary* (Lanham, MD: University Press of America, 2003). This is one of the few books to study the difference between male and female seminarians, based on research at one particular unnamed seminary.

4. Rami Shapiro, *Perennial Wisdom for the Spiritually Independent: Sacred Teachings—Annotated & Explained* (Woodstock, VT: Skylight Paths Publishing, 2013).

5. Twenty-three percent of U.S. adults are religiously unaffiliated, called the "nones" or the "spiritually independent," with a growing number of adults who designate themselves as "spiritual but not religious." "America's Changing Religious Landscape: Christians Decline Sharply as Share of Population; Unaffiliated and Other Faiths Continue to Grow," Pew Research Center, May 12, 2015, http://www.pewforum.org/2015/05/12/americas-changing-religious-landscape/.

6. Samuel G. Freedman, "Secular, but Feeling a Call to Divinity School," *New York Times*, October 15, 2015; http://www.nytimes.com/2015/10/17/us/more-students-secular-but-feeling-a-call-turn-to-divinity-schools.html?

experiences, our recommendations apply to the needs of all students, not just women. Justice for one is justice for all. In addition, unless men are advocates for women, based on their awareness of female seminarians' perspectives, the seminary and church will not change.

Part of the challenge for this enterprise is to avoid developing widely divergent tracks focused on different groups (for example, students of color, men, women, and nonheteronormative persons) or based on vocational calling (for instance, parish, specialized ministry, graduate teaching, nonprofit organizations, etc.). While specialized courses are important, we need a core curriculum and seminary ethos that benefit and enrich the whole community.

In the first part of this chapter, the following components of theological education will be described: institutional structures, finances, student body, faculty, curriculum, and Christian community. Included here will be how each component is changing and developing, leading to new paradigms and challenges. The second part of the chapter will present a whole-person theological education model and address how it relates to the components of theological education mentioned above and is called for by the challenges and complexities that women are experiencing in their ministries, as described in the previous chapters.

Although this chapter will include general remarks and information about theological education, much of the material is based on our research of PTS women's perspectives and on our experience at PTS.[7] In addition, we also rely on books on theological education, ATS material, and examples from several other seminaries. We realize that PTS is somewhat different from its sister seminaries, so we have tried to take this into account in our descriptions and recommendations. Our hope is to foster conversations with other seminaries that are instituting so many creative and interesting programs, as well as with persons generally interested in theological education.

COMPONENTS OF THEOLOGICAL EDUCATION

Institutional Structures

One of the struggles for seminaries is whether their primary identity is as a school of religion, a training ground for future clergy, or a Christian

---

7. This research is based on the Survey and over sixty years of combined teaching experience at PTS (forty-three years for Katharine Doob Sakenfeld and eighteen years for Abigail Rian Evans). In addition, Evans has taught in seminaries in Washington, DC; Virginia; California; and Campinas, Brazil.

community. Most of them become a hybrid of all three, with some emphasizing one aspect more than another. Seminaries that focus on training clergy will typically ask applicants to describe their call to ministry, but arriving students may discover a hybrid context. PTS, for example, emphasizes its connection to the Presbyterian Church with an ecumenical perspective, as well as its core MDiv program and strong PhD program. This leads to individual students sometimes believing that their vocational interests may not be primary. Those headed to the parish may believe that the seminary is more interested in PhD students, while those headed for graduate school may believe that it is overly geared to parish ministry. It is a challenge for a seminary to serve multiple goals effectively. When schools offer a clear statement of focus, students can make choices about which seminary to attend based on these emphases.

There are a number of structures for seminaries, including university divinity schools, freestanding nondenominational seminaries, and consortia of schools. We are focusing principally on denominational seminaries, which historically were scattered geographically throughout the United States for two main reasons: a desired geographic proximity for students, and differences in theological and worship beliefs. For example, Presbyterian churches sent their members most often to nearby seminaries, and regional synods in the Presbyterian structure had a strong sense of responsibility for their seminarians. Despite the ease of travel now, attending seminary close at hand is still a strong pattern. In an extensive ATS survey, seminarians rated geographic proximity as "somewhat important" in their selection of a seminary, perhaps more important than denominational affiliation. Other factors were academic quality, faculty, and theological fit.[8]

In the 1980s and 1990s, some denominational seminaries discussed how to differentiate themselves, and the idea of a "niche" seminary emerged. Rather than competing against one another for the same pool of students, seminaries highlighted their particular programs and curricula to attract students with similar interests. They pointed to a variety of emphases: vocational focus (e.g., the parish, academia, specialized ministry, urban ministry); type of student (e.g., students of color, second-career students); type of affiliation (e.g., strong denominational or university affiliation); and institutional structure (e.g., catering to residential or commuter students). These seminaries do not exclusively serve one population or offer only narrowly focused courses, but many

---

8. "Entering Student Questionnaire: 2015–2016 Profile of Participants," Association of Theological Schools, table 19, http://www.ats.edu/uploads/resources/student-data/documents/total-school-profiles/esq-total-school-profile-2015-2016.pdf. Reasons for preferring geographic proximity may include a lack of residential housing at some seminaries or a student's inability to move because of family, job, or financial costs.

are known for providing a welcoming environment for those seeking a certain type of education. Few seminaries, however, have brought women seminarians to the forefront of the entire seminary ethos. For example, courses in feminist theology seem to have been more a result of the particular faculty hired than an intentional institutional shift. This is curious upon reflection, since some seminary student bodies are at least half female.

Recent Trends

One recent development has been the *retooling of denominational seminaries.* The pool of mainline denominational students has shrunk. The decline in membership of the mainline churches is a familiar story, resulting in a smaller pool of students to attend their denominational seminaries. For example, the PC(USA) lost 22.7 percent of its members from 1997 to 2011.[9] PTS until the early 2000s was 50 percent Presbyterian, but in 2015 it was only 32 percent Presbyterian. A decrease in the percentage of PC(USA) students has been experienced by other Presbyterian seminaries as well. According to a 2010 survey of PC(USA) candidates for ministry, only 58 percent were attending a PC(USA) seminary.[10] Based on anecdotal evidence, the large percentage of Presbyterian candidates attending non-Presbyterian seminaries is due to financial considerations and geographic proximity, particularly for second-career students.

Some persons are raising the question whether, in the face of shrinking resources, some seminaries should merge with their sister denominational seminaries. Do we wait for natural attrition, or do we have a proactive plan to consolidate them? Several seminaries are finding creative ways to diversify their pool of students and offerings. For example, Lutheran Seminary in Philadelphia and Gettysburg Seminary are in the process of becoming "one school with two campuses and multiple points of access."[11]

Another recent trend has been the *decentralization* of theological seminaries. This has two aspects: geographic decentralization and distance online courses. Some schools have established satellite locations to attract nearby students: for example, Fuller Theological Seminary, Union Presbyterian Seminary, Reformed Theological Seminary, and Gordon-Conwell Theological

9. "2010–11 Board of Pensions Demographic Study," Presbyterian Church (U.S.A.), 4, https://www.pensions.org/AvailableResources/BookletsandPublications /Documents/DemographicStudy_2010-2011.pdf.

10. Ibid., 44. The 2002 "Assistance Survey" referenced in Figure 38 references all active ordained PC(USA) clergy, not just candidates.

11. "Pennsylvania Lutheran Seminaries Declare Intent to Form 'New School of Theology,'" Evangelical Lutheran Church in America, January 19, 2016, https://www .elca.org/News-and-Events/7810.

Seminary. Decentralization also plays a role when students commute from increasingly greater distances, so that in-class hours are often consolidated into once-a-week, or even less frequent, meeting times. Online courses are one of the most important trends, as seminaries offer more and more online courses and even degrees. This may often lead to the use of rented rather than permanent buildings, and someday it may lead to virtual-reality seminaries.

Finances

Currently many theological seminaries are facing a financial crisis. There are two sides of the crisis: increased costs and reduced income.

Increased Costs

Numerous factors are leading to increase in seminary budgets:

- Increased regulation typical of all higher education, which results in more complex administrative structures.
- Higher salaries for administrators with specialized expertise.
- Rising costs of physical plants. This is the case both for older buildings, which are costly to maintain, or more expensive residential housing, student centers, refectories, and so forth.
- Rising costs of fringe benefits for faculty, staff, and students, especially health insurance premiums.
- Many new support programs for students, such as counseling, computer services, and academic support.
- Increased need to offer financial aid to students, as they carry large college debt into seminary and do not have significant projected future income. The 2016 average college student debt load was $37,172.[12] In addition to the college debt, a seminarian also acquires seminary debt. About half of all 2015 MDiv graduates reported over $10,000 of seminary-acquired debt, and about half of those had over $40,000 of seminary debt.[13] Some examples of denominational data are also available. The average United Methodist MDiv student debt in 2015 was $35,761, plus an average college debt of $13,542, totaling $49,303. (For perspective, the median entry-level pastor's salary plus housing in 2015 was $49,742.)[14] A small study of 259 students by the Evangelical Lutheran Church in America

---

12. "A Look at the Shocking Student Loan Debt Statistics for 2016," Student Loan Hero, https://studentloanhero.com/student-loan-debt-statistics-2016/#.

13. Daniel Aleshire and Stephen Graham, "State of the Industry: ATS Webinar 2015," PowerPoint slide #26.

14. "Average Debt for a United Methodist M.Div. Graduate Reaches $49,303," United Methodist Church, http://www.gbhem.org/article/average-debt-united -methodist-mdiv-graduate-reaches-49303.

showed an average seminary debt of $32,677 in 2013.[15] And in a 2010 survey of 1,168 Presbyterian candidates for ministry, 47 percent reported student debt from seminary.[16]

These increasing expenses have resulted in major increases to the institutions to educate each student. The cost to ATS seminaries has risen from a 1980 average of $5,300 per full-time equivalent student (2015 equivalent $15,245 after inflation[17]) to $26,000 per FTE student in 2015.[18] This is a 70 percent increase beyond the expected increase due to inflation.

Reduced Income

At the same time that costs are increasing, sources of income are declining:

- Denominations that founded seminaries have drastically reduced their support or give nothing at all (individual church members, however, still support seminaries by pledges, wills, and bequests). For Presbyterian seminaries, the support had already dropped to less than 5 percent of the schools' budgets by 1990.[19]
- Shrinking student bodies, with concomitant reduced tuition income.
- Excessive drawdown on endowments for operating expenses, which reduces future income.

It should be noted, however, that the cost charged to a seminarian (annual tuition and fees) is still quite modest compared to other professional schools. The 2015–2016 average annual tuition and fees for a U.S. MDiv degree was

15. Adam DeHorek, "Stewards of Abundance: Extent, Causes, and Consequences of Seminarian Debt and Efforts to Reduce It," Evangelical Lutheran Church in America, 7, http://www.ats.edu/uploads/resources/current-initiatives/economic-challenges -facing-future-ministers/financial-issues-research/elca-stewards-of-abundance-final -report.pdf.

16. "2010–11 Board of Pensions Demographic Study," Presbyterian Church (U.S.A.), 41.

17. Calculated according to the CPI (Consumer Price Index) inflation calculator provided by the U.S. Department of Labor, http://www.bls.gov/data/inflation _calculator.htm.

18. In 1980 there were 197 schools educating 49,611 students and spending $264 million. This means that they spent $5,300 per student. In 2015 there were 270 schools educating 72,116 students and spending $1.87 billion. This means that they spent $26,000 per student. "Fact Book on Theological Education 1980–81," Association of Theological Schools; "2015–2016 Annual Data Tables," Association of Theological Schools.

19. Joseph P. O'Neill, "Denominational Funding of Protestant Theological Education (1994)," Auburn Center Background Report, No. 1, p. 1.

$15,356,[20] compared to $35,272 for law school (2013)[21] and $46,911 for medical school (2015–16).[22]

In discussing this difficult economic situation, we are not suggesting that the increased costs, including discretionary expenditures, are unnecessary or ill advised. Yet increased costs and shrinking dollars require a reallocation of resources, which may result in smaller faculties and support staff, selling of buildings and land, fewer or smaller scholarships, and in some cases, seminaries completely closing. There are so many fixed costs of buildings and tenured faculty that reducing expenditures is a challenge. ATS reports that "more than 50 percent of freestanding ATS schools have expenses that exceed their income."[23] While solutions for the economic challenges facing theological schools are not within the purview of this book, any recommended changes in theological education need to take into account these economic realities.

Student Body

Probably the most seismic change in seminaries concerns the student body. Twenty-first-century seminarians are vastly different from the all-white male cohorts who lived at seminaries in the nineteenth and up to the mid-twentieth century; the shift has been gradual, but it has accelerated in the last several decades. It is represented by the increased number of women, second-career students, persons of color, and the small but new group of the "nones." It is reflective of the huge demographic shifts in the United States, especially the increase in the Hispanic population, which historically had a low membership in mainline Protestant denominations. This increased diversity has encouraged seminaries to examine the constituency of their faculty, curriculum, physical plant, and other aspects of theological education.

In terms of women students, there were, of course, the pioneer women,

---

20. "2015–2016 Annual Data Tables," Association of Theological Schools, table 4.1. This figure is a weighted average for programs of all sizes in ATS schools in the United States.

21. "Data from the 2013 Annual Questionnaire: ABA Approved Law School Tuition History Data," http://www.americanbar.org/content/dam/aba/administrative/legal_education_and_admissions_to_the_bar/statistics/lawschool_tuition_averages_by_year_public_private.xls. This figure is a weighted average for various categories of schools. These data are the most recent available.

22. "Tuition and Student Fees Report," Association of American Medical Colleges, table 1, https://services.aamc.org/tsfreports/report_median.cfm?year_of_study=2016. This figure is a weighted average (not including health insurance).

23. "2015 Annual Report," Association of Theological Schools, 3, http://www.ats.edu/uploads/resources/publications-presentations/documents/2015-annual-report%20FINAL.pdf.

such as the first woman theological student Antoinette Brown, who finished her Oberlin College theology studies in 1850 but was not formally granted a degree until decades later, when she received honorary MA and DD degrees.[24] (See appendix A for other milestones of American women in ministerial leadership.) It should be noted that the lead denomination historically to educate female seminarians was the Unitarian/Universalists, who today have 60 percent female clergy.[25]

As the ordination of female clergy became a reality in the old mainline denominations and later in other churches, beginning in the 1980s–1990s women poured into the seminaries in significant numbers. This phenomenon was concurrent with the rise of feminist, womanist, and *mujerista* liberation movements. Many of these women were ready to challenge the church in order to claim their rightful place among the clergy. They encountered huge resistance and prejudice, however, against their serving as local church clergy. There were few women mentors or role models for them to follow. Some men did step forward to remove the barriers to women's assuming clergy leadership in local churches, as attested in the stories in this book.

The next new group was students of color, who entered predominantly Anglo seminaries and brought an important new perspective as well as demands not only for curricular changes but also for transformation of the whole seminary ethos.[26] These institutions, to a large extent, were not aware of the white privilege under which they had operated. The sense that they were prejudiced came as shock to many of them, and there was a resistance to change, a resistance that is still not fully overcome. As pointed out in the previous chapter, unlike white women who had scarcely been in seminaries or pulpits, the African American community had a long tradition of distinguished, powerful women preachers (albeit not typically ordained), educated either by their churches or at historic black seminaries. Multicultural offices, antiracism initiatives, and other programs are springing up everywhere to encourage the celebration of the gift of racial ethnic diversity.

---

24. "Antoinette Brown Blackwell," *Dictionary of Unitarian and Universalist Biography*, http://uudb.org/articles/antoinettebrownblackwell.html.

25. "State of the Ministry," Unitarian Universalist Association, May 18, 2016, 14, http://c.ymcdn.com/sites/www.uuma.org/resource/resmgr/Docs/StateofMinFinal.pdf.

26. Ibid., 6. White enrollment declined about 17 percent from 2005 to 2011, but African American enrollment increased by 7 percent during that same period, and Hispanic enrollment increased by a dramatic 26 percent. Despite continuing growth, overall Hispanic enrollment remains relatively small. Hispanic enrollment in U.S. ATS member schools in 2011 was 5.3 percent of total enrollment (compared to 60.5 percent white); by 2015 Hispanic enrollment had risen to 6.5 percent (compared to a decrease to 56.5 percent for whites). "2015–2016 Annual Data Tables," Association of Theological Schools, table 2.12-B.

There has been a significant change in the age range of seminarians: while the majority of seminarians in the 1960s had just graduated from college, the average age increased to about thirty-five at the turn of the twenty-first century. Since 2003, the cohort in the 30–49 age range has been decreasing, and in 2011 the 20–29 and 50-plus cohorts were the fastest growing groups.[27] In 2015 28 percent of women enrolled in MDiv programs at ATS schools were age fifty or older.[28]

Financial factors will continue to influence who comes to seminary. Here we refer not only to the cost of seminary education but also to the shrinking number of positions available to seminary graduates. For example, in the PC(USA) in June 2016, 1,785 persons were seeking positions, while only 528 church-related positions were advertised (although many of the seekers were presumably currently in positions).[29]

Faculty

Beginning with the liberation movements in the 1960s, there has been more demand from students to have a larger role in the selection of faculty, and even staff, in institutions of higher learning. Seminaries have not been immune from this demand. In our research of PTS alumnae, several commented on the importance of faculty in creating a welcoming learning environment for all students. There is need for more women faculty, especially women of color.

As in higher education generally, so also in seminaries as a whole, the increase in female faculty has not always kept pace with the increase of women students. In 2015 24 percent of full-time faculty at all ATS member schools were women.[30] As noted in chapter 9, the total enrollment of female students in all degree programs in all ATS schools was 33.4 percent in that same year. At PTS in 2016, 42 percent of the students were women, and 32 percent of the faculty were women.

Of course, individual schools vary widely in the number and percentage of female faculty. Overall, the pool of women applicants for faculty positions

27. Barbara G. Wheeler, Anthony T. Ruger, and Sharon L. Miller, "Theological Student Enrollment: A Special Report from the Auburn Center for the Study of Theological Education," August 2013, 7, http://auburnseminary.org/wp-content /uploads/2016/05/Theological-Student-Enrollment-Final.pdf.

28. "2015–2016 Annual Data Tables," Association of Theological Schools, table 2.14-A.

29. "Applicants and Positions Report," Presbyterian Church (U.S.A.), https://clc .pcusa.org/reports/ApplicantsAndPositions.aspx?ReturnUrl=%2fadmin%2fLogin.aspx.

30. "2015–2016 Annual Data Tables," Association of Theological Schools, table 3.1-A.

remains proportionately smaller. And yet, since many women with appropriate credentials do not find or retain positions, faculty search committees must continue to face the question of their definitions of "qualified." There have been strides in recent years toward a more diverse faculty, but there remains a long way to go. What theological foundation of justice is operative in the effort to move toward inclusion? Do schools operate from a philosophy of compensatory justice, where faculty are recruited to compensate for the prejudice and exclusion of the past? Or do they instead look to the Rawlsian theory of justice as fairness, where everyone has equal opportunity based on skills, experience, and education that fit the criteria for a highly specialized need in the faculty? Of course, one can define "highly specialized need" not solely by subject expertise but also by being part of an underrepresented population in a seminary department or faculty as a whole.

We return to the economic realities facing seminaries vis-à-vis the hiring of new faculty. As student bodies shrink, so do the faculties, leading to intense competition among applicants for faculty positions. Not all seminaries have the luxury of specialized faculty; for example, in practical theology the areas of Christian formation, homiletics, speech, pastoral theology, and congregational ministry may be covered by only two or three faculty members rather than one for each area. This means that diversity is measured partly by the ability to teach in several subject areas. In light of financial constraints, many seminaries are hiring increasing numbers of adjunct faculty for specialized courses to meet students' interests and needs.

Curriculum

Currently most of the discussion concerning curriculum mirrors the focus on goals, outcomes, and skill sets at university and professional schools. Accrediting bodies for seminaries now look for measurable-outcomes language in curricula at all levels, from overall curriculum to individual courses. We are not criticizing this shift, but too much focus on curriculum can limit a coherent philosophy of theological education.

Planning the Curriculum

Historically, the mission of a seminary has been set by the board of trustees, the president, and the faculty. The curriculum then flows from the mission of the institution and the kind of seminary it purposes to be. Given this structure for implementing change, which often moves at a glacial pace, what roles are students taking in planning or influencing courses offered at a seminary? This question is especially relevant if curricular changes are one answer to our question of how women's experiences should reshape theological education.

Certainly student advocacy in some schools has encouraged curricular changes related to cultural diversity and faith in the public square. Students may also request individual faculty members to offer new courses, or they may shape curricula through participating in developing position descriptions for new faculty, which will influence the types of courses that will be available. In some cases professors open the planning of the course to students once they are enrolled in the course: a fully codesigned course. We note that women have often led the way in participating in course changes and new curricular directions.

Meeting Diverse Curricular Needs

A key question concerning curriculum is how we meet the needs of certain categories of students without undercutting the importance of an integrated curriculum. Several approaches through the years have attempted to address this question:

- Different tracks but a core curriculum that is required of everyone. Students may form cohorts with entrepreneurial tracks such as youth ministry or urban ministry.
- Language-specific degrees—for instance, for some years New York Theological Seminary has offered the MDiv degree in English, Korean, and Spanish; most faculty are bilingual in English and one of the other languages.
- More freedom in electives with fewer required courses and a more flexible curriculum.
- Courses in specialized areas such as gender, multicultural, and/or racial ethnic concerns within multiple subject areas of the curriculum. While such courses do address the needs/interests of particular students, such topics should ideally be incorporated as well into all core/required courses so that all students have some exposure to them.
- Certificates in specialized areas (e.g., youth ministry, interim pastorates), which can be done concurrently or upon completion of the MDiv.[31]

Practical Ministerial Skills and Theological Foundations

Several studies cite students' desire for more "practical" courses within the MDiv curriculum. For example, Barbara Finlay writes, "For a substantial group of students, seminary education seems 'too academic,' and they would prefer more practical experience in actual ministry."[32] In our Survey, this tension between "practical" and other courses is reflected in participants'

31. Enrollment in "professional" MA programs, which are not under consideration in this discussion, increased from 14 percent of students in 1992 to 20 percent in 2011. Barbara G. Wheeler and Anthony T. Ruger, "Sobering Figures Point to Overall Enrollment Decline," *In Trust*, Spring 2013, 7.

32. Finlay, *Facing the Stained Glass Ceiling*, 22, 120.

answers about theological education. The respondents spoke highly of the rigorous academics at PTS, especially in biblical studies, history, and theology, which gave them a firm foundation for ministry. The practical theology courses offered were ranked highly, as were field education placements and clinical pastoral education. One respondent captured the sentiment of many: "Although there are many things they can't teach you in seminary, I was blessed to study with professors who had a love of pastoral ministry and their specific area of expertise. I also learned where to find the information I needed once I was in a congregation."

On the other hand, Survey respondents expressed a need for more classes in administration, management, finances, pastoral care, conflict management, and leadership or dealing with sexism; based on our experience, these areas are of equal interest to men. It seems as if PTS students have long raised the issue of needing more "nuts and bolts" courses in seminary. For example, one respondent wrote, "Academically, great preparation. Not so great on how to take care of myself, where to find support, what to do in relation to church politics, how to handle conflict, and practical things like working with funeral directors, what to do in the case of a problem with a staff member who is also a church member, what to do when volunteers fail to show up and you're left holding the bag." While recognizing the importance of foundational courses, PTS students have desired more applied courses in the practice of ministry. However, this view most often emerges retrospectively when they are thrust into the parish and do not know how to create a budget, work with conflicted churches, or lead a local church governing council effectively.

Seminaries employ various strategies as they seek to balance the needs for a solid theological foundation and for practical courses on the skills of ministry. In the past, some seminaries addressed this challenge by requiring an additional yearlong internship as part of the MDiv degree. It seems that this requirement has generally been eliminated as a degree requirement, presumably because of logistical and cost concerns for students, especially those with families. Today this need is often addressed by faculty who integrate the practical work of ministry into courses on Bible, church history, or theology, or by the addition of required practical theology courses.

Some denominations still maintain the internship year as an ordination requirement. In the Evangelical Lutheran Church in America, for example, a full-year internship remains a requirement for ordination (although the internship is not an MDiv graduation requirement in Lutheran seminaries).[33]

---

33. "Evangelical Lutheran Church in America Candidacy Manual," Evangelical Lutheran Church in America, 23, http://download.elca.org/ELCA%20Resource%20Repository/Candidacy_Manual_2012.pdf.

The internship is normally the third year of a four-year seminary experience. As of 2016, the ELCA is engaging in a process of review that may allow more flexibility (for example, taking some online classes while on internship or taking summer courses) in order to shorten the program to three years.[34]

Recent Trends

One recent development has been a movement to offer *dual degrees.* Historically, dual-degree programs were for different forms of ordained ministry; now, bivocational ministry is the byword. Beginning about two or more decades ago, dual-degree programs were being added to some seminary curricula (for instance, MDiv/MSW, MDiv/MBA, MDiv/MA [in counseling or Christian education]) as one way to address the shifting needs of clergy to work in new, nonparish settings such as nonprofit organizations. Is this a wave of the future for seminaries? Some schools offer an internal dual degree, such as PTS's four-year MDiv/MA in Christian education. Examples of schools offering dual degrees involving other institutions include PTS (MDiv/MSW Rutgers) and Union Theological Seminary in New York (MDiv/MSSW Columbia University). Seattle Pacific University offers a dual MDiv/MBA degree through its seminary and its own School of Business and Economics.

For dual degrees involving other institutions, several factors affect the feasibility of such offerings: the proximity to colleges and universities that offer courses to make such joint degrees possible; job placement statistics of dual-degree graduates; and tuition and other costs to the students. Programs that are not internal to a school may require extensive administrative time from seminary staff, including ongoing negotiations with the partner school, vetting prospective candidates, and related paperwork; the administrative overhead may sometimes be disproportionate to the number of students enrolled for the dual degree. At PTS, the joint MSW/MDiv program was started around 1980. The number of students enrolled per year has fluctuated from one to nine, with a spike to fourteen applicants in 2016.[35]

Feasibility questions aside, the central question is the desirability of such dual-degree programs. Dual-degree programs (and related certificate programs) may provide graduates with more options for bivocational ministries. Such programs also offer to all students, but especially to many women with families, qualification for positions that, unlike local parish settings, offer set work schedules and/or flexible hours.

A second curricular trend is the increase in *certificate programs.* Recently

---

34. Dennis T. Olson (PTS Professor), in discussion with the authors, May 20, 2016.

35. This information was provided by the PTS registrar in May 2016.

many seminaries have begun offering multiple specialty focus MA and certificate programs. Certifications are offered in clinical pastoral education, marriage and family counseling, lay ministry, youth ministry, and the like. The focus of this chapter is on the MDiv degree, so we do not discuss the proliferation of one- and two-year MA degrees that are independent of the MDiv option. It is noteworthy, however, that specialty "certificates" and "concentrations" are being incorporated as an option within some MDiv programs, functioning somewhat analogously to a "major" in undergraduate degrees. PTS, for example, offers certificates in black church studies and in theology, women, and gender. Luther Seminary offers various concentrations, including congregational mission and leadership; children, youth, and family ministry; and parish nursing. In addition, there are some MA programs that emerged out of clinical pastoral education work and that offer licensure as a professional counselor. An emerging question is whether seminaries should expand their curricula, for instance, by offering certificate programs for ruling elders commissioned as pastors or lay pastors (some presbyteries now offer this training).

A third development reflects a new mode of delivering the curriculum: *online degrees*. The decentralization of education with nonresidential students may be the most dramatic institutional shift in theological education. In fact, PTS may be one of only a limited number of seminaries that remain predominantly residential (defined as students living in school-owned housing). In 2015 only 25 percent of seminary students in ATS schools lived on or adjacent to campus; 50 percent were local commuters, and 25 percent were long-distance commuters.[36] The general desire of students to complete their seminary education close to home suggests that online programs that can be done from home will continue to be attractive to students. It thus seems likely that more online degree programs may lead to further reductions of totally residential and local commuter seminaries.[37]

Online seminary courses are a relatively new phenomenon, with some seminaries shifting to them for predominantly economic reasons. As these courses develop, seminaries have been considering how the new delivery formats may require changes in course content and style of teaching. Many seminaries offer some online classes; a few now offer totally online degrees. As of 2016, 139 ATS member schools (slightly over 50 percent of all schools) were

36. "2015 Annual Report," Association of Theological Schools, 12.

37. According to the ATS survey cited in note 8, which represents 174 schools and 6,196 entering students in 2015, when asked about the importance of factors determining their decision on which school to attend, "close to home/work" showed an average of 2.7, which represents a response close to "somewhat important." (See "Entering Student Questionnaire: 2015–2016 Profile of Participants," table 19.)

approved to offer "comprehensive distance education" programs consisting of six or more online classes,[38] and eighteen member schools were approved to offer fully online MDiv degrees.[39]

For some students, an online degree program may make seminary education more accessible and affordable. Does this facilitate more participation of second-career women and provide flexibility for women with small children? There are obviously pedagogical as well as practical arguments to support the online model; for instance, some students learn better when they can think through a question and post an asynchronous online response rather than having to jump into a classroom live conversation. But there are potential losses with the absence of a more traditional on-campus structure, and the effectiveness of online MDiv programs remains under review. ATS is currently in the midst of a major four-year (2015–2018) Educational Models and Practices Project, designed to review these questions with anticipation of revising the standards for the MDiv degree in light of the findings.[40]

Seminary as Christian Community

One important component of a seminary is the community of students, faculty, and staff who become a support network and spiritual companions, as well as future mentors. For this reason, ATS has traditionally required at least one year of on-campus experience in its basic MDiv program unless residency exceptions are granted.[41] As we will suggest later, developing not just facts and academic knowledge but also insight, discernment, and wisdom requires very different strategies in a predominantly online or part-time commuter learning environment. While maintaining our focus on the MDiv context in a predominantly Christian student body, we recognize that seminaries have differing expectations and requirements for the faith traditions of their faculty members and admitted students. Some Christian seminaries have faculty and students only of the Christian tradition while others have a more religiously diverse population.

The seminary educational experience can be challenging. Many students

38. "Schools Offering Six or More Courses Online," Association of Theological Schools, http://www.ats.edu/member-schools/member-school-distance-education.

39. "Approved Exceptions and Experiments," Association of Theological Schools, http://www.ats.edu/member-schools/approved-exceptions-and-experiments.

40. "Explore, Assess, Affirm: The ATS Educational Models and Practices Project," Association of Theological Schools, http://www.ats.edu/uploads/resources/current-initiatives/educational-models/publications-and-presentations/ats-educational-models-brochure.pdf.

41. "Degree Program Standards," Association of Theological Schools, A.3.1.3, http://www.ats.edu/uploads/accrediting/documents/degree-program-standards.pdf.

feel overwhelmed while pursuing rigorous academic degrees and need the support of other students. Students generally evaluate their experience of the seminary community as very positive, wonderful, and caring. Community is particularly important in supporting students through the faith challenges, deconstructionism, and vocational discernment that are part of the seminary experience. For decades, students at PTS have cited the most important and positive part of their theological education as living in a Christian community. Statements from our story contributors in the previous chapters (e.g., Blanchard, Buckner, Kim) illustrate this emphasis. Likewise, in their Survey responses PTS alumnae noted the importance of fellow students to their theological experience. Respondents made comments such as "developing friendships and a collegiality among a diverse student body continues to energize and offer feedback even today."

As professors at PTS, we certainly observed that course discussion sections and informal small groups built lifelong friendships as students bonded over "the Bible boot camp" or the General Ministries course or other required courses, which sometimes turned upside-down their previous theological and biblical beliefs. A strong majority of our Survey respondents wrote about how their residential seminary experience enhanced their faith journeys. "Witnessing the passion, the anguish, the joy of my sisters and brothers . . . changed my perspective entirely," said one respondent. Many said this occurred within the classroom or in relationships with faculty. Others were encouraged by their peers outside of the classroom. "The best moments of seminary were . . . in the quad, over dining tables, in the dorms and apartments. It is there where we hashed out our faiths," one respondent wrote. A few spoke directly about their positive relationships with international students, and some highlighted chapel and other spiritual practices on campus.[42] In addition, the residential campus with faculty living in proximity provided friendships between faculty and students that continued for decades after graduation.

A residential campus, however, is not without its challenges, as living in such close proximity can be a two-edged sword. Expectations are high among many students that they are joining some ideal Christian community in which all their spiritual and emotional needs will be met. Some students anticipate a perfect covenantal or intentional community. Students may come with an idealized view of Dietrich Bonhoeffer's life together as reflected in his call to Christian community, but they forget his warning: "Those who love their dream of a Christian community more than they love the Christian community itself become destroyers of that Christian community even though their

---

42. The Survey, questions 36–39.

personal intentions may be ever so honest, earnest, and sacrificial."[43] They may come with expectations of life on a transcendent plane, based on conversion experiences at church camps or having lived in intentional communities. Not unlike the disciples at the Mount of Transfiguration, they want to capture permanently their mountaintop moment. Then they discover that seminary is not a perfect paradise of Christian harmony. Some seminarians are caught up in fierce competition for good grades comparable to the competition in law or medical schools; some experience theological divides and separations based on gender, racial ethnic identity, nationality, and other differences. In addition, students who are part of any minority in a seminary community may experience being marginalized or treated like the "other."

Some groups of students have been particularly marginalized in seminaries, or perhaps they are present but with no voice. For example, the gay/transgender community has often been made invisible. Potential applicants with disabilities have often been daunted by attitudinal and architectural barriers in theological institutions. In fact, their numbers are so few in some seminaries that they have no support or student group. Certainly we need a sign that reads, "That all may enter." Their voices for inclusion are just beginning to be heard and to change the environment of seminaries. These changes in the student body have created some points of solidarity among those groups who have been made to feel like the "other." This reality is reflected in the fact, for example, that PTS joint events are sponsored by the Women's Center, the Association of Black Seminarians, and the LBGTQ campus organization.

As our Survey participants indicated, there is also the reality that a residential community in some cases inhibited or challenged their faith journeys. This may have occurred in the classroom, or because of a cultural disconnect between faith and actions in the seminary community, or because of a lack of spiritual support on campus. Some women also recounted their encounters with sexism and racism at PTS as a challenge or hindrance to their faith. The predominance of male perspectives at seminary was also mentioned as impacting their faith. Finally, a few respondents were simply neutral about how seminary affected their faith journey.

Is a residential campus necessary for community, or can community be generated in other creative ways? In our experience, support networks have traditionally been developed among students through their classes, residences, and other programs and events at the school. Students often meet for coffee or meals after class, or attend the same church, or serve on faculty and student committees that provide interaction that can foster networks and friendships.

---

43. Dietrich Bonhoeffer, *Life Together: Prayerbook of the Bible*, vol. 5 of *Dietrich Bonhoeffer Works* (Minneapolis: Fortress Press, 1996), 36.

Students may also form Bible study or support groups among themselves. For many students, however, what constitutes a community has dramatically changed with the advent of social media. Facebook friending, texting, and twittering mean instant contact and sharing of ideas and experiences. In fact, even when students are in physical proximity with one another, social media are sometimes the preferred means of communication. These new online networks may more and more replace face-to-face groups for some purposes.

How can students' spiritual growth, emotional resiliency, and preparation for leadership (and maturity in dealing with people generally) be nurtured for that 25 percent of seminarians who are currently long-distance learners, as well as for those part-time students who commute to campus only for courses offered in block scheduling? Anecdotal evidence suggests that many students do form strong relationships via technology with classmates whom they have met only online, and many programs require at least brief intensive periods when a cohort of students meets in person to set such relationships in motion. Students may also have significant support from home congregations where they are living and working, and individual professors may choose to make themselves available for extensive individual "office hours" in distance formats. Can such a mix of options yield results comparable to that of a local residential seminary community? We look forward to the results of the ATS study that is considering these questions.

A VISION FOR THEOLOGICAL EDUCATION
FOR THE WHOLE PERSON

Having examined briefly the current picture of seminaries, we now turn our attention to a new vision for theological education that might reshape it for the twenty-first century. We need a coherent philosophy of theological education, not simply annexing courses to the curriculum but rather examining its raison d'être, educating for a variety of vocations to serve in Christ's name. Our thesis is that seminaries need to educate the whole person—body, mind, and spirit—in the context of a community. Since health from the Judeo-Christian perspective involves all these aspects, education should include them in order to prepare effective pastors, educators, and specialized ministers, and to develop leaders ready for new and changing ministries. What we have learned about women's experience in ministry underscores the importance of broadening of the task of theological education to include the cultivation of knowledge, wisdom, virtue, spirituality, and healthy living. This redefining of theological education can have positive implications for men as well as for women, for the church, and for those called to all kinds of ministry.

There is no doubt that the ethos of a seminary has the power to shape the values, lifestyles, and theology of many of its students. The seminary should foster a context for human flourishing. The ethnographic study by Jackson W. Carroll et al. of two seminaries, one evangelical and one mainline, certainly lends support to this perspective. A seminary's culture comprises its "shared symbolic forms, worldviews and beliefs, ritual practices, ceremonies, art and architecture, language, and patterns of everyday interaction."[44] The authors state that "most students' views, values and, it appears, habits are reshaped by the ideas and behaviors the school promotes, but students do not entirely surrender the commitments, opinions, and tastes that they came with. Their goals, outlook, language, and manners when they leave are a melding—often painfully forged in intense engagements with each other and with those who represent the school—of what they brought with them and what the school has insistently set before them."[45]

This and other studies certainly illustrate the importance of the type of community, curriculum, and values that we strive for in theological education. Each one of the components of theological education could be shaped by this whole-person theological education perspective. Hence, the task of theological education is much broader than historically conceived. It is ironic that many seminaries provide future ministers with knowledge of church history, Bible, theology, Christian education, and preaching, but leave them largely on their own to develop a moral, spiritual, and healthy physical and mental life. Given the time pressure of academics, is it possible to give attention to these cocurricular aspects? We believe that it is not only possible but necessary.

Heretofore the concern for a more integrated understanding of theological education stemmed from the desire to equip seminarians for the stresses of the pastorate. Now a bigger challenge may be for our graduates to find a church position or other avenues of ministry. We need to be thinking bivocationally and educating for resilience and flexibility in the face of uncertainty and unemployment, equipping our graduates for these new realities.

Historically, seminaries have treated their students as disembodied heads, with a somewhat gnostic view of the body. The life of the mind was not seen to include the health of the mind, and it is only in recent years that seminaries have offered organized mental health services such as counseling centers. When seminaries were founded, piety and learning were linked and a student's

---

44. Jackson W. Carroll, Barbara G. Wheeler, Daniel O. Aleshire, and Penny Long Marler, *Being There: Culture and Formation in Two Theological Schools* (New York: Oxford University Press, 1997), 5.
45. Ibid., 222.

spiritual life was considered important. Yet during the 1960s through the 1980s this link, especially in many Protestant seminaries, was lost, and students were left on their own to develop a devotional life and spiritual practices. Clergy ethics and the moral life were assumed rather than integrated into the learning environment. (Certainly there were many exceptions, but we are describing general trends in theological education.) Beginning in the 1990s, there was a turn from this single-minded focus on disembodied learning, though there have always been seminaries interested in a more wholistic approach. Programs in spiritual formation appeared in Protestant seminaries; the vision of education for the whole person presented here expands upon this trend.

Theological education should include the fostering of wholistic healthy lifestyles that can be carried into future ministry. If seminaries encourage physical fitness, mental acuity, spiritual depth, and high moral standards for seminarians, it may help to prevent clergy burnout, loss of vocational focus, and poor physical health. The components of this whole-person vision are as follows: growing in the intellectual life; pursuing physical, emotional, and mental health; deepening the spiritual life; and cultivating the moral life in community.

Growing in the Intellectual Life

The life of the mind, rightly so, has dominated theological education. Yet it has often consisted of an accumulation of facts rather than an understanding of the Christian faith and the wisdom of which Proverbs speaks (Prov 1–4). The book of Proverbs reminds us that our pursuit should be for God's wisdom, not our own. Proverbs 3 especially highlights pursuing God's wisdom—the Truth of Life, the goal of all learning. When we realize the limits of our own insights, then we turn to God for wisdom. James H. Charlesworth and Michael A. Daise provide an exposition of how we understand God's wisdom, both in the Jewish Wisdom literature and in its flowering as *logos* in the Gospel of John. Personified by the feminine in both the Hebrew and Christian Scriptures and the Jewish Wisdom Scriptures, Wisdom "is both 'a reflection of eternal light' and 'a spotless mirror of the working of God.' She is nothing less than 'an image of his goodness.' She passes into human souls 'and makes them friends of God (Wisdom of Solomon 7:25–27).'"[46] Wisdom cannot be synthesized because it is defined by life experience; it does not command but persuades. Wisdom, like the *logos*, existed before the creation of life and of

---

46. James H. Charlesworth and Michael A. Daise, *Light in a Spotless Mirror: Reflections on Wisdom Traditions in Judaism and Early Christianity* (Harrisburg, PA: Trinity Press International, 2003), 2.

earthly and interstellar space. Both Jesus and Wisdom symbolize light and mirror (John 8:12: "'I am the light of the world'"). Lady Wisdom is sent into the world as is Jesus, from above.[47]

Based on the pursuit of wisdom, theological education is not just gathering information but also invites the integration of knowledge, which leads to wisdom. In our discussion of curriculum we focused on the relationship of ministry skills and foundational material for a well-rounded theological education. Here we make the slightly different point that insight and integration are at least as important as the command of facts. An important step may be to reduce departmental silos, in addition to fostering interdisciplinary conversation.

Dwayne Huebner writes,

> Education happens because human beings participate in the transcendent. Education—the "going beyond" of what we are at any moment—indicates that we are in, but not of, the world. Participation in the transcendent is not recognized because adult human beings ground educational ends in human standards and expectations. Augustine's vision "Lord, you have made us for yourself, and our hearts are restless until they find their rest in you" is dusted over and dirtied by images of human progress and achievement. But the dust is blown away by the winds of human failure and the dirt is washed away by the tears of pain—whether of sickness, separation, or death.[48]

How the curriculum enriches the intellectual life is key, but it also must create a thirst for knowledge, a desire to unmask the false gods of society, such as the worship of grades rather than learning. Another aspect of the intellectual life is the knowledge that we and the world belong to God. Dorothy Bass and Craig Dykstra point out that Christian practices take us into new ways of being and knowing, with God directing this enterprise.[49] This marriage of piety and learning, which John Calvin noted long ago, should mark seminaries.

The type of learning offered in seminaries is important. Theology as praxis fosters long-term effectiveness for the practice of ministry. This focus not only brings theology to the context, but theology also arises from the practice of ministry; the dialogical relationship between the two is where real learning takes place. In many seminaries the field education programs provide

---

47. Ibid., 92–96.

48. Quoted from Raymond R. Roberts, "Is Public Education Hopeless?" *The Presbyterian Outlook*, April 26, 1993, 7.

49. Craig Dykstra and Dorothy Bass, "A Theological Understanding of Christian Practices," in *Practicing Theology*, ed. Miroslav Volf and Dorothy C. Bass (Grand Rapids: Eerdmans, 2002), 13–32.

that intersection, modeling theology as praxis. The case study approach also enhances learning, as medical, business, and law schools have long recognized. A number of seminary professors use real church or hospital cases to help students apply their theoretical learning to practical situations. In our experience, women students are particularly drawn to this approach. Our claim is not that all women prefer such an approach, but that, generally speaking, this may be more the case. As we educate students, we need to help them integrate the theoretical and practical to understand how God is at work in the world.

Furthermore, the way we learn and what we consider important to learn are central. Examples include feminist approaches to biblical courses, which forefront the hidden women of Scripture and nontraditional interpretations of familiar texts, and homiletics classes where personal stories and experiences are applauded rather than discouraged. Since 78 percent (137 respondents) of PTS women in our survey stated that their ministry style was different because they were women, we should take this situation into account in reshaping theological education; just offering women's courses is not enough. Furthermore, all students, and not just women, should be "conscientized" (i.e., brought to existential awareness) with regard to feminist perspectives on theology, the Bible, and other subjects. Part of the challenge is to educate male students about gender issues and the importance of full inclusion of women in all forms of ministry. However, there needs to be not only conscientization of seminarians and faculty about women's perspectives but also changes in teaching methodologies, course content, and faculty composition.

In the Survey, when asked the question "What changes could be made to theological education to better equip women for ministry?" 50 percent of the responses addressed one or more subjects under the practical theology umbrella. Other changes were mentioned in the free-form survey answers. Some desired to hear from more female and nonwhite perspectives in the classroom; others felt that learning about diversity, multiculturalism, and cross-cultural ministry would be beneficial. Incorporating more courses on spiritual formation was also mentioned. Some said that a degree in law or business would be helpful. These themes are also reflected in the stories in this book.

Regarding this issue of educational changes, a good number of respondents focused on concerns involving women as a minority in ministerial leadership. Mentoring was suggested as a beneficial relational option. Specific models included a cohort or networking system, relationships with working female pastors while in seminary, or more access to female faculty and staff. In addition, a few alluded to a class that could deal with specific issues that female pastors encounter, such as pregnancy, modesty concerns, and singleness. Although a few did not think any changes to theological education were necessary for women specifically, the majority addressed special challenges women face in ministry because of their gender. Thus, as seminarians women need to have opportunities to develop resiliency for these future challenges.

Pursuing Physical, Emotional, and Mental Health

As we turn to consider the role of seminaries in students' physical, emotional, and mental health, it is important to remember that none of us will reach perfect health this side of eternity. In our earthly life, each person has periods of greater and lesser health; the length of these periods and their coming and going varies greatly from one individual to another. Persons with ongoing physical or mental illness often show an amazing amount of courage— enduring difficult treatments or experimental medications in their struggle to live life as fully as possible in spite of limitations imposed by their illness. Especially those with mental illness have to face the stigma that tragically is often connected to their illness. So health is a goal and not a state, a vision that guides us as we journey toward it. From the perspective of Christian theology, all of us are broken, and it is how we face this reality that binds us together; we are only whole as we share in the brokenness of others. Thus, the question here is not about achieving perfect health but rather how seminaries can help to encourage healthier lives now, for the good of future ministers and the church.

In the past we may have assumed that clergy are healthier than the general population in all aspects. However, this is not necessarily the case. They too are subject to the stresses of modern society. Stress, some would say, is a contemporary addiction that touches not only individuals but also society as a whole.[50] The church and seminaries are not immune from this illness. Ann Wilson Schaef has labeled workaholism the designer drug of the church.[51] Seminaries should resist workaholic patterns rather than fostering them. Stress and its effects can have serious implications for seminarians and clergy, their work performance, and their overall physical and emotional health. While some amount of stress is effective for accomplishing tasks, the risk of overwork is high. Stress and workaholism are behavioral addictions and reflect how extensive addictive lifestyles and patterns are in our society.

50. Gerald G. May, *Addiction and Grace: Love and Spirituality in the Healing of Addictions* (New York: HarperOne, 1988).

51. Ann Wilson Schaef, *When Society Becomes an Addict* (New York: HarperOne, 1998).

A growing number of studies show the relationship between stress and weakened immune systems, which can lead to an increased risk for upper respiratory tract infections and autonomic, cardiovascular, and immune-system-related illnesses (though there is not always a direct correlation, as other factors come into play). Many of these studies focus on university and graduate students during exam times and other times of extreme stress. What these studies suggest is that sustained stress can have an impact on our health.[52] Often seminary curricula are so demanding, with few breaks, that students complain of living under constant pressure. The paper chase is as evident in seminary as in medical and law schools, and some students equate any grade less than B+ as a sign that God has not called them into ministry. These stressors, if allowed to continue in seminary, will simply be exacerbated in ministry.

Studies have shown that clergy have been faced with physical, mental, and emotional challenges for decades, and this leads many to leave the ministry. A 1999 study of Presbyterian clergy shows that among the 14 percent who left the ministry between 1990 and 1997, the reasons for leaving were as follows. Negative reasons: conflict with head of staff or supervisor, burned out, health problems, unclear and unrealistic expectations from others, unsupportive congregation, work seemed unimportant, not being paid enough to pay off student loans, and racial discrimination. Other reasons: sense of completion of their call, wanted to spend time with young children, followed their spouse to a new location, needed more time with family, and no longer felt called to ordained ministry.[53]

An Evangelical Lutheran Church in America (ELCA) report states, "The church's professional leaders must adopt a better health and wellness discipline or the ELCA will be in jeopardy. We must change our ways to keep this church viable." The data from this 2006 study indicate that "about 71 percent of pastors and other leaders have risk factors because of poor nutrition; 69 percent are overweight; 64 percent are at risk for the consequences

52. Suzanne C. Segerstrom and Gregory E. Miller, "Psychological Stress and the Immune System: A Meta-Analytic Study of 30 Years of Inquiry," *Psychological Bulletin* 130, no. 4 (2004): 601–30, http://sites.northwestern.edu/foundationsofhealth/files/2013/03/04-PsychBull-Psych-stress-human-immune-sys-meta-analysis.pdf; Gregory E. Miller, Edith Chen, and Eric S. Zhou, "If It Goes Up, Must It Come Down? Chronic Stress and the Hypothalamic-Pituitary-Adrenocortical Axis in Humans," *Psychological Bulletin* 133, no. 1 (2007): 25–45, http://sites.northwestern.edu/foundationsofhealth/files/2013/03/07-Psych-Bull-If-it-goes-up-must-it-come-down.pdf.

53. "Ministers Ordained in the 1990s: A Look at Clergy Who Have Left the Ministry" (Louisville, KY: Presbyterian Church [U.S.A.], 1999).

of high blood pressure, and 63 percent indicated they have poor emotional health."[54]

The reasons for clergy stress noted in the previous studies still pertain today: overwork, dealing with too many or conflicting expectations, working constantly with needy people, confusing the masks we wear with the person we are, not knowing if we have really accomplished anything, groping for a relevant faith, and living with pressing personal or family needs.[55] This picture of clergy is important to understand. As much as possible, seminaries should keep in mind the future stressors that persons in ministry will face. Can seminaries prepare students for every exigency? Of course not—but a preventative approach is important in principle.

Perhaps not surprisingly, research is documenting the interplay between levels of stress and satisfaction in ministry. "The challenge for congregations and their spiritual leaders becomes how to increase the clergy's satisfaction with their ministry and decrease pastoral stress."[56] Factors contributing to such dissatisfaction include "poor overall health, weak professional self-concept, insufficient pay, and lack of clergy support."[57] To prevent stress that eventually leads to burnout or even leaving the ministry, the congregation should provide ministers with the freedom to step away from responsibilities and pursue self-care.[58] As seminaries foster a culture of self-care, their graduates will be better able to grasp its importance and to communicate it to their congregations or other employers.

There are signs that churches are beginning to note the importance of wholistic health for clergy. The PC(USA) Assistance Program is helping to counter clergy stress by providing ways for pastors to receive spiritual, vocational, health, and financial education and training. To achieve this goal, the assistance program offers CREDO conferences for PC(USA) clergy. The conferences are "intentional Christ-centered communities; a work of the heart, mind, body, and spirit; a living stream with a sustainable spirit; a four-step life

54. "Almen, Hanson Announce Plans for Future," *The Lutheran,* December 2006, 51.

55. Donald P. Smith, *Empowering Ministry: Ways to Grow in Effectiveness* (Louisville, KY: Westminster John Knox Press, 1996), 141.

56. David Briggs, "Mental Health of Clergy Requires Balancing Stress and Success," U.S. Congregational Life Survey, February 12, 2013, http://www.uscongregations.org/beyond-the-ordinary/mental-health-of-clergy-requires-balancing-stress-and-success/.

57. Patricia M. Y. Chang, "Assessing the Clergy Supply in the 21st Century," Pulpit & Pew Research on Pastoral Leadership, 2004, 22, http://pulpitandpew.org/sites/all/themes/pulpitandpew/files/ClergySupply.pdf.

58. Briggs, "Mental Health of Clergy."

cycle process of identity, discernment, practice, and transformation."[59] The PC(USA) board of pensions also sponsors well-being conferences for clergy and their spouses.

In the face of the stresses of student life, and to better prepare students for the stresses of their future work, seminaries can foster healthy lifestyles, which include care of one's physical and emotional health. The body as the temple of the Holy Spirit is one of the teachings of Pauline theology, but there are many roadblocks to embracing this understanding. Christians still are very ambivalent about the body and often sacrifice their physical health on the altar of success and career. Caring for our bodies involves adopting a certain lifestyle. Romans 12:1–2 becomes the classic text—"Present your bodies as a living sacrifice"—in an effort to honor God (*liturgia*).

Our relationship to food is one part of developing healthy bodies. What we eat has spiritual ramifications: what some call choosing "soul food" over fast food. Feasting, fellowship, and celebrating are highlighted in the parables, for instance, of the messianic banquet, which depicts the kingdom of God. God created a variety of foods for our enjoyment. Partaking of the largesse of the earth can be a form of gratitude to the Creator who made it. As we learn more about what foods are good and help sustain all of God's people, we care for ourselves by emphasizing those foods. Disregard of diet is not inconsequential; neither undereating nor overeating is appropriate. Diet figures largely in the Old Testament, with prohibitions about what cannot be eaten. The New Testament approaches clean and unclean foods differently: "'All things are lawful,' but not all things are beneficial" (1 Cor 10:23). What we eat may affect others (1 Cor 8:9–11), as Paul discusses not causing our weaker brother or sister to stumble.

Despite our health consciousness, 72 percent of American males are overweight or obese, whereas 85 percent of male associate pastors are overweight or obese. The percentage of female associate pastors who are above normal weight is about the same as the general female population (67 percent). These female associates are less likely to be obese than the general female population (26 percent versus 36 percent), but still 41 percent of female associate pastors fall in the BMI overweight category (25.0–29.9).[60] It is clear that it matters what we eat.

Food is important, but fasting can also be part of the rhythm of life. Feasting and fasting are both biblical. Fasting helps to clear the mind and focus

---

59. Board of Pensions of the Presbyterian Church (U.S.A.), CREDO Assistance Program, http://www.pensions.org/PlansAndPrograms/AssistanceProgram/CREDO/Pages/default.aspx.

60. Joelle Kopacz, "Weighty Issues," U.S. Congregational Life Survey, March 13, 2012, http://www.uscongregations.org/beyond-the-ordinary/weighty-issues/.

on God. It can take the extreme form of the holy anorexics such as Teresa de Avila or be part of the seasons of the Christian life. This is different, however, from eating disorders. "In the United States, 20 million women and 10 million men suffer from a clinically significant eating disorder at some time in their life."[61] Anecdotal evidence suggests that eating disorders are also a problem among women in seminary. The book *The Cost of Competence* labels eating disorders in women as "somatic anxiety syndrome." This syndrome is based on the myth that thin women are competent and successful, while curvaceous women are not. This false perception goes as far back as the 1920s with the flappers, when women wanted to look more like men.[62] It is the healthy, fit body that is important, not whether we are thin. We need to remember the Aristotelian virtue of temperance, the golden mean—moderation in all things, and with regard to food, eating in a sacred manner. Some seminaries are now developing a focus on the importance of food, agriculture, and the environment, both for individuals and for the planet.

Another growing problem at some seminaries is the abuse of alcohol. In college, students may have used alcohol to cope, and they simply carry those patterns into seminary. For other students coming from very conservative colleges, it may be the first time that they drink. More recent studies continue to affirm the reality that students who use alcohol are more likely to miss class and have poorer academic performances. Research studies on alcohol use among students are generally done on college campuses, but now may be the time to conduct such studies at seminaries.[63] Seminaries who receive federal funding for students are required to develop policies and programs for prevention and intervention around alcohol and drug abuse. In addition, students may be affected by extended family and friends who are battling addiction.

Caring for the body also involves exercise—walking, standing, and stretching. For some, more vigorous exercise increases metabolism, assists weight loss, reduces stress, and, by the release of endorphins, promotes a sense of well-being. Wellness centers can be available at some seminaries, or access can be provided to community aerobic, yoga, and fitness classes; to weights and exercise equipment; and to complementary health care practitioners.

61. "Get the Facts on Eating Disorders," National Eating Disorders Association, https://www.nationaleatingdisorders.org/get-facts-eating-disorders.
62. Brett Silverstein and Deborah Perlick, *The Cost of Competence: Why Inequality Causes Depression, Eating Disorders, and Illness in Women* (New York: Oxford University Press, 1995).
63. "College Drinking," National Institute on Alcohol Abuse and Alcoholism, https://www.niaaa.nih.gov/alcohol-health/special-populations-co-occurring-disorders /college-drinking.

Such resources are not simply niceties but could be considered part of the whole theological education experience.

There is also a new approach to body care and physical movement that links it with prayer and meditation—something Eastern religions have known for a long time. As Bruce Epperly writes, "Moving in the spirit is one of life's ordinary pleasures. Prayer and spiritual formation are not restricted to reading scripture, sitting in meditation, or going to church. Today, persons are learning about 'body prayer' (movements that accompany certain spoken or chanted prayers) as well as using their exercise time as a time of prayer and meditation."[64]

Another very important aspect of health is emotional and mental well-being, which is part of a wholistic understanding of health. Here we are focusing on the importance of a positive and life-affirming view that helps to lessen the effects of the challenges everyone experiences. We all have periods of feeling discouraged and depressed, but we recognize that this is different from clinically diagnosed mental illness, which in fact is a problem among seminarians and clergy. According to a Presbyterian Panel in 2006 (the most recent available), 14 percent of clergy self-report being affected by a serious mental illness.[65] In theological education what we need is not judgment but support for those who are struggling with this illness. Unfortunately, mental illness has often carried a stigma in our society, and even more so in the church. This means that clergy have not always sought mental health care for fear that their congregations will believe that they are not spiritually sound. Society does not yet fully accept the truth that mental illness is a disease no less than cancer, diabetes, or heart problems. Seminaries need to address these misconceptions not only for the good of future clergy but also for the wider community and church.[66]

Deepening the Spiritual Life

The cultivation of the inner spiritual life also should form part of theological education. The heart of the spiritual life of any residential seminary is

64. Bruce Epperly, *Spirituality & Health, Health & Spirituality: A New Journey of Spirit, Mind, and Body* (Mystic, CT: Twenty-Third Publications, 1997), 31.

65. "Mental Illness," Presbyterian Panel (Presbyterian Church [U.S.A.], 2006), A-6, www.presbyterianmission.org/ministries/research-services/presbyterian-panel/.

66. Stewart D. Govig, *In the Shadow of Our Steeples: Pastoral Presence for Families Coping with Mental Illness* (Binghamton, NY: Haworth, 1999); Amy Simpson, *Troubled Minds: Mental Illness and the Church's Mission* (Downers Grove, IL: InterVarsity, 2013); Susan Gregg-Schroeder, *In the Shadow of God's Wings: Grace in the Midst of Depression* (Nashville: Upper Room Books, 1997).

its worship life—where students come together to praise God through word and song. Regular chapel services can help shape the inner life of the community and produce a framework for individual spiritual practices. Students also often form their own Bible study groups, class study groups, and support groups, which are possible even in nonresidential contexts. Women, who often have felt marginalized in seminary, have found such spiritual groups or an *anam cara* (soul friend) to be lifesaving. Attention to the spiritual life also includes supporting a student's sense of call and creating a climate of nurture and discernment as to where God is leading.

Spirituality in general is one of the most popular topics today. Denominations as well are beginning to address issues of spirituality. The Spiritual Formation program of the PC(USA) publishes a newsletter, *Hungry Hearts*, which focuses on the centrality of cultivating the spiritual life. At minimum, as Frederick Buechner suggests, the spiritual dimension is to listen to the sounds of your life, for they are Christ speaking to you.[67]

Seminaries can offer opportunities for students to practice the spiritual disciplines of *lectio divino*, praying the psalms, meditation, silent retreats, and soaking prayer, to name a few. Structuring Sabbath times into the semester schedule is paramount. In the current American context, the observance of the Sabbath is a countercultural move. Sabbath flies in the face of our material and consumer-driven society. Yet we need space and time to recharge our inner being, not only to hear God's voice but also to reflect on what God would have us be and do. Keeping the Sabbath may mean setting aside several hours daily for prayer and reflection or one whole day free of work. For example, PTS until the late 1960s held no Monday classes in recognition of the fact that students were working in churches on Sundays. This schedule was discontinued for a variety of curricular reasons. Although a return to this approach may not be practical, students need space in their personal schedules to cultivate their inner lives—the lifeblood of theological education. Fostering such opportunities for commuter or online students may be a particular challenge. Are their needs different because (theoretically) they participate in their local churches and already have existent support structures?

In light of this renewed interest in spirituality and spiritual formation, seminaries are recognizing the importance of incorporating these matters into their programs, both curricular and cocurricular. A few examples of the different ways they have done this are described below.

Bethel Seminary incorporates a variety of formal and informal structures and programs related to the whole of a student's experience. Its Center for

67. Frederick Buechner, *The Sacred Journey* (San Francisco: Harper & Row, 1982), 77–78.

Spiritual and Personal Formation offers interdisciplinary courses, marriage and family studies, mental health counseling, pastoral care, and spiritual and personal formation. The faculty and administration are dedicated to the vision of making Bethel Seminary a place where people are growing toward personal holiness and wholeness.[68]

Columbia Theological Seminary, working in partnership with Pittsburgh Theological Seminary, offers a certificate in spiritual formation that can be added to the MDiv course requirements or taken as a stand-alone program. The requirements for the certificate include a pilgrimage (e.g., a trip to the Holy Land, the Isle of Iona, or Ghost Ranch), a practicum, and an immersion experience. Completion of this certificate requires a series of residencies in which students are engaged in plenary sessions and experience supervised practice of spiritual direction, worship, and time for study and reflection.

Louisville Presbyterian Theological Seminary offers a variety of approaches to spiritual formation: community worship three days each week; informal groups for learning and practicing spiritual disciplines; formal individual and group sessions with certified spiritual directors; courses designed to explore spiritual formation academically and experientially; discernment groups in which students offer one another spiritual direction; field education opportunities with congregations that teach students how to identify and plan for a congregation's spiritual needs; retreats throughout a student's seminary experience (orientation, class retreats, contemplative retreats at monastic communities); an outdoor prayer labyrinth; and periodic common meals.[69]

Luther Seminary's Healthy Leaders program seeks to assist students in self-care and wellness. This program discusses the impact of students' lifestyles and seeks to minister to them through discussion of the following elements of well-being: career, social, financial, physical, community, intellectual, and spiritual. Accompanied by a parish nurse, students are encouraged to identify healthy behaviors that enable them "to be good stewards of their God-given gifts and model healthy lifestyles for those they will serve in the parish and community." The school also gives students the opportunity for spiritual care groups, led by PhD students and faculty, or to join in spiritual direction by group or individual choice. Included in these offerings is the ability to take spiritual retreats for spiritual renewal and growth.[70]

Princeton Theological Seminary sponsors a Wholistic Health Initiative

68. *2016–2017 Academic Catalog*, Bethel University, http://catalog.bethel.edu /bethel-seminary/course-descriptions/center-spiritual-personal-formation/.

69. "Spiritual Formation," Louisville Presbyterian Theological Seminary, http:// www.lpts.edu/community/campus-life/spiritual-formation.

70. "Healthy Leaders Program," Luther Seminary, https://www.luthersem.edu /healthy_leaders/.

under the Department of Student Life. Within this department the Office of Student Counseling offers counseling, spiritual direction, wellness life coaching, a lending library, self-assessment services, and various support groups. PTS has made counseling affordable on campus, at Trinity Counseling Service, and through the Student Health Benefit Plan, which offers a roster of forty therapists and fifteen spiritual directors. Both the spiritual direction and the counseling services are widely used by students, spouses, and couples. Counseling cases in 2014–2015 included one hundred females, eighty-five males, and fifteen couples (from a student body of about four hundred). Fitness classes are offered through the Department of Student Life.[71] The seminary also offers daily chapel services, with a full-time director of the chapel as well as a director of music. Several faculty teach courses on spirituality and health, spiritual discipline, and formation. There is also a dual-degree program combining the MDiv and MA in spiritual formation and mission. A rising number of these dual-degree students are getting certified through a partnership with PTS and Oasis Ministries (www.oasismin.org) to be spiritual directors.

San Francisco Theological Seminary offers a wide range of opportunities under the umbrella of the Program in Christian Spirituality. These opportunities include, but are not limited to, an MDiv concentration in Christian spirituality, a diploma in the Art of Spiritual Direction or Spiritual Formation Studies, a DMin with an emphasis in Christian spirituality or spiritual direction, and an MA/PhD in Christian Spirituality through the GTU/SFTS partnership.[72]

Cultivating the Moral Life in Community

What can seminaries do to provide the context and necessary guidelines for students to flourish in their moral lives? Given time constraints and curricular demands, how can we address the cultivation of the moral life? We have discussed community as one of the key components of theological education. At its heart, we need a moral community. A moral code is not simply a set of rules and prohibitions or orthodox theology but a moral environment where all persons deserve dignity and respect, where there are no marginalized persons or strangers, where justice rules and even the appearance of impropriety is avoided—a community, however, where grace rather than the law is

---

71. Nancy Schongalla Bowman (PTS Director of Counseling Services), in discussion with the authors, April 28, 2016.

72. "Program in Christian Spirituality," San Francisco Theological Seminary, http://sfts.edu/academics/program-in-christian-spirituality/.

dominant. It is a place for forgiveness, repentance, restoration, and courageous conversations, especially around sexism, systemic racism, and treating
some as "the other."[73] Part of the mission statement of seminaries should
reflect this call for a moral community that provides the context for human
flourishing.

In our research, numerous women seminarians in various settings have
found this moral community lacking. They have experienced sexual harassment by fellow students, faculty, and field education supervisors. They may
represent a small number—but even one is too many. As well, female seminarians have sometimes been treated as invisible in the classroom at best or
with hostility at worst. They do not always feel encouraged or affirmed, and
in past decades they were even accused of coming to seminary only to catch
a husband. Numerous schools offer programs to counter these problems and
prejudice. For example, Columbia Theological Seminary, Duke University
Divinity School, Perkins Divinity School at SMU, the Graduate Theological Union, McCormick Theological Seminary, Yale Divinity School, and the
University of Chicago Divinity School offer courses and programs in sexuality, theology, and women's and gender studies.

At PTS, the first response to these concerns was the student-led formation
in 1972 of the Women's Center; women students came to the only women
faculty members, Freda Gardner and Katharine Sakenfeld, for support
toward becoming a recognized student organization. The Women's Center
today continues its important consciousness-raising advocacy and programming in support of PTS women students. Its work toward gender equality
has included ongoing advocacy for inclusive language for God as well as for
human beings. At the request of Freda Gardner and other women faculty, a
faculty Committee on Women in Church and Ministry was established in the
late 1970s. A decade later, a request by women faculty led to the establishment in 1989 of the Women in Church and Ministry lectureship, to ensure
that at least one distinguished woman would lecture on campus each year
and to ensure that one lectureship would focus on women; this lectureship
has continued uninterrupted to the present, even as now other lectureships
frequently have women speakers.

Most recently, the seminary has established the Women in Ministry (WIM)
Initiative and the Center for Theology, Women, and Gender (CTWG).
WIM, founded in 2011, honors all women associated with PTS since its
founding and also offers ongoing support to and advocacy for women in their

---

73. Yolanda Pierce, "Before the Healing Can Begin: Race, Racism, and Beloved
Community" (Alumni lecture, Princeton Theological Seminary, Princeton, NJ, May
18, 2016).

different ministries in service to God, the church, and the world. It is led by cocoordinators and a twenty-member committee that are organizing (especially for alumnae) conferences, events, women's networking, mentoring, and archival library collections. The seminary has honored women in ministry by dedicating a large, light-filled, public room on the third floor of the library as a hub for study, networking, events, and programs, and for telling the story of women's leadership in Christian ministry.

The CTWG was founded in 2015 under the Office of Academic Affairs with a faculty director and the following mission statement:

> The CTWG promotes the flourishing of all persons, especially those marginalized by both church and society due to their gender identity. It celebrates, supports, and advocates for women and sexual minorities in the church and the world by critically examining the continuing challenges facing them, and by drawing upon the resources of the Christian tradition, as well as the best in scholarship in other fields, in order to address these challenges. It takes, whenever possible, an intersectional approach to issues of gender, race, class, and disability, among other categories of analysis, believing that enduring change only takes place through attention to the complex interplay of these categories. In all of these areas, the Center advocates for change so that the church might better reflect the body of Christ, and witness more faithfully to the transforming power of Christ in the world. It also offers a Certificate in Theology, Women, and Gender Studies for M.Div. students.

Some believe that seminaries, by virtue of their raison d'être as religious organizations, are moral communities. But as noted above, that is not always the case. In addition, clergy ethics have been under fire, especially over the last decade, with the scandals of pedophilia among Roman Catholic priests, sexual misconduct lawsuits in churches and seminaries, and declining honesty ratings for clergy. According to one Gallup survey, clergy honesty is at an all-time low. In a survey in December 2015, only 45 percent of people surveyed ranked clergy as having "very high/high" ethical standards.[74] After Gallup began taking these surveys in 1977, the highest ranking was reached in 1985, when confidence in clergy stood at 67 percent.[75]

Now more than ever before, seminaries should address clergy ethics. Clergy ethics involves more than learning how not to be sued or taking classes

---

74. "Honesty and Ethics Rating of Clergy Slides to New Low," Gallup, http://www.gallup.com/poll/166298/honesty-ethics-rating-clergy-slides-new-low.aspx?g_source=clergy&g_medium=search&g_campaign=tiles; "Honesty/Ethics in Professions," Gallup, http://www.gallup.com/poll/1654/honesty-ethics-professions.aspx.
75. Ibid.

about sexual harassment and misconduct. Only as we develop a moral compass can we systematically address issues of sexual misconduct, financial improprieties, and churches conflicted because of a pastor's lack of ethical conscience and behavior. Moral ideals are what we strive for, though we may never obtain them. One word of caution—there is a certain arrogance and self-righteousness that can creep into the pursuit of virtue, potentially destroying those very virtues that we are seeking. The true possession of a virtue is inseparable from our motive and intent. According to Aristotle, virtue is to be cultivated for the sake of one or another particular trait. For example, if we pursue the virtue of honesty simply because we are afraid of being caught and not because we cherish honesty for its own sake, we do not really have that virtue. The test for clergy is doing something because it is the right thing to do.

Ministers should conduct their lives as a seamless garment between their personal and professional lives. Hence, if a pastor preaches love on Sunday but beats his wife or neglects her children on Monday, it should be grounds for dismissal. Does this sound too harsh? It is interesting that sexual misconduct is not tolerated, yet other unethical behavior is not targeted as clearly unacceptable. The studies of wife abuse among clergy are frightening, as are the studies on financial irregularities.

Seminarians and clergy should be held to a higher standard of morality, and even the appearance of wrongdoing should be avoided. The building of moral character results from a set of mind and heart, a perspective, a rigorous analysis of choices and options. Although we all live under the severe mercy of God and are far from perfect, cultivating the moral life in seminary is paramount for ethical future clergy.

Being moral has to do with four things: harmony between individuals, harmony within oneself, harmony with life, and harmony with God. It is noteworthy that many seminaries have rules against plagiarism, cheating on exams, drunkenness, and the like, but not necessarily a moral code as part of their student life handbooks or a description of what constitutes the moral ethos of their seminary community. It is not only the morality of our students that is important, but likewise that of the entire campus community, faculty, administration, and staff. It is interesting that there are major discussions about the importance of virtuous physicians, and for decades there have been required courses in ethics in medical schools, especially to stave off the commercialization and commodification of health care. Surely the fostering of the moral life should be equally if not more important in a theological community. The ethos of the seminary goes a long way in the development of moral character. Seminaries who care equally for the grounds crew and the president, the staff, students, administrators, and faculty speak loudly as to what is prized and cultivated.

The moral life, however, is not just connected with personal individual morality but also expands to include concerns about global poverty, hunger, environmental issues, and stewardship of the earth.[76] We have a moral obligation as seminary communities to discuss these global challenges with a love for justice and equity for the use of God's resources.

To summarize, women's experiences testify to a more wholistic vision of ministry. This vision encourages us to embrace theological education for the whole person, for the benefit of both women and men. It includes fostering intellectual excellence, encouraging healthy lifestyles, deepening the spiritual life, and developing moral sensitivity. The call to seminaries is to lift up the devotional, liturgical, contemplative, and mystical; and to strengthen and energize their communities to seek the needs of others. Ministry, social action, service, and justice all come together. Holding together mind, heart, body, and activities in education during seminary will lead to wholistic, healthy, integrated ministry after seminary. The goal of theological education is to foster the flourishing of the whole person within the life of the community. It will take intentional planning and sustained effort over time for any seminary to create an ethos in which all constituencies, including students, value this approach. But the effort will be worthwhile insofar as this focus on the whole person helps to lead not just students, but also their future congregations and others, into the abundant life that God has promised.

---

76. For their fiftieth reunion, the PTS Class of 1963 reflected on how seminaries need to change, and they put forward these concerns (John Richard Powers, ed., "What Does the Seminary Need to Do to Prepare Its Graduates for the Challenges They Will Face?" [written report to Princeton Theological Seminary president, October 2013]).

Conclusion

We are living in exciting times for women in America society; women are moving from the assembly line to the boardroom, from secretary to lawyer, from health aide to medical doctor. We have even witnessed the first woman candidate nominated by a major political party run for president of the United States. In the majority of Protestant churches, tokenism for women is being replaced by acceptance at all levels of leadership, both ordained and lay. God is an "equal opportunity employer," and the church is finally beginning to realize this truth, as women are no longer satisfied with living on the fringes of the church but are asserting their rightful place, moving from the pew to the pulpit. We are pleased, through this book, to reflect some of these important changes. By now, many younger women who have come from women-led congregations and have female doctors and lawyers may wonder if there is still a problem. Yet although the stained-glass ceiling is cracking, it is not gone. As in other liberation movements, prejudice may take subtler forms, lurking and ready to pounce when least expected.

The birth of this book came from Princeton Theological Seminary's desire to honor, celebrate, and support women associated with the seminary through every generation. Today as in the past, these women are on the frontiers of change—sometimes in dramatic ways but often choosing unsung paths. Their stories of ministry, often carried out amid struggle and challenges, testify to God's grace and presence in their lives. Their courage inspires us to use our own gifts and graces. As we delved deeper into their witness, we recognized first that the understanding of ministry was expanding to include the work of all Christians, and second, that female clergy were emphasizing a new style of leadership—shared leadership with less disparity between leader and

259

follower, a change from a hierarchal view of authority. This latter shift then led us to a vision for whole-person theological education that would better equip not only women but also men as they prepare to serve God, the church, and the world.

The goal of this book will be accomplished only if all of us join in a common effort to implement change and a broader vision for the betterment of all God's people. We will rejoice if this effort sparks more occasions and venues for sharing women's stories of their ministries, especially those of unheralded women who are serving God in Christ's name in all corners of the globe. We hope that the reflections here will serve as an invitation for all of God's people to join in conversations about justice, inclusion, and equality not only for women but for all who have been treated as the "other." Our prayer is that the church will find its prophetic voice, to transform society so that positive values are applauded, the interests of others replace self-interest, diversity is celebrated, and honor is bestowed not just on the powerful but on the least of these.

FAITH OF OUR MOTHERS, LIVING STILL

Commissioned by Princeton Theological Seminary

♩ = 110

1. Faith of our moth - ers, liv - ing still,
2. Faith of our sis - ters, serv - ing still,
3. Faith of our daugh - ters, hop - ing still,
4. Faith of our fam' - lies, grow - ing still,

through gifts de - rid - ed, calls de - nied,
with towel and ba - sin, cup and bread,
ven - tur - ing path - ways yet un - trod,
var - ied in gen - der, class, and race,

striv - ing un - daunt - ed through the years,
tend - ing earth's needs with pa - tient care,
part - ners in wit - ness to the world,
patch - work of pat - terns, shapes, and hues,

TEXT: Mary Louise Bringle, 2017
MUSIC: Sally Ann Morris, 2017
Text and Music © 2017 GIA Publications, Inc.
For congregational reprint permission, including overhead projection,
   contact OneLicense.net, 1-800-663-1501.

BETSEY STOCKTON
8.8.8.8.8.8
Alternate tune: ST CATHERINE

till   bolt - ed   doors   have   o - pened   wide:
till   hurts   are   healed   and   hun - gers   fed:
seek - ing   a   liv - ing,   mov - ing   God:
vast   as   the   man - tle   of   God's   grace:

faith   of   our   moth - ers,   firm   and   strong;
faith   of   our   sis - ters'   art   and   skill,
faith   of   our   daugh - ters,   bold   and   true,
faith   of   our   fam' - lies,   grow - ing   faith,

voic - es   long   si - lenced   rise   in   song!
lov - ing   with   heart   and   mind   and   will;
rest - less   till   Christ   makes   all   things   new;
we   hon - or   you   in   life   and   death.

Appendixes

Appendix A

Time Line

*Selected Milestones of American Women
in Ministerial Leadership*[1]

1637   As a part of the antinomian controversy, Anne Hutchinson is banished from the Massachusetts Bay Colony for leading religious meetings in her home and for promoting a doctrine of "free grace."

1721   Jane Fenn Hoskens and Elizabeth Levis, Quaker women living in Pennsylvania, begin to work together as ministers, traveling throughout the mid-Atlantic and northeast regions for several years. Hoskens's spiritual autobiography, which records her forty-plus years of public ministry, is published in 1771.

1743   A church council that includes Jonathan Edwards chastises Bathsheba Kingsley, a Congregationalist woman from Massachusetts who traveled as an itinerant evangelist. The council forbade Kingsley from speaking in public, though it encouraged her to host private religious meetings with other women in her home.

1759   Sarah Wright Townsend, a Long Island schoolteacher who had been an "exhorter" in earlier revivals, begins to preach regularly at a Separate Baptist church in her home community, which she does for over a decade.

1774   Ann Lee, leader of the United Society of Believers in Christ's Second Appearing (also known as "Shakers"), arrives in America

---

1. These facts were gathered from a variety of historical sources on women in American history.

from England. While preaching in public and conducting extensive missionary work, she promotes social equality between men and women.

1812 Ann Hasseltine Judson travels to India, where she and her husband, Adoniram Judson, work as missionaries. Later, while serving as a missionary in Burma, she translated the books of Daniel and Jonah into Burmese, as well as the Gospel of Matthew into Thai—the first Protestant to do so.

1815 Clarissa Danforth becomes the first woman ordained as a Free Will Baptist, preaching throughout northern New England for years.

1819 Jarena Lee becomes the first woman to be authorized to preach by Richard Allen, founder of the African Methodist Episcopal Church.

1822 Betsey Stockton, an emancipated slave, sets sail with a team of missionaries to Hawaii (then known as the Sandwich Islands). Endorsed by the American Board of Commissioners for Foreign Missions, she was the first single, American woman sent overseas as a missionary.

1827 Harriet Livermore preaches in the House of Representatives chamber of the U.S. Congress, which she did on three later occasions.

1837 Phoebe Palmer begins leading the "Tuesday Meeting for the Promotion of Holiness" in her home. She is regarded as one of the founders of the nineteenth-century Holiness movement.

1843 Mary Ann Aldersey leaves her missionary work in Java and travels to Ningbo, Zhejiang (in China), where she becomes the first Christian missionary woman to serve in the country.

1850 Antoinette Brown completes her coursework at Oberlin College's Theological Department, becoming the first woman to receive a seminary education, but she is not formally granted a degree. Much later, she was awarded honorary MA (1878) and honorary DD (1908) degrees.

1853 Antoinette Brown becomes the first woman to be ordained as a mainstream Protestant minister in the United States, serving a small Congregational church in South Butler, New York, for one year. Later in life she became a minister in the Unitarian church.

1863 Olympia Brown becomes the first woman to be ordained in the Universalist denomination.

1867 Amanda McFarland and her husband, David, open a mission to Native Americans in New Mexico. A decade later, after her husband's death, McFarland moved to Fort Wrangell, Alaska, and assumed the leadership of a mission school there. She was the first Euro-American woman to reside in that region.

1874 The first national convention of the Women's Christian Temperance Union is held. Under the nineteen-year presidency (1879–1898) of Frances Willard, the union became a powerful force for religion-based social reform.

1888 Clara Hale Babcock becomes the first woman ordained in the Christian Churches/Disciples of Christ through the Restoration or Stone-Campbell Movement.

1894 Itinerant evangelist Julia A. J. Foote becomes the first woman to be ordained as a deacon in the A.M.E. Zion Church.

1908 Aimee Semple McPherson founds the Foursquare Church, an evangelical Pentecostal denomination.

1950 Mary Ely Lyman becomes the first woman professor at Union Theological Seminary in New York City and the first woman to hold a full professorship at a U.S. seminary.

1956 The Presbyterian Church in the U.S.A. and the United Methodist Church approve the ordination of women as clergy.

1964 The Presbyterian Church in the U.S. approves the ordination of women as clergy.

1970 The American Lutheran Church and the Lutheran Church in America (which would merge to form the ELCA in 1986) approve the ordination of women as clergy.

1976 The Episcopal Church in the United States of America approves the ordination of women to its three orders of bishop, priest, and deacon.

1980 The Reformed Church in America authorizes the "Proposal to Maintain Peace in Diversity in the RCA Concerning Women as Church Officers," officially approving women's ordination while also providing a conscience clause for those within the denomination who object to the practice. The General Synod of the RCA voted to remove this clause in 2012.

2011   The Evangelical Presbyterian Church votes to allow presbyteries to ordain women, if they so choose.

Appendix B

Time Line

Women's Ordination and Ministerial
Leadership in the Presbyterian Church

In addition to the Presbyterian Church (U.S.A.) the following time line includes the four denominations that preceded the formation of the PC(USA): Presbyterian Church in the U.S.A. (PCUSA), United Presbyterian Church in North America (UPCNA), Presbyterian Church in the U.S. (PCUS), and United Presbyterian Church of the U.S.A. (UPCUSA).

1832 The General Assembly (G.A.) of the PCUSA states, "Meetings of pious women by themselves, for conversation and prayer, whenever they can conveniently be held, we entirely approve. But let not the inspired prohibitions of the great apostle to the Gentiles, as found in his epistles to the Corinthians and to Timothy, be violated. To teach and exhort, or to lead in prayer, in public and promiscuous assemblies, is clearly forbidden to women in the Holy Oracles." This is the first statement of its kind from the General Assembly.

1864 The PCUS officially organizes and is largely comprised of congregations from the Presbyterian Church in the Confederate States of America, founded in 1861.

1875 The G.A. of the UPCNA approves the formation of the Women's General Missionary Society, the first national organization for women in the Presbyterian Church.

1906 The UPCNA opens up the office of deacon to women.

1912 The G.A. of the PCUSA states in Overture 362, "From the Presbytery of Chemung, asking a definite deliverance upon the question of the acceptance of women by a Presbytery as candidates for the ministry. The following answer is recommended: That while the Assembly gives its hearty endorsement to the broad work now being carried on by the godly women of our Church, We deem it inexpedient to have a Presbytery receive under its care women as candidates for the ordained ministry." In this year, the Presbytery of Chemung took Rachel Gleason Brooks under its care as a "student of theology."

1918   Lillian Herrick Chapman is licensed to preach within the bounds of the Chemung Presbytery, so that she could supply the pulpit of North Presbyterian Church in Elmira, New York, while its pastor was serving as a chaplain in World War I. The following year her licensure was rescinded.

1920   PCUSA G.A., responding to overtures, asks presbyteries to vote on ordination of women as elders and as deacons.

1921   PCUSA overture to ordain women fails narrowly in presbyteries; G.A. sends a new overture to presbyteries for ordination of women as deacons.

1922   PCUSA presbyteries approve ordination of women as deacons.

1927   Katharine Bennett and Margaret Hodge present "Causes of Unrest Among Women of the Church" to the 1927 General Council of the PCUSA. It is the first critical analysis of the issue within the PCUSA written solely by women. An excerpt from the document reads, "Woman asks to be considered in the light of her ability and not of her sex. She recognizes that being as one woman said, 'the first generation out of the kitchen,' she has much to learn, but she cannot be a 'new woman' in all phases of her life and willingly accept the position accorded to her in the church. Her mind rebels even if her heart keeps her tongue quiet."

1929   PCUSA again submits to presbyteries alternative overtures on the ordination of women: (A) as ministers and elders; (B) as elders only; (C) as licensed evangelists.

1930   PCUSA ordination of women as both ministers and elders is defeated by presbyteries; ordination as elders only is approved (158–118–7); licensing fails by 3 votes (of presbyteries).

1946   On recommendation of General Council, PCUSA G.A. sends to presbyteries the overture that "the office of minister may be either men or women." In addition, the G.A. sends an overture that would enable presbyteries to grant local commissions for teaching and preaching to qualified men and women, to be known as "lay preachers."

1947   Presbyteries defeat the first overture (100–128–8) and ask that presbyteries vote on ordaining women as ministers. However, presbyteries pass the second overture, regarding "lay preachers," by a vote of 138–93.

1953   PCUSA Presbytery of Rochester submits Overture 3, requesting that women be ordained as ministers, to the 165th General Assembly. In response, the G.A. appoints a special committee of seven persons—three ministers and four ruling elders, two of whom are women—to write a report on the issue and present it to a future G.A.

1955   PCUSA G.A. reviews the special committee report, which found no theological barrier to the ordination of women and maintained that such action would contribute to the growth of the church. Following the recommendation of the committee, the 167th G.A. sends an overture to approve ordination of women as ministers to the presbyteries for a vote in the following year.

1956   PCUSA presbytery vote is 205–35 to add to Form of Government, under the heading "Of Bishops or Pastors, and Associate Pastors," "Both men and women may be called to this office." Margaret Towner becomes the first woman ordained as a PCUSA minister.

1956   PCUS committee recommends a proposal that women be ordained as elders and deacons, and G.A. sends the proposal to presbyteries (G.A. vote: 234–226).

1957   PCUS presbyteries defeat the proposal (39–44).

1958   The PCUSA and the UPCNA merge to form the United Presbyterian Church in the U.S.A. (UPCUSA).

1963   PCUS Assembly, on the urging of two special committees, recommends *Book of Church Order* changes to make women eligible for all church offices.

1964   PCUS presbyteries approve the ordination of women as deacons, elders, and ministers. Rachel Henderlite becomes the first woman minister ordained in the PCUS.

1971   Lois H. Stair is elected as moderator of the 183rd General

Assembly of the UPCUSA, becoming the first woman elected as a G.A. moderator in the history of the American Presbyterian Church.

1979   The UPCUSA resolves that ordination as minister is to be denied to anyone who refuses to ordain women. Also, UPCUSA changes the Form of Government to mandate that women be represented on the session and the board of deacons.

1983   The UPCUSA and the PCUS merge to form the reunited PC(USA), which adopts UPCUSA policies on the ordination of women.

1994   According to a study by the Hartford Institute for Religion Research, 19 percent of PC(USA) pastors at this time are women.[1]

2002   According to a PC(USA) report, 27 percent of the PC(USA) active ministers (teaching elders) were women.[2]

2014   PC(USA) Statistical Services reported that 37 percent of the PC(USA) active ministers (teaching elders) were women.[3]

---

1. "A Quick Question: What Percentage of Pastors Are Female?" Hartford Institute for Religion Research, http://hirr.hartsem.edu/research/quick_question3.html.
2. Ida Smith, "Women Rule?" Presbyterian Church (U.S.A.) Blogs, http://www.pcusa.org/blogs/presbyterians-by-the-numbers/2014/5/19/women-rule/.
3. Ibid.

Appendix C

History of Women Faculty at PTS[1]

Summary of the number of women faculty since the founding of PTS.

> Visiting/Guest Professors, Lecturers, Adjuncts, and Other Unranked Faculty: 81
> Ranked Faculty: 36
> Total: 117

(Ranked faculty are defined as full-time faculty members who participate in faculty governance, having been appointed to their position by the faculty with concurrence of the president and the board of trustees.)

Names of all women faculty, in chronological order by date of first appointment, through summer 2017:

Jessie Dell Crawford
> *Guest Professor of Christian Education (part time) 1946–1950*

Bertha Paulssen
> *Visiting Lecturer in Psychology 1949–1951*

Dorothy Fritz
> *Visiting Lecturer in Christian Education 1950–1952*

Jean Cassat
> *Assistant Instructor in Christian Education and Field Work Supervisor 1951–1953*

1. The information below is compiled from PTS academic catalogs, archives, and the academic dean's office.

Dorothy Faye Kirkwood
Assistant Instructor in Christian Education and Field Work Supervisor 1953–1956

Harriet Prichard
Instructor in Christian Education 1957–1959
Assistant Professor 1959–1961

Freda Ann Gardner
Assistant Professor of Christian Education 1961–1977
Associate Professor 1977–1985
Professor 1985–1992
Thomas W. Synnott Professor Emerita of Christian Education (granted upon retirement in 1992)

Virginia J. Damon
Visiting Lecturer in Speech 1964–1967, 1988–1990
Assistant Director of Speech 1968–1985

Elizabeth Gordon Edwards
Instructor in New Testament 1970–1973
Lecturer 1977–1980
Assistant Professor 1980–1998

Katharine Doob Sakenfeld
Instructor in Old Testament 1970–1971
Assistant Professor 1971–1976
Associate Professor 1976–1987
Professor 1987–1992
William Albright Eisenberger Professor of Old Testament Literature and Exegesis 1992–2013
Director of PhD Studies 1984–2009

Joyce Hyacinth Elaine Bailey
Visiting Lecturer in Christian Education 1970–1971

Ruth Dannemann
Instructor in New Testament 1974–1976

Thelma Cornelia Adair
Visiting Lecturer in Christian Education 1974–1978

Margaret Ruth Eddy
Visiting Lecturer in Pastoral Theology 1975–1979

Sandra Read Brown
Instructor in Pastoral Theology 1976–1982
Assistant Professor 1982–1987

Doris Krimper Donnelly
Visiting Lecturer in Theology 1976–1978
Visiting Lecturer in Theology and Christian Education 1978–1985

Lois Gehr Livezey
Instructor in Christian Social Ethics 1977–1983
Assistant Professor 1983–1988

Mary Lane Potter
Instructor in Theology 1978–1981

Kathleen Elizabeth McVey
Assistant Professor of Church History 1979–1986
Associate Professor 1986–1992
Joseph Ross Stevenson Associate Professor of Church History 1992–1993
Professor 1993–2017

Anna Arnold Hedgeman
Visiting Lecturer in Religion and Society 1979–1980

Rena Karefa-Smart
Visiting Lecturer in Church and Society 1981–1982

Dolores Madeline Pelletier
Visiting Lecturer in Pastoral Theology 1981–1982

Elizabeth Anne Gaines
Instructor in Old Testament 1982–1985

Suzanne Pogue Mott Rudiselle
Visiting Lecturer in Preaching 1982–1983

Martha Lee Wiggins
Visiting Lecturer in Christian Education 1982–1983, 1986–1987

Evelyn Delaney
Visiting Lecturer in Communication 1983–1986, 1987–1990

Susan Horowitz
Visiting Lecturer in Communication 1983–1984

Jane Dempsey Douglass
Fredrick and Margaret L. Weyerhaeuser Professor-Elect of Historical Theology 1984–1985
Hazel Thompson McCord Professor of Historical Theology 1985–1998

Carol Marie Noren
Instructor in Preaching 1984–1985

Mary Claire Boys
Visiting Lecturer in Christian Education 1984–1985

Jacquelyn Grant
Visiting Lecturer in Theology 1984–1985

Judith Eileen Sanderson
Assistant Professor of Old Testament 1985–1991

Clarice Jannette Martin
Instructor in New Testament 1985–1986
Assistant Professor 1986–1992

Elena Malits
Visiting Lecturer in Theology 1985–1986

Maureen Shaughnessy
Visiting Lecturer in Christian Education 1985–1987

Christine Marie Smith
Instructor in Homiletics 1986–1987
Assistant Professor 1987–1991

Marie Harris
Guest Professor of Christian Education 1986–1987

Christine Cozad Neuger
Assistant Professor of Pastoral Theology 1987–1992

Carol Eichling Lytch
Visiting Lecturer in Preaching 1987–1988, 1989–1990

Margaret Ann Sanders Krych
Visiting Lecturer in Christian Education 1988–1989

Marianne Sawicki
Guest Professor of Christian Education 1989–1990

Christina Ann Baxter
Guest Professor of Theology 1989–1990

Barbara A. Bate
Visiting Lecturer in Preaching 1989–1990

Grace Darling Cumming Long
Visiting Lecturer in Ethics 1989–1990

Nancy Jean (Janine) Duff
Assistant Professor of Christian Ethics 1990–1992

Associate Professor 1992–2009
Stephen Colwell Associate Professor of Christian Ethics 2009–

Pamela Jean Holliman
Visiting Lecturer in Pastoral Theology 1990–1991

Evelyn Rothchild
Visiting Lecturer in Pastoral Theology 1990–1991

Sally Green Willis-Watkins
Visiting Lecturer in Speech 1990–1991

Nancy Lammers Gross
Visiting Lecturer in Preaching 1991–1992
Visiting Lecturer in Speech Communication 1996–2001
Associate Professor of Speech Communication and Ministry 2001–2003
Arthur Sarrell Rudd Associate Professor of Speech Communication in Ministry 2003–
Dean of Student Life 2006–2012

Barbara Lundblad
Visiting Lecturer in Preaching 1991–1992

Abigail Rian Evans
Associate Professor of Practical Theology 1991–1999
Charlotte W. Newcombe Professor of Practical Theology 1999–2009
Director of Field Education 1992–1996
Coordinator of the Clinical Pastoral Education Program 1993–1997
Academic Coordinator of Field Education 1997–2007

Elsie Anne McKee
Archibald Alexander Associate Professor of the History of Worship 1991–1994
Professor 1994–1999
Archibald Alexander Professor of Reformation Studies and the History of Worship 1999–

Beverly Roberts Gaventa
Associate Professor of New Testament 1992–1995
Helen H. P. Manson Professor of New Testament Literature and Exegesis 1995–2013

Julie Ann Duncan
Assistant Professor of Old Testament 1992–1996

Carol Lakey Hess
Assistant Professor of Christian Education 1992–1999

Lucy Bregman
Visiting Lecturer in Pastoral Theology 1992–1993

Susan Jane Dunlap
Visiting Lecturer in Pastoral Theology 1992–1993
Visiting Lecturer in Pastoral Care 1993–1994

Gloria Carter Taylor
Visiting Lecturer in Christian Education 1992–1993

Delores S. Williams
Visiting Lecturer in Theology 1992–1993

Catherine Agnes Ziel
Visiting Lecturer in Homiletics 1992–1993

Leonora Tubbs Tisdale
Assistant Professor of Preaching 1993–1995
Assistant Professor of Preaching and Worship 1995–1997
Associate Professor 1997–1999
Elizabeth M. Engle Associate Professor of Preaching and Worship 1999–2001

Kenda Creasy Dean
Visiting Lecturer in Speech 1993–1996
Visiting Lecturer in Christian Education 1995–1997
Assistant Professor of Youth, Church, and Culture 1997–2004
Associate Professor 2004–2010
Professor 2010–2013
Mary D. Synnott Professor of Youth, Church, and Culture 2013–
Director of the Tennent School of Christian Education 2000–2008

Elizabeth Anne Frykberg
Visiting Lecturer in Christian Education 1993–1994

Antoinette Irene Goodwin
Visiting Lecturer in Pastoral Care 1993–1994
Visiting Lecturer in Pastoral Theology 1998–1999

Nancy Hurd Schluter
Visiting Lecturer in Ministry 1993–1998

Deborah van Deusen Hunsinger
Assistant Professor of Pastoral Theology 1994–2000
Associate Professor 2000–2007
Professor 2007–2009
Charlotte W. Newcombe Professor of Pastoral Theology 2009–

Mercy Oduyoye
  John A. Mackay Visiting Professor of World Christianity 1994–1995

Janet Lynn Weathers
  Assistant Professor of Speech Communication in Ministry 1994–2001

Alyce Mundi McKenzie
  Visiting Lecturer in Preaching 1994–1995, 1997–1999

Marilyn Chandler McEntyre
  Visiting Lecturer in Literature and Theology 1995–1996
  Adjunct: Pastoral Theology 2011–2012

Kathy Jane Nelson
  Visiting Lecturer in Ministry 1996–1998
  Visiting Lecturer in Field Education 2005–2006

Ellen Tabitha Charry
  Margaret W. Harmon Associate Professor of Systematic Theology 1997–2010
  Margaret W. Harmon Professor of Systematic Theology 2010–2017

Sally Freedman
  Visiting Lecturer in Semitics 1997–1998

Felicia Y. Thomas
  Visiting Lecturer in Ministry 1997–1998

Phyllis Trible
  Visiting Lecturer in Old Testament 1997–1998

Joyce MacKichan Walker
  Visiting Lecturer in Christian Education 1997–1999, 2003–2004
  Adjunct: Presbyterian Polity 2013–2017

Jacqueline Evangeline Lapsley
  Instructor in Old Testament 1998–1999
  Assistant Professor 1999–2004
  Associate Professor 2004–
  Director of the Center for Theology, Women, and Gender 2015–

R. Marie Griffith
  Visiting Lecturer in History 1998–1999

Carol A. Wehrheim
  Visiting Lecturer in Christian Education 1998–2001, 2002–2003

Kathy Lynn Dawson
  Visiting Lecturer in Christian Education 2000–2001

Kristin Emery Saldine
Visiting Lecturer in Ministry 2000–2001
Minister of the Chapel 2001–2006

Eunny Patricia Lee
Instructor in Old Testament 2001–2004
Assistant Professor 2004–2011

Sally Ann Brown
Assistant Professor of Preaching and Worship 2001–2006
Elizabeth M. Engle Assistant Professor of Preaching and Worship 2005–2007
Associate Professor 2007–

Jennifer Wiley Legath
Visiting Lecturer in Church History 2003–2004

Leanne Sue Simmons
Visiting Lecturer in Pastoral Care 2005–2006

Virginia Berglund Smith
Visiting Lecturer in Field Education 2005–2006

Alison Irene Young
Visiting Lecturer in Christian Education 2005–2007
Adjunct: Practical Theology 2007–2009
Adjunct: Education and Formation 2009–2017

Bo Karen Lee
Instructor in Christian Education 2006–2007
Assistant Professor 2007–2008
Assistant Professor of Spirituality and Historical Theology 2008–2013
Associate Professor of Spiritual Theology and Christian Formation 2013–

Katie (Donna) Day
Visiting Lecturer in Congregational Ministry 2006–2007

Katrina B. Olds
Visiting Lecturer in Church History 2006–2007

Yolanda Pierce
Elmer G. Homrighausen Associate Professor of African American Religion and Literature 2007–2017
Liaison with the Princeton University Center for African American Studies 2007–2013
Director of the Center for Black Church Studies 2013–2017

Sara E. Brooks
Adjunct: Church History/History 2007–2008

Karla Koll
Adjunct: Mission, Ecumenics, and History of Religions 2007–2008

Rebekah Massengill
Adjunct: Practical Theology 2007–2009

Jill L. McNish
Adjunct: Practical Theology 2007–2009

Carla J. Works
Adjunct: New Testament 2007–2008

Celia M. Chazelle
Adjunct: Church History 2008–2009

Angela Dienhart Hancock
Adjunct: Practical Theology 2008–2009

Karina Ramins
Adjunct: Worship 2008–2009

Angela Reed
Adjunct: Education and Formation 2008–2009

Lisa Cerami
Adjunct: Church History 2009–2011

Caroline Walker Bynum
Adjunct: Church History 2010–2011

Angella M. Pak Son
Adjunct: Pastoral Care 2011–2013, 2016–2017

Erin Rafferty
Adjunct: Practical Theology 2012–2013
Adjunct: Ecumenics 2014–2015

Esther Schor
Adjunct: Old Testament 2012–2013

Lisa M. Bowens
Instructor in New Testament 2013–2014
Assistant Professor 2014–

Katherine Douglass
Adjunct: Education and Formation 2013–2014, 2016–2017

Sonia Waters
Adjunct: Pastoral Care 2013–2014
Assistant Professor of Pastoral Theology 2014–

Marilyn McCord Adams
Adjunct: Philosophy 2014–2016

Yvette Joy Harris
Postdoctoral Teaching Fellow: Speech 2014–2016
Lecturer in Speech Communication in Ministry 2016–

Melanie Howard
Adjunct: New Testament 2015–2016

Erin E. Fleming
Adjunct: Old Testament 2015–2016

Christina Harker
Adjunct: New Testament 2015–2016

Ruth P. Workman
Adjunct: Education and Formation 2015–2017

Elizabeth Bloch-Smith
Adjunct: Old Testament 2016–2017

Nancy McWilliams
Adjunct: Pastoral Care 2016–2017

Margarita Mooney
Associate Professor of Congregational Studies 2016–

Christiane Marie Lang Hearlson
Adjunct: Education and Formation 2016–2017

Appendix D

Geographical Spread of PTS Alumnae

There are a total of 3,059 active alumnae worldwide (out of a total of 11,106 active alumni/ae, men and women, worldwide). In the United States (including territories) specifically, there are a total of 2,875 active alumnae. All fifty states are represented by PTS alumnae.[1]

STATES WITH 40+ ALUMNAE

New Jersey 508	Minnesota 76
Pennsylvania 296	Georgia 75
California 229	Michigan 74
New York 190	Maryland 60
North Carolina 130	Massachusetts 56
Virginia 105	Indiana 49
Texas 99	Tennessee 46
Washington 95	Colorado 44
Florida 90	Kentucky 42
Ohio 88	Connecticut 40
Illinois 83	

1. All information was supplied in April 2016 by Lorelei Zupp, associate director of Development Operations at PTS.

OTHER COUNTRIES REPRESENTED BY ALUMNAE

Africa

Egypt 2

Ghana 2

South Africa 2

Nigeria 1

Total Africa 7

Americas (North, Central, Caribbean, South)

Canada 24

Costa Rica 2

Argentina 1

Bahamas 1

Brazil 1

Guyana 1

Trinidad and Tobago 1

Uruguay 1

Total Americas (outside U.S.) 32

Asia and Pacific

South Korea 17

Taiwan 10

Malaysia 9

India 7

Burma/Myanmar 5

Japan 5

Hong Kong 4

Australia 3

Indonesia 3

New Zealand 3

Philippines 3

Fiji 1

Nepal 1

Pakistan 1

Singapore 1

Thailand 1

Total Asia and Pacific 74

Europe and Mid-East

Germany 19

Scotland 14

England 11

Hungary 6

Switzerland 6

Netherlands 3

France 2

Northern Ireland 2

Sweden 2

Czech Republic 1

Ireland 1

Italy 1

Latvia 1

Lebanon 1

Total Europe and Mid-East 70

Appendix E

PTS Alumnae by Denomination[1]

Among the 2,822 active alumnae who have reported their denominational affiliation, approximately 56 percent listed the PC(USA) as their denomination.

Denomination	Total Number of Alumnae
Presbyterian Church (U.S.A.)	1,580
United Methodist Church	221
United Church of Christ	101
Episcopal Church	95
Evangelical Lutheran Church in America	84
Baptist (United States)	66
American Baptist Churches	55
Presbyterian Church (Abroad)	53
No Affiliation	52
Roman Catholic	51
Nondenominational	47
Reformed Church in America	40
Southern Baptist Convention	23

1. All information was supplied in April 2016 by Lorelei Zupp, associate director of Development Operations at PTS.

Denomination	Total Number of Alumnae
African Methodist Episcopal Church	22
Korean Presbyterian Church in America	15
Mennonite Church	15
Christian Reformed Church	13
Baptist (Abroad)	11

In addition, eighty-six denominations are represented by fewer than ten alumnae.

Appendix F

PTS Alumnae in Different Areas of Ministry[1]

Among 1,673 active alumnae who are currently employed and who have reported their area/field of work, approximately 50 percent are working in congregational ministry.

Career Field	Number of Alumnae Currently Serving
Congregational Ministries	816
College or University (faculty/staff/chaplains)	196
Medical (including hospital chaplains)	156
Seminary (faculty/staff/chaplains)	155
Business	60
Nonprofit	58
Preschool/Elementary/Secondary Education	45
Denominational Middle Governing Bodies	33
Denominational Higher Governing Bodies	17
Military Service	17
Government	16
Law/Legal System (including prison ministry)	12

1. All information was supplied in April 2016 by Lorelei Zupp, associate director of Development Operations at PTS.

Career Field	Number of Alumnae Currently Serving
Government—Other/Service Organizations	2
Other	90
Unknown	940
Retired	349

Appendix G

PTS Women in Ministry
Alumnae Survey[1]

Created and written by Abigail Rian Evans and Katharine Doob Sakenfeld, 2015 (see introduction for information about development and administration of the Survey).

SECTION I: PROFILE

1. Age range (*click the appropriate category*)

2. Marital status (*click the appropriate category*)

3. Number of children: _____

4. Ethnicity (Categories from the U.S. government's Office of Management & Budget) (*check all that apply*)
   - ☐ American Indian or Alaska Native
   - ☐ Asian
   - ☐ Black or African American
   - ☐ Latino/a or Hispanic
   - ☐ Native Hawaiian or other Pacific Islander
   - ☐ White
   - ☐ Other _____

5. Nationality
   - ☐ USA
   - ☐ Other _____

1. This survey has been reformatted for publication in this book.

6. Education (*check all that apply*)

Select Degree	Name of Institution	Year
☐ BA	_____	_____
☐ BS	_____	_____
☐ MDiv	_____	_____
☐ ThM	_____	_____
☐ MTS	_____	_____
☐ MACE	_____	_____
☐ MSW	_____	_____
☐ MBA	_____	_____
☐ MFA	_____	_____
☐ MHA	_____	_____
☐ MPA	_____	_____
☐ MEd	_____	_____
☐ Master of Arts—Other	_____	_____
☐ Master of Science—Other	_____	_____
☐ PhD	_____	_____
☐ ThD	_____	_____
☐ DMin	_____	_____
☐ EdD	_____	_____
☐ JD	_____	_____
☐ Doctoral—Other	_____	_____
☐ Professional—Other	_____	_____

7. Certifications

Name of Certification	Certifying Institution
_____	_____
_____	_____
_____	_____
_____	_____
_____	_____

8. Please check association(s) you have with PTS

☐ Administrator
☐ Alum
☐ Faculty
☐ Friend
☐ Trustee

☐ Other

If you answered "other" above, please indicate the association:

_____

9. Current Denomination: _____

10. Prior Denomination (if applicable): _____

11. What was your reason for changing denominations (if applicable)?

_____

_____

12. Ordination

Are you ordained?   ☐ Yes   ☐ No

13. If you are currently ordained, please provide the following details:

Office   Year Ordained

☐ Clergy   _____

☐ Deacon   _____

☐ Elder   _____

☐ Other   _____

If you answered "other" above, please indicate the office to which you
are ordained here: _____

14. *If you would like to share any additional comments related to your current denomination and/or change of denomination, please do so here:*

_____

_____

SECTION II: WORK AND VOLUNTEER HISTORY

15. For each position in your PRIOR PAID work history (excluding any present
positions), please select the area and the principal position you held in that
area.

- Please indicate approximate rounded number of total years involved.
  (Indicate 1 for anything less than 1 year.)
- Please begin the list with your most recent prior paid position, and note
  that dates should be entered in mm/dd/yyyy format.

Area/ Position/ Begin Date/ End Date/ Number of Years Involved
*[Note: in electronic form, respondents selected Area and Position from drop-down
lists of categories used in the PTS Alumni/ae Database.]*

_____

_____

_____

_____

16. Please provide any additional information about your response to question 15 (or additional positions).

_____

_____

17. Current employer(s)? (e.g. parish, nonprofit, business, hospital, government, self-employed, other—not specific name of employer)
    (Note: please indicate "retired" or "unemployed" if applicable)

_____

18. *If you need to clarify your answer to Question 17 above, please do so here:*

_____

_____

19. What is the title of your current position(s), if applicable?
    Check all additional information that applies.

Position	Paid	Unpaid	Full-time	Part-time
_____	☐	☐	☐	☐
_____	☐	☐	☐	☐
_____	☐	☐	☐	☐

20. How many years have you served with this employer? _____

21. What was your title in your immediate past position (if applicable)?

_____

22. How many years did you serve in your most recent past position? _____

23. Did you at any point create your own paid position/agency? ☐ Yes ☐ No
    If yes, please elaborate on your answer:

_____

_____

24. Are you currently seeking a position? ☐ Yes ☐ No
    If yes, in what area?

_____

_____

25. Please list volunteer activities in which you have participated during the last five years:
    Check all additional information that applies.

Activity	Church Related	Non-Church Related
_____	☐	☐
_____	☐	☐
_____	☐	☐

26. *If you would like to clarify any of your comments in this section of the survey (Section II: Work and Volunteer History), please do so here:*

_____

_____

SECTION III: ATTITUDES TOWARDS MINISTRY

27. Please answer questions 27, 28, and 29 with the following understanding of ministry in mind (see cover letter):

> *"Ministry here applies to anyone who has been baptized in the Christian faith and who understands her vocation as service to God and others."*

How do you understand your current paid or volunteer position as ministry?

_____

_____

28. How did you first experience your call to ministry?

_____

_____

29. How has your understanding of your call to ministry changed over time?

_____

_____

30. Were you the first woman to hold your current position or a previous position?

☐ Yes   ☐ No

31. What kinds of support or obstacles have you encountered in responding to your call and/or in your work?

_____

_____

32. Is there anything about your ministry or leadership style that you think is unique to your being a woman?

☐ Yes   ☐ No

Please elaborate on your answer:

_____

_____

33. In what respects, if any, does being a woman enhance or inhibit your ministry in your current position?

_____

_____

34. How would you describe your faith journey and your experience of spiritual companionship along the way?

_____

_____

35. *If you would like to share any additional comments related to this section of the survey (Section III: Attitudes Towards Ministry), please do so here:*

_____

_____

SECTION IV: IMPACT OF THEOLOGICAL EDUCATION

36. How well did your theological education in the classroom equip you for your ministry?

	1	2	3	4	5		N/A
very poorly	☐	☐	☐	☐	☐	very well	☐

Please comment on your answer:

_____

_____

37. What changes in theological education might better equip women in ministry, especially for those going into your field of work?

_____

_____

38. How did your seminary experience, broadly understood, enhance and/or challenge your faith journey?

_____

_____

39. *If you would like to share any additional comments related to this section of the survey (Section IV: Impact of Theological Education), please do so here:*

_____

_____

Index of Scripture

Index of Names

Index of Subjects